Facilitator's Guide for the

LifeGuides Program

on Alcoholism and Other Family Problems

Joseph A. Muldoon

Community Intervention™, Inc.
Minneapolis, Minnesota

Joseph A. Muldoon

Joseph A. Muldoon is a licensed psychologist with 17 years' experience in the treatment, training, and writing on problems related to adolescent drug abuse. He is the primary author of *Effective Employee Assistance* (CompCare Publications, Minneapolis) and *One Step Ahead: Early-Intervention Strategies for Adolescent Drug Problems* (Community Intervention™, Inc., Minneapolis. He is also the author of the Community Intervention™ Insight Class Program™. He received his master's degree in psychology from the University of Minnesota and has worked as a psychologist for the Hennepin County Court system in Minneapolis and for the Jamestown Adolescent Chemical Dependency Treatment Center in Stillwater, Minnesota. He has also served as supervisor of counselors for Face-To-Face Health and Counseling in St. Paul and as a community organizer for VISTA in the southern United States.

ISBN 0-945485-17-4

Inquiries, orders and catalog requests should be addressed to the publisher.

Community Intervention ™, Inc.
529 South Seventh Street, Suite 570
Minneapolis, MN 55415
Call toll free 1-800-328-0417
In Minnesota call 1-612-332-6537

Printed in the United States of America

Table of Contents

LifeGuides Exercises and Background Material

Opportunities to Help— Not Obligations to Fulfill

The LifeGuides Program provides many different routes to the same ends. The resources listed under each subject area present many options for planning a curriculum. The asterisks indicate subject matter or exercises that have related material in the participant guidebooks.

PHASE I: Becoming Aware

Start-up at the Beginning of the Year

Personal Safety

Communication and Listening Skills

What's a "Normal" Family?

Drug and Alcohol Use: What's Normal, What's Not?

Alcoholism and Drug Dependence: When Use Goes Out of Control

Shock Waves: How Alcoholism Affects the Family

Something to Think About: Participants' Risks for Future Problems

Phase II: Taking Care

Denial: Dance of Deception

Debbie, Tom, and Carol

Debbie, Tom, and Carol have a lot in common. Debbie is bright, personable, and popular. Her grades are excellent and she excels in extracurricular activities. Her cheerful facade masks strong feelings of inadequacy, which make her try harder to please the people around her.

Tom is disruptive in the classroom and trouble on the streets. He scorns extracurricular activities and is an unreliable employee of a local, fast-food establishment. His grades are low, his school attendance is poor, and he tends to blame everyone else for his problems. He is angry much of the time.

Carol, though plagued by constant depression, gets to class every day. Her schoolwork is far below her potential, but average for her class. Because she is so very shy, she finds it hard to make friends. She feels very lonely, both at school and at home. Carol is hardly noticed by adults or her peers.

Neither Debbie nor Carol has ever been referred for counseling or psychotherapy. Tom has seen the school psychologist and the school counselor, and has been assigned both a social worker and a probation officer.

One more detail. Debbie, Tom, and Carol all lack support and guidance from the adults in their lives. Debbie's father is alcoholic. Tom's father is tyrannical and abusive. Carol's parents are divorced. She lives with her mother, who is depressed much of the time.

Despite the vast differences in their outward behaviors and their chosen peer groups, this lack of adult support and guidance binds Debbie, Tom, and Carol closer to each other than to many of their chosen friends. Their personal experiences are similar, and they suffer from many of the same painful feelings. All three are at high risk for drug abuse, depression, and other disruptive personal problems.

Debbie, Tom, and Carol are also uniquely equipped to **help** each other — if educators and other concerned adults can identify them and bring them together.

The goal of the LifeGuides Program is to bring together children from alcoholic and other disrupted family environments, in the most supportive and productive way possible.

Introduction

Debbie, Tom, and Carol, the three young people described on the previous page, share a common bond. The people whom they should be able to rely on to help them through the difficult years of adolescence will not, or cannot, give them the guidance and support they need.

The LifeGuides Program is designed for people like these three children — junior and senior high school students whose school performance, relationships, or emotional development are adversely affected by the lack of caring, competent adults in their lives. Children whose families are disrupted by parental alcoholism, their parents' marital conflicts, physical or emotional abuse, or other family problems can all benefit from a LifeGuides class.

The LifeGuides Program process is very flexible. Class facilitators can refer to a number of clearly described participant needs and class objectives to help them decide which subject areas and related exercises should be emphasized in a given week. By monitoring the learning and behavioral changes participants manifest both during class and in the general school environment, facilitators can shape the curriculum to meet the changing needs of the young people involved.

Classes typically meet once a week for a single class period. Unlike more structured curricula, such as the Insight Program developed by Community Intervention, Inc., the LifeGuides Program is open-ended and may last for an entire school year. Some participants will be enrolled in the class for two or more years.

The LifeGuides materials allow facilitators to implement the class in a manner compatible with their own training and unique areas of competence. Some may take a structured, didactic approach, emphasizing the information most needed by participants at each step in the process. Others will prefer a free-flowing style in which experiential exercises, class discussion, and feedback among participants and facilitators take up most class time.

Although schools are the most common providers of the LifeGuides Program, social service agencies, court systems and medical facilities can offer it as well. The curriculum can be implemented using the following basic materials:

- **The LifeGuides Facilitator's Guide.** This provides necessary background information, program procedures, and guidelines for exercises in the three LifeGuides Phases.
- **The Participant's Guidebook for Phase I, Becoming Aware.**
- **The Participant's Guidebook for Phase II, Taking Care.**
- **The Participant's Guidebook for Phase III, Moving On.**

The participant guidebooks contain materials for some, but not all, of the exercises described in the facilitator's guide. Many of the exercises require either no printed material or materials that are found in any classroom. In addition, the facilitator's guide includes recommendations for films, audio tapes, and background reading.

The LifeGuides Program has its roots in the "Concerned Persons Groups" offered by schools and social service agencies around the country. These support groups for children of alcoholics were developed by educators and social service professionals in response to the serious unmet needs of their students and clients. The name "Concerned Persons Groups" was borrowed from the model used by chemical dependency professionals when attempting to help families intervene with and motivate an alcoholic to accept treatment. As it is used in school programs, the name is a bit of a misnomer. It implies that the class or support group is focused on changing the drinker, not the participants. As the LifeGuides materials make abundantly clear, the goals of the program focus on providing support to participants and assisting them in taking steps to improve their self-esteem, behavior in school, academic performance, personal relationships, and emotional development. Any change in the behavior of a parent or anyone outside the class is a fortuitous, though not uncommon, by-product of the process. For these reasons, the term "Concerned Persons Group" is not appropriate.

Thanks to Our Contributors

Jim Crowley, President of Community Intervention™, Inc., and a long-time advocate of the LifeGuides model, has been a driving force in the development and completion of this project. His innumerable meetings with community activists and educators around the country provided insights concerning the needs of LifeGuides facilitators and participants alike. Drawing on his experience as an educator and program consultant, Jim made many suggestions that helped keep the material as practical and useful as possible.

JoAnne Terry guided the production of the Lifeguides materials from rough draft manuscripts all the way to typesetting and printing. Her common sense, eye for detail, and organizational skills kept the project moving as fast and efficiently as was humanly – and humanely – possible.

As with all of Community Intervention's training programs and publications, the LifeGuides Program materials are based on the experiences and insights of those who work daily with young people in student assistance programming. Our contributors have

years of experience working with children from alcoholic and other disrupted family environments. The following people have reviewed the LifeGuides curriculum and made extensive revisions and contributions:

Mike Andert, Referral Coordinator, Minnetonka Senior High School, Minnetonka, Minnesota.

Kirsten Dawson, Chemical Education Coordinator, Moundsview School District, St. Paul, Minnesota.

Susan Kaplan, Chemical Awareness Program, Minneapolis Public Schools, Minnesota.

Jan Ryan, Coordinator for the Desert Sands Unified School District Chemical Awareness Network (CAN), Indio, California.

Thanks also to the following people who offered suggestions and comments on the project: Ray Bryson, Coachella Valley Unified School District, Thermal, California; Judy Zervas, Robbinsdale Public Schools, New Hope, Minnesota; Mandy Little, Irondale High School, St. Paul, Minnesota; Katia Petersen, Prevention/Intervention Specialist and Consultant, Minneapolis, Minnesota; Karen Paray, Barbara Mahoney, Pat Mersy, Mary Hoopman, and Polly Ryan, Minneapolis, Minnesota, School District; Cinda Sheldon, Hudson High School, Hudson, Ohio; Mary Goodwin, Cindy Baer, and Dianne McCartney, Roosevelt High School, Kent, Ohio; Lorraine Caswell, Tallmadge High School, Tallmadge, Ohio; Carol Ranney, Cuyahoga Falls High School, Cuyahoga Falls, Ohio; Jan Wilger, Palm Desert High School, Indio, California; and Doug Hull, Sheffield Middle School, Lorain, Ohio.

Students in Need

Although they do not often admit it, young people need a lot of help from adults to get along. They need love, protection, support, and guidance. For the most part, these needs are fulfilled by a child's immediate or extended family.

But when no one is meeting these needs, young people must fend for themselves. And fending for oneself at an early age can be overwhelming. A twelve-year-old who feels responsible for protecting his three-year-old sister from a drunken father must summon every bit of energy he can. A fourteen-year-old who has no one to protect her from the sexual advances of adults can become exhausted from the effort.

For millions of children, the lack of competent, caring adults in their lives is an everyday reality. These children are not getting what they need from their families or other adults because of alcoholism, their parents' marital conflicts, abuse, abandonment, or other problems.

Many of the methods used to help these children through the LifeGuides Program were developed specifically for children of alcoholics. The peculiar progression of alcoholism and society's reaction to this devastating disease provide children of alcoholics with remarkably similar experiences. These common experiences, however, are not UNIQUE experiences.

Professionals working with children of alcoholics began to recognize that these youths are similar to children from other types of disrupted families. They also realized that literature and services for children of alcoholics could benefit other people as well. Recognition of this commonality is reflected in the titles of two books for children of alcoholics: *Once Upon a Time — Stories from Adult Children of Alcoholic **and Other Dysfunctional Families*** (Dean, 1987) and *Guidelines for Support Groups: Adult Children of Alcoholics **and Others Who Identify*** (Woititz, 1986). (Our emphasis.)

Whether or not parental alcoholism is present, then, children from homes disrupted by marital discord, physical abuse, emotional abuse, or sexual abuse will have much in common with children from alcoholic homes. And all can benefit from the Life-Guides Program.

At Least a Third of All Students Are Affected by Serious Family Disruption

"Many Youth Affected by Family Problems," on page 10, gives some insight into the scope of the problem schools and others face. For instance:

- Thirty-eight percent of white and 75% of black children may experience the dissolution of their parents' marriage by the time they are sixteen years old.

- Fourteen percent of all children live in single-parent homes with divorced or separated parents.

- Twenty-two percent of all children under age 18 live in single-parent homes.

- About 20 - 25% of all students have alcohol problems in their homes.

Although these percentages overlap because many of these problems occur within the same families, it would seem safe to assume that at least a third of all students come from families that have, at one time or another, experienced serious problems. Examples of just how family problems interfere with education are given in "Family Conflict and School Problems," page 14.

Many Youth Affected by Family Problems

Divorce and Separation

In 1987, Congress held a special hearing on divorce in America. The resulting publication, *Divorce: The Impact on Children and Families,* provided the following statistics on the number of children affected by divorce and separation:

- Thirty-eight percent of white children born to married mothers may experience the dissolution of their parents' marriage by the time they are 16 years old.
- Seventy-five percent of black children born to married mothers will have the same experience.

Single-Parent Homes

The same Congressional report revealed that:

- Twenty-two percent of all children under the age of 18 live in single-parent homes.
- Fourteen percent of children under the age of 18 live in single-parent homes with parents who were separated or divorced.

Youth With Alcoholic Parents

According to a 1987 Gallup survey, about one-fourth of all American homes have been affected by alcohol-related family problems. When people were asked, "Has drinking ever been a cause of trouble in your family?", 24% of those interviewed answered "yes." This is twice the 1974 level and is the highest reported level of problem drink-

ing since Gallup started asking the question in 1950.

Student assistance programs find that almost half of the troubled students they deal with are affected by parental alcoholism.

The experience of the Minneapolis, Minnesota, Public Schools is typical of the student assistance program evaluations reviewed in the development of the LifeGuides curriculum. In the 1983–1984 school year, the Minneapolis program served 1,919 students (*One Step Ahead,* page 119). The reasons for referral were divided into four general categories related to drug use:

- Problems related to the student's own use of chemicals, 54%.
- Problems related to someone else's use of chemicals, 43%.
- Problems related to own and others use, 9% (included in each of the two preceding categories).
- Problems not related to drug use, 13%.

Most student assistance programs can expect to identify a similar rate of problems related to another's use of chemicals.

A number of studies indicate that a very large proportion of the youths in the juvenile justice system have parents with drinking problems.

A 1986 review of intake information from a residential treatment

facility for adjudicated male offenders indicated that alcoholism was by far the most frequently reported problem facing the families of these boys (O'Gorman and Ross). More than 55% of those in placement came from homes where there was an alcoholic parent or other adult. They also found that 18% of the families had been investigated by child protection services for child abuse or neglect.

Another study focused on a statewide population of adolescents who had been placed in state-subsidized residential facilities for pre-delinquent and disturbed children (Lund and Landesnan-Dwyer, 1979). Of the total population of clients, 29.1% had lived with a parent who was considered to be alcoholic.

One-fifth of high school students have a family member who has received drug counseling or treatment.

In a survey of 11,000 students in Minnesota (Benson et al., 1983), 23% of all twelfth graders indicated that some member of their family had a problem with alcohol or other drugs at the time of the survey and 20% indicated that a family member had had professional counseling or treatment for chemical abuse or dependency. This finding is similar to that reported by Woodson (1976), who found that 16% to 23% of a sample of college students had an alcoholic parent.

Alcoholism And Domestic Abuse...
What's The Connection?

The relationship between domestic abuse and alcoholism is complex. In a thorough and critical review of the alcohol/family violence literature, two writers examined the ideology, research methodology, and conclusions drawn by various researchers (Hamilton and Collins, 1981). They discounted, for various reasons, many studies that purported to show a clear connection between high rates of alcohol abuse and domestic violence. Even so, the authors came to the following tentative conclusions:

■ **Drinking often precedes acts of family violence.** Estimates of the percentage of family violence incidents in which alcohol use was present prior to or during the event ranged from 6% to 67%. This percentage tended to be lower in cases of child abuse than in wife beating. A speculative estimate of the percentage of child abuse incidents where alcohol use was present would be less than 20%. For wife beating alone, an analogous estimate would be between 25% and 50%.

■ **Both spouse abusers and child abusers are more likely to abuse alcohol than the general population.** Estimates of the percentage of problem drinkers involved in family violence have ranged from 0% to 93%. Alcoholism was more characteristic of wife abusers than of child abusers.

■ **The highest rates of abuse are found in "moderate-to-heavy" drinkers** rather than "heaviest" drinkers; the lowest rates are found among those who drink the least.

The rate of alcoholism will vary among the populations of abusers being served and will often be quite high. For example, a methodologically sound study of child abusers in a military population found that alcoholism or alcohol abuse was a factor in 68% of the families (Behling, 1979).

The rate of child abuse among particular groups of alcoholics will also vary. Certain treatment centers, because of their referral sources or admissions criteria, may end up with high rates of child abuse among their alcoholic clients.

The Dynamics of Alcohol in Domestic Violence

Few people would deny that there is a relationship between alcohol abuse, domestic violence, and child abuse, but just how alcohol fits into the picture is a matter of some debate. Three of the most frequently cited patterns are:

■ Alcoholism as a stress-inducer. Since long-term difficulties with alcohol tend to create problems in relationships and finances, the alcoholic or spouse may feel pent-up frustration and rage, which is then directed at another family member. Release from stress may sometimes occur under the influence of alcohol and sometimes not.

■ Alcohol as a disinhibitor. Alcohol is presumed to remove inhibitions against aggression, violence, and sexual abuse.

■ Alcohol as an excuse. Consciously or unconsciously, the alcohol user expects that, among his friends, family, ethnic group, and in American society as a whole, alcohol intoxication will excuse his behavior or at least mitigate his guilt. This is where professionals in both alcoholism and domestic abuse treatment could have a direct and immediate impact. Alcoholism, blackouts, and so forth should not be accepted as valid excuses for repeated abusive behavior.

In any given case, alcohol use could act in all three ways — as a stress factor, a disinhibitor, and an excuse. An alcoholic whose problems with the drug are creating stress may feel more comfortable expressing anger when drinking. He may then decide, consciously or unconsciously, to start drinking when he needs to release pent-up frustrations. He may also say, truthfully or falsely, that he blacks out when he drinks and thus has no memory of his actions. Let the helping professional be aware.

What Happens in Alcoholic and Other Disrupted Family Environments

Appendix A lists a number of different books on parental alcoholism, divorce, loss, personal safety, suicide, and other issues relevant to LifeGuides participants. This additional background reading will help prospective LifeGuides facilitators develop a deeper understanding of the experiences of participants.

Whenever a youth's family is in turmoil, there is a greater likelihood that he or she will experience some or all of the following: emotional neglect; inconsistent and unpredictable behavior by a parent; family conflict; non-fulfillment of parental responsibilities; unstable living conditions; loss of a parent due to separation, divorce, or abandonment; and negative messages from peers and adults outside the family.

Emotional Neglect

In a study of 50 children of alcoholics (Booz-Allen and Hamilton, 1974), emotional neglect and family conflict were the most frequently cited problems. Emotional neglect was usually associated with the "quiet drunk" who sits by him- or herself, stares at the television, and drinks beer or cocktails. Emotional neglect of the children is also probably the most common complaint in families where parents are depressed or distracted because of marital problems.

Inconsistent and Unpredictable Behavior by a Parent

The vast majority of youths in support groups for children of alcoholics report that their parents are inconsistent and unpredictable. The parents might be warm and friendly one minute, vicious and attacking the next. They might promise to attend a school event and then not show up. One night they might be helpful and concerned about homework, then the next night, totally disregard their children's need for help. Parents distracted by their own personal problems, such as depression or marital conflicts, also tend to be unreliable.

Family Conflict

Ask children from disrupted family environments what bothers them most about their home lives and the most likely response will be their parents' fighting. Children frequently report being awakened by the sound of their parents' arguments. This is extremely painful to them. They become so upset that they cannot study, sleep, or concentrate when in school. Physical violence becomes even more likely when a family is troubled by alcoholism.

Non-fulfillment of Parental Responsibilities

In many alcoholic homes, not only can the alcoholic not carry out parental responsibilities, but neither can the overburdened, distraught, and exhausted spouse. The children often go to extraordinary lengths to compensate for their parents' shortcomings.

Some parents, in addition to failing to fulfill their parental duties, actively pressure their children to undertake adult responsibilities. They burden their children by telling them the details of their sex lives or their spouse's extramarital affairs. They may complain about financial problems and look to their children for advice.

Unstable Living Conditions

Many troubled families move around a lot. This may be related to poverty and the need to find work, alcoholism, mental illness, and many other issues. The family may hope that a change in geography will change their fortunes. The children may be left with relatives while the parents are out on a binge, in jail, or in treatment for chemical dependency or mental illness.

Some families with a long history of physical or emotional abuse have a pattern of leaving a community whenever local child protection services start investigating them.

Loss of a Parent Due to Separation, Divorce, or Abandonment

When parents are in conflict, separation, divorce, or abandonment are always possibilities. Separation and divorce are more frequent in alcoholic families than in the general population. In addition, alcoholism can lead to the death of a parent either from the disease itself or from related accidents or illness.

Frequently, loss of a parent is the most obvious problem presented by children from disrupted family environments. They are devastated because a parent has left them. Except in cases of sudden death, there is usually a period of family disruption related to this loss that has had a powerful, negative impact on the child. Identifying the nature and effects of this period of disruption can be an important function of the LifeGuides Program. Participants are usually more willing to focus on the loss than on the issues leading up to that loss.

Negative Messages From Peers and Adults Outside of the Family

The attitudes of both young people and adults in our society serve to intensify the suffering of children from disrupted family environments. Children of alcoholics, in particular, may be subject to name calling, rejection by peers, ridicule, and being chased, especially when they are in elementary school.

Adults contribute to the pain by inflicting all their biases about alcoholism on the children. They may assume that all children of alcoholics are raised in an immoral environment. They may consider a family with an alcoholic parent "lower class" or "shiftless."

Ministers may call alcoholism a sin, while doctors frequently do not call it anything at all. They diagnose and focus only on the symptoms of alcoholism, not the disease itself.

Children of divorce often face similar prejudices. Some adults don't want their children associating with children from "broken homes," causing children of divorce to lose their friends.

Relatives will often ignore these problems so vigorously that it becomes clear to the children from disrupted families that they have something to be deeply ashamed of. Schools, for the most part, hold strictly to a "code of silence": they either do not know or will not discuss the prevalence and the impact of family problems on the students in their schools.

The Immediate Effects of Alcoholism and Other Family Problems on the Children

Children from drug-abusing or other high-stress families often tend to change themselves to fit a dysfunctional system in which their own needs are never met. Instead of becoming more confident, more aware of their feelings, and more able to express those feelings, they come to believe that they don't count, that they are not worthwhile. They learn to close themselves off from all emotions in order to fend off their feelings of helplessness, pain, confusion, and guilt. They tend to rely on repetitive behavior formulas instead of experimenting with a range of responses.

Among the most poignant findings of researchers is that many children of alcoholics fear they are losing their minds:

"Nothing they saw or heard made sense. Children do not understand how there could be a bloody rampage in the house at night and the next morning no one acts like anything has happened; how the mother can allow the father to drink up the family budget when the children have holes in their shoes and no warm clothes; how the parents and society insist that children love and respect their parent(s) when the parent is never lovable and frequently disgusting. The environment is so inconsistent, irrational and unresponsive that some children begin to conclude they are the crazy ones. It is not just the inconsistency and abusive behavior of the alcoholic that creates this feeling; it is also the apparent acceptance of such behavior by the non-alcoholic parent." (Booz-Allen and Hamilton, op.cit.)

One of the main goals of the LifeGuides Program is to help participants affirm their own perceptions of reality and to trust their feelings.

Effects on School Behavior

Research has shown that family problems have a direct and significant effect on school performance. For example:

- A study on children of divorce revealed that ongoing parental conflict was clearly associated with lower grades, less social competence with peers, more behavioral problems, and self-perceptions by the children that they were less intelligent and less popular than their classmates (Brody, 1987).

- Of 41 youth who had an absenteeism rate of at least 20% and who also manifested signs of fear and anxiety:
  - Forty-three percent indicated that their parents had persistent relationship difficulties.
  - Half reported that they felt better when they were away from home.
  - Forty-three percent indicated that they felt sad most of the time (Ficula et al., 1983).

- In a study of 117 guidance counselors (Burke and Wolpin, 1985), "Family difficulties were among the top two problems they considered threatening to public education."

- Younes and Web (1976) found that "familial and social disruption exert a significant negative effect on children's school performance."

- "Broken homes and absent fathers" have been related to poor school achievement (Gwinn, 1976).

- A review of the literature lead one author to conclude that children of alcoholics tend to be academic underachievers (Fialkov, 1985). Two other researchers report that children of alcoholics often manifest low self-esteem, depression, and school problems (Clair and Genest, 1984).

Family Conflict And School Problems: Case Examples

These are examples of the effects of family problems on the school-related behavior of children. They are all real-life cases, offered by student assistance counselors.

Laura, twelve years old

When Laura insisted on leaving class many times each day to call home, the frustrated teacher called an early-intervention counselor. As it turned out, the girl was worried about her infant brother; if her mother was still passed out by mid-morning, the baby would be alone, crying and hungry. The frequent phone calls were attempts to wake her mother and allay her own fears that her mother might be dead.

Valerie, fifteen years old

Although Valerie's mother and her mother's boyfriend were addicts, Valerie was able to cope with the help of a support group as long as her mother was not using. She had been in the group at school for three years and was doing well. She attended group faithfully, was in a dance troupe, was passing all her subjects, and had a job. When her mother started using again, however, things deteriorated rapidly. Her mother sold the furniture and telephone to buy drugs. Valerie started fighting more with her mother and was finally kicked out of the house. She stopped coming to school because she was so exhausted, staying at the houses of friends and acquaintances. She felt constant stress because of her vulnerability to sexual assault at other people's houses. Her grades plummeted and she dropped out of school.

Juan, sixteen years old

Juan's father is a binge drinker. He gets drunk, goes straight, gets drunk, and then goes straight again. When his father is drinking, Juan withdraws into a fantasy world. At school, he daydreams, drifts away, and does not attend to his school work. He doesn't talk about the real problems his father's drinking causes, but makes up excuses as to why he skipped school, came late, or didn't do his homework. He once told a story about a band of robbers who came into his house and whom he singlehandedly drove off the premises.

Mark, fourteen years old

Mark's father was abusing him sexually. He was not doing well in school, but he was passing. He eventually was removed from his home and put in foster care. Paradoxically, it was when he was removed from his home that he began to have even more trouble in school. Through a school-based support group for students from disrupted families, he was able to look at how his feelings of loneliness and abandonment were affecting his school work. Simply by being with young people who had also been placed in foster care, he did not feel so isolated and so depressed.

Similar Symptoms for Different Problems

Those who work with troubled youth find that, despite a wide variation in the kinds of problems young people are struggling with, they manifest many of the same symptoms and behaviors. Published literature and non-published training materials on adolescent drug abuse, suicide, child abuse, and parental alcoholism all cite a core group of behaviors most of which can be manifested both at home and in the school environment. They include:

- Poor grades, truancy.
- Avoidance techniques, such as always sitting in the back of the class, never answering questions, avoiding eye contact with the teacher.
- Withdrawal from others; increased isolation and loneliness, problems with peer relationships.
- Sudden change in behavior or performance: compliant and passive one day, aggressive and demanding the next; changing from being cooperative to being argumentative and given to temper tantrums and verbal abuse.
- A new or increased unwillingness to assume responsibilities.
- A general defensiveness about behavior, attitudes, opinions, mistakes, or friendships.
- Increased problems with discipline, such as violations of curfew, use of foul language, and being disrespectful to parents, siblings, and teachers.
- Mood swings: elated, expansive, friendly, gregarious one moment; depressed, withdrawn, pessimistic, and reticent the next.
- Inability to sit still, easily agitated, low frustration tolerance.
- Poor concentration, preoccupation.
- Extreme fatigue, lethargy.
- Boredom, apathy, disinterested in everything.
- Physical complaints — stomachaches, backaches, headaches, etc.
- Sleep problems: insomnia or excessive sleepiness; sleeping in class.

Although normal adolescents show many of the behaviors, children with several concurrent and more extreme manifestations of these behaviors are likely to be facing some personal crisis in their lives.

The Needs of LifeGuides Program Participants

A review of the experiences of children from disrupted family environments will point to many immediate and long-term needs. These needs can be broken down into two categories: **basic needs** that go beyond the LifeGuides Program, and which must be met in the broader community as well as in class; and the **need for guidance and support from skilled professionals**, which facilitators have more control over and which can be met to a great extent through the LifeGuides Program.

Basic Needs

Basic needs pertain to the **general context** in which a LifeGuides class takes place. Facilitators have only partial influence over these factors, but they can, and must, monitor how well participants are doing in each area. Facilitators can also help participants become aware of which of their basic needs are not being met and how they might go about meeting those needs. These basic needs include:

- **Protection** from physical, emotional, or sexual abuse, as well as from danger due to accidents or illness.
- **Rest and relief** from the tension of living with parents who may be fighting, frightening them, or giving them too many responsibilities. Children need breathing space that allows them time for reflection and for having fun.
- **Complementary parenting** when parents are not fulfilling their duties to their children. Children need the love, support, care, affection, comfort, nurturing, and trust associated with parenting.
- **Healthy relationships.** Children need to experience healthy relationships at an early age to be able to love, trust, express affection, and survive pain. They need to experience a positive interaction with an adult of the same sex as an absent or impaired parent. They also need healthy relationships with their peers.
- **Respect** from their family, friends, and community. Children need respect for their rights, feelings, opinions, and individuality.
- **A positive peer and community environment**. Young people need and deserve a caring community, where they do not have to feel shame because of a parent's impairment.
- **The right to seek help**. Obviously, a child who is being physically or sexually abused has the right to seek help from community agencies. Children with

very serious but less obvious problems, such as living with emotional abuse, may not have services readily available to them. Some schools will not allow children into support groups unless they first obtain parental permission. Although the facilitators of the LifeGuides Program cannot circumvent local statutes or school policies, children who are being abused need strong advocates who can help them get the help they are entitled to.

Need for Guidance and Support from Skilled Professionals

The knowledgeable guidance and support provided by skilled professionals is not the same as the complementary parenting described previously. Any warm, caring, nurturing person who is concerned about a youth can provide complementary parenting whether or not that person is aware of the youth's background. Children from disrupted family environments also need guidance and support from professionals who are both aware of their problems and willing to take some specific steps to help alleviate those problems.

During their daily, weekly, or other ongoing work with young people, LifeGuides facilitators, as well as other educators and social service professionals, can provide guidance and support in the following ways:

- **Let them know that they are not alone.** They need to know that others share their experiences and understand their feelings.

- **Validate their perceptions and interpretations of their experiences.** They need help in sorting out their confusion. Someone must explain to these children that they are not crazy, even though they might feel as if they are. They need to be told that they are reacting to adults who downplay or ignore the severity of their own problems, deny that certain events ever took place, and behave inconsistently.

- **Help them gain some perspective on how their parents' drug use or other behaviors have affected them.** It has often been said that children from alcoholic families fall into predictable, unhealthy patterns of behavior. For example, some become overly responsible to compensate for the irresponsibility of a parent, while others act out constantly to get attention from an otherwise inattentive parent. The LifeGuides Program classes can help participants identify and consider ways of changing their patterns of behavior.

- **Absolve them of blame.** Participants often need to be convinced that their mother's or father's drinking is not their fault and that they can't cause, control, or cure it. Some must be reminded again and again that they are not at fault for the divorce, marital problems, neglect, and physical or sexual abuse in their families.

- **Help them separate the parent from the problem behavior.** Alcoholics may be very caring, concerned people when they are not drinking. A depressed, neglectful father may be capable of very nurturing behavior when his depression passes. Participants need to hear that a parent's drunkenness or other behaviors are not signs that their parent does not love them and that, furthermore, parents may be worthy of love despite some of their disruptive behaviors.

- **Offer them hope.** Some participants must be told that alcoholism is a disease from which their parents can recover. Others will need to know that the initial turmoil of divorce will eventually reach a more stable and tolerable resolution.

- **Urge them to take care of themselves.** Participants need to be encouraged to do positive things for themselves. They also need help to stop taking responsibility for duties rightfully belonging to others.

- **Provide them with a safe outlet for dealing with their anger.** Many participants will be very angry at their parents. This anger tends to be expressed in destructive and inappropriate ways unless children are given a safe outlet for it.

- **Explain their risks related to chemical dependency.** Children of alcoholics need to know that they are at high risk of becoming chemically dependent or for marrying a chemically dependent person. Those who are about to leave home tend to believe that their troubles will soon be over. They must learn that they are more likely to encounter certain problems than are children raised in families in which alcoholism was not an issue. Facilitators should let all participants know that family problems can make them vulnerable to drug abuse and unhealthy relationships.

- **Build their self-esteem.** All concerned adults should try to raise the self-esteem of these children in any way possible. For many, simply having an adult listen closely to them can boost their self-esteem.

- **Help them cope with their daily lives.** Because of the many stresses on LifeGuides participants, even minor tasks, such as getting to school on time, may be very difficult. Educators and social service professionals should not pity participants for their problems or allow them to perform below their potential. They should, however, be aware that participants may need some extra assistance in order to accomplish routine or simple tasks. This information is summarized in the "Checklist of Participants' Needs" on page 49, in the LifeGuides Interview section. Regular review of this checklist throughout the LifeGuides process will help facilitators decide which needs should be addressed and what methods should be emphasized for each participant as well as the class as a whole.

Opportunities to Help, Not Obligations to Fulfill

The many needs of LifeGuides participants cannot be met in a single session, a school quarter, or an entire year of LifeGuides classes. Nor is it the responsibility of LifeGuides facilitators to meet all these needs. Rather, they should be aware of participants' needs and look for opportunities to help meet them. Facilitators should follow the maxims of the self-help groups: take it "one day at a time," and "let go" when they have done all they can within the context of their role as facilitators.

Don't wait for a program to be in place before offering this type of assistance to young people. The needs described here can be met in a variety of ways by any adult who comes into contact with youths from disrupted families. If students speak of parental alcoholism, divorce, or family conflicts, adults can explain to them that they are not alone, that many other children suffer from the same problem. Adults can also help young people sort out their perceptions, thoughts, and feelings so they can better decide what is real in regard to family issues.

Facilitators and others providing support should remember that meeting these needs does not depend on changing the parents in any way. In fact, children **must not wait** for their parents to change before starting to improve their own lives.

These Needs Serve as the Major Criteria for Admission to the LifeGuides Class

No diagnosis is necessary or even appropriate when accepting a youth for the LifeGuides Program. Although signs of family disruption will be clear in many cases, the exact nature and degree of that disruption may not be known to the facilitators. Rather than gathering more data about the family — which may not be appropriate for a school-based program — facilitators should ask themselves, "Would this youth benefit from a class that helps to meet these needs?" If the needs of a youth are similar to those described above, the youth should be offered a chance to participate. Whether the youth's family experiences are identical to those of other participants does not matter as much as how the youth has been affected by those problems.

Self-help Groups Can Fill Some of These Needs, Some of the Time

Many of these needs are addressed in Al-Anon, Alateen, Emotions Anonymous, or ACOA (Adult Children of Alcoholics) groups. These self-help groups, however, are only a partial answer and only reach a small minority of children of alcoholics. The LifeGuides Program differs from Al-Anon in several ways:

- The LifeGuides Program provides trained facilitators. These people are not only aware of the problems related to parental alcoholism, but also of the need for intervention for other problems when necessary.

- The facilitators are professionals in the context within which the LifeGuides Program takes place. For instance, classes held in schools are facilitated by educators who are familiar with the problems of the school environment and who can make the issues discussed in the LifeGuides Program more immediately relevant to the educational setting.

- There is much more emphasis on referral to outside resources when necessary.

Treatment for the Parents is Not Sufficient

Helping the parents does not automatically mean the children will get help. Treatment of an alcoholic, for instance, does not solve the problems of children of alcoholics. Children are constantly learning family rules and guidelines for survival and growth. When the drinking in an alcoholic home stops, the children cannot go back to "normal" ways of operating, because they do not know what "normal" is. They haven't learned the rules for "normal" behavior.

A school counselor who contributed to this curriculum noted that most of the students he saw in his school support group for the children of alcoholics did not benefit greatly from their parents' chemical dependency treatment. "Treating the parents' alcoholism certainly takes care of the more obvious problems, such as the parent lying down drunk on the living room floor," he said, "but it often does not have a strong impact on the child's feelings. I remember one student I talked with, the daughter of an alcoholic. The father went for treatment, but the daughter continued to have the same feelings once her father was sober as she did when he was drinking.

She was still angry about some of the things he had done. Her self-esteem was still low because of a long history of emotional neglect. The changes that happened for the father didn't happen for her."

Cork (1969) compared conditions for children whose parents had stopped drinking to those whose parents were still drinking. She found that "there was surprisingly little difference for the children from the homes where the drinking had stopped when compared to the homes where drinking was still going on. There is still a great deal of tension in the homes and a lot of depression. In only one family did things change radically because the father had stopped drinking."

Structure of the LifeGuides Program

Assisting children from disrupted family environments is obviously a process, rather than an event. More importantly, though, it is a cyclical process. Participants will comprehend information given them during the early sessions of the LifeGuides Program differently when it is repeated later in the process. Their patterns of perceiving and interacting with the world, which they learned from their families, are deeply entrenched. Information provided to a young person who is just starting to deal with these issues will have a limited — although important — impact; as the youth learns more about how families are affected when a parent becomes impaired, the same basic information will be seen from a new perspective. Therefore, while lessons must not be tediously repetitive, information must be brought up several times.

The LifeGuides Program consists of three phases, each touching on key issues in a different way.

- **Phase I: Becoming Aware**
- **Phase II: Taking Care**
- **Phase III: Moving On**

Below is a brief synopsis of each of the three phases, described by "subject areas" rather than classroom sessions. As will be explained in "Planning a LifeGuides Class," page 61, facilitators and program planners can choose which subject areas to emphasize within each phase. In addition, there are several exercises within each subject area to choose from.

Many of the content areas described below are found in a variety of primary and secondary prevention programs. The material prepared for the Life-Guides Program, however, has been tailored to meet the needs of children from alcoholic and other disrupted family environments. Information offered in this guide will help the facilitators present material and direct the process for maximum effectiveness with LifeGuides participants.

Subject Areas for Phase I: Becoming Aware

Phase I, Becoming Aware emphasizes the knowledge participants need to comprehend the problems they face. After several sessions spent introducing new participants to the process and to each other, participants begin learning specific information about families. The effects of parental impairment, especially impairment due to alcoholism, are described, and participants' risks for problems with drugs and in relationships are considered. In Phase I, much more than in Phases II and III, **information** about families and the problems that affect them is intended to be a major agent of change for participants. The basic subject areas covered in Phase I are:

- **Start-up at the Beginning of the Year.** Participants review summer vacation, get acquainted with new and experienced participants, and take a look at where they stand emotionally and socially.

- **Personal Safety.** Facilitators and participants review objective and subjective data regarding personal safety at home, on the streets, and in school.

- **Communication and Listening Skills.** Barriers to clear communication are reviewed, and techniques for clear, useful feedback are described.

- **What's a "Normal Family?"** Participants learn that "normal families" are not perfect, but there are still some basic needs that must be met.

- **Drug and Alcohol Use: What's OK? What's Not?** The first stages of chemical use — experimentation and social use — are described. Participants try to distinguish between acceptable and unacceptable adult alcohol use.

- **Alcoholism and Drug Dependence: When Use Goes Out of Control.** The third and fourth stages in the process of addiction are described: harmful involvement and chemical dependency. The concept of alcoholism as a disease is presented and the implications of that concept are considered.

- **Shock Waves: How Alcoholism Affects the Family.** Participants learn how family roles change as parental alcoholism progresses and how members start to use denial to cope. The parallels between the effects of parental alcoholism and other impairments are considered.

- **Something to Think About: Participants' Risks for Future Problems.** Research about the effects of parental alcoholism on children is presented in a simple, straightforward manner. Participants' increased risk for future problems in relationships, regardless of the presence of drug problems, is also presented.

Subject Areas for Phase II: Taking Care

Taking Care focuses on two areas: first, helping participants consider honestly and courageously how their family problems affect their behavior, feelings, and self-concepts; and second, teaching them coping techniques to help them handle their feelings and problems on a daily basis. In this phase, then, facilitators are not necessarily focused on long-term changes in participants' lives. Some participants will be under such pressure that avoiding depression will be sufficient success for the week. In Phase II, a youth may learn about the concept of detachment, but the emphasis on practicing detachment will be left to Phase III, Moving On. The basic subject areas covered in Phase II are:

- **Denial: Dance of Deception.** The many textures of denial—in quality and degree—are explored.

- **Enabling: The Helping That Hurts.** Participants learn the concept of enabling and are given many examples to consider. They also learn that enabling in order to cope with stress at home or in school is very acceptable and often necessary.

- **Feelings: Where They Come From, Where They Take Us.** Facilitators describe the language of feelings and help participants get in touch with how they currently feel about their lives. The concept of shame is introduced and explored.

- **Anger and Conflicting Feelings.** Facilitators describe the many direct and indirect ways that anger is expressed. Participants learn that it is natural to have conflicting feelings about parents, families, school, and other issues.

- **Self-esteem: Liking Ourselves.** Building self-esteem is a major goal of all the LifeGuides classes. The sessions devoted specifically to this issue focus on helping participants get in touch with how they feel about themselves, including what they consider to be their strongest and weakest abilities and attributes.

- **Coping with Daily Challenges.** The class considers all the details of daily life that can overwhelm vulnerable youth. Suggestions for coping with daily challenges and reducing stress are presented.

Subject Areas for Phase III: Moving On

Moving On contains exercises similar to those found in the many "life skills" prevention curricula currently available. The information and exercises presented here, however, are tailored to meet the needs of children from alcoholic and other disrupted family environments. The basic subject areas covered in Phase III are:

- **Family Roles: Rigid and Restricting or Guidelines for Growth?** Facilitators describe the family roles that children from alcoholic and other disrupted family environments tend to fall into.

- **Codependency and Codependent Behaviors: Too Close for Comfort?** Codependent behaviors are described. Participants reflect upon whether or not their own behaviors indicate codependency.

- **Detachment: Letting Go to Catch On.** The concept of detachment is described, and some techniques for achieving detachment are taught. The class discusses how to let go of resentments, anger, and regret. Forgiveness is also discussed.

- **Interpersonal Skills: Finding Fulfillment in Relationships.** Participants assess their current relationships, learn how to make new relationships, and consider the pitfalls and benefits of their intimate relationships.

- **Assertiveness Skills: Standing Up for Yourself.** The differences between non-assertive, assertive, and aggressive behaviors are described. Facilitators help participants consider how their behaviors may be related to the behaviors modeled by their parents. Helpful ways of dealing with conflict are presented.

• **Taking Care of Business: Problem-solving, Decision-making and Goal-setting.** Facilitators explain how goal-setting, decision-making, and time-management skills can make the lives of participants more fulfilling.

• **Taking Care of Ourselves, Having Fun.** Participants review their daily lives and see if they are doing the things they need to do to enjoy themselves and renew their spirits.

The LifeGuides Interview and Opening Exercises

There are two other important components to the LifeGuides Program, the LifeGuides Interview and the Opening Exercises.

LifeGuides Interview. It is through the LifeGuides Interview, a one-to-one interview with a facilitator, that young people first learn in detail what the program is about. As these children listen to descriptions of the issues that will be discussed in class and answer the facilitator's inquiries as to how those issues apply to their lives, "the lights may go on" and they may start the process of change. Simply by learning that the facilitator is aware of the problems they face, prospective participants recognize that they are not alone.

Opening Exercises: Check-ins and Warm-ups. The check-ins and warm-ups are more than ways to loosen a class up before the "real work" begins. In the LifeGuides process, opening exercises are chosen carefully to make sure that the key issues of children from alcoholic and other dysfunctional families are reviewed regularly.

Rationale for Intervention

There are at least four compelling arguments in favor of schools becoming involved in early intervention with children from disrupted family environments:

- The direct effects of family problems on children's personal and educational growth and development.
- The relationship between family problems and student drug abuse.
- The special opportunities schools have to help.
- The relationship between adult alcoholism and child abuse.

Personal and Educational Growth and Development

The problems of LifeGuides participants tend to wax and wane, but are disruptive nonetheless. A bright student may do well half the time, but have difficulty concentrating and be too depressed to study when his parents are in a period of constant fighting. He may do A-level work when things are going well and C-level work when things are bad. The fact that he gets an average grade of B may lead educators to mistakenly think this person is not too strongly affected by family disruption.

Even those whose academic achievement has not been noticeably affected may encounter serious problems in emotional, personal, and social development. These children merit assistance too. It is the rare school that would maintain it was interested only in the academic achievement of its students.

"Effects on School Behavior," on page 13 in the "LifeGuides Overview" section, offers examples of the impact of family problems on school performance.

Sometimes school staff, administrators, or people in the community need further evidence of the relevance of family problems to school behavior. Case examples of local youths whose school work was affected by family problems will usually have a strong impact on skeptics.

The Relationship Between Family Problems and Student Drug Abuse

There is an especially close relationship between parental alcoholism and student drug abuse (See "The Children of Alcoholics Face a High Risk of Having Drug Problems," page 116). Conversely, heavy drug users are more likely than most students to be from troubled homes. Any school or agency that works with drug users, then, will inevitably identify children from troubled homes.

Few people today question that schools should be involved in prevention and intervention for drug and alcohol use. Certainly, schools alone cannot solve the drug problem, but they must be involved if any progress at all is to be made. On this basis alone, schools and any other system or agency that addresses the drug use of youths will inevitably be faced with the issue of family problems and their effects on children.

Special Opportunities to Help

There is a difference between the schools' responsibilities and the schools' opportunities to help. For example, some people may question whether it is the schools' responsibility to identify drug users, chemically dependent youth, and children of alcoholics who are showing no behavioral problems in school. Few would dispute, however, that the schools have a rare opportunity, unmatched by any other agency or institution in the community, to identify these youths.

For many youths, the school environment is the only place — EVER — in which concerned adults will actively seek to address any issue that may be interfering with their growth and development. After high school, employers, the Armed Services, and college personnel will be less focused on them as persons and more focused on them as performers. It is in the elementary and secondary schools where they are most likely to get help for what may be the most important issue in their lives.

Preventing the Need for Recovery

Most material written about the children of alcoholics focuses on services for ADULT children. In this context, the term "recovery" is used rather than "prevention." While the LifeGuides Program is also concerned with recovery to some extent, its main concern is prevention.

Adult children of alcoholics frequently have much to regret: they regret the pain they endured, the shame they felt, the childhood they let slip by while taking care of or worrying about family problems. There are thousands of adults in AL-Anon, Alcoholics Anonymous, and ACOA (Adult Children of Alcoholics) groups getting help for problems related to parental alcoholism. For many of them, it wasn't until their first, second, or third divorce; their deep depressions; their incessant career problems; or their lifelong problem of finding ways to simply enjoy themselves that they came to the conclusion that they needed help. And then it may have taken several more months or years for them to find the courage to actually get that help.

In the LifeGuides Program, youths are given an opportunity to prevent much of this pattern. They learn to take care of themselves and to actively break free of bonds which keep them away from their peers and enjoyable activities. They are given some of the nurturing not available at home. They are shown how to relax so they don't burn out from a state of constant tension.

The Program, then, is part prevention, part early intervention, and part recovery. Participants are **recovering** from the slings and arrows of the outrageous fortune they have already endured. The Program helps **intervene** in a current problem and focuses on stopping behaviors that, if continued, could turn into major, lifelong issues. The LifeGuides program may **prevent** many of the typical stresses of participants.

The Relationship Between Adult Alcoholism and Child Abuse

"Alcoholism and Domestic Abuse...What's the Connection," on page 11, addresses the complex relationship between these two issues. Although few would deny the relationship, how and when the use of alcohol leads to abuse is still debated. In any case, LifeGuides facilitators will encounter participants who experience the combined problems of alcoholism and abuse in their families.

Benefits of the Class Setting

The LifeGuides Program is presented as a **class** for young people who need the information and guidance it offers. The class setting offers several benefits over a one-to-one guidance-counseling setting, including:

• **Breaking the isolation of participants**. Obviously, people are not alone with their problems when they meet, talk to, and work with others with similar problems. The examples offered by participants add to and clarify material offered by the facilitators. Each participant's questions and the reactions to those questions by other participants contribute to the entire group learning experience.

• **An appropriate emphasis on information**. The class setting reminds participants that there is information to be learned. Children from disrupted family environments have a lot to **learn** about families and how certain family problems can affect them. Being taught this vital information can help them understand and predict their experiences and feelings, which may otherwise seem haphazard and dangerously unstable.

• **Protection**. Class members can offer each other ideas on how to stay safe in their homes and on the streets. Some of them will be "street-wise." They can help each other out and share experiences.

• **Healthy relationships**. The relationships developed in the class setting can serve as guidelines for developing healthy relationships outside of the class.

• **Respect**. Not only do participants receive respect from one or two facilitators, they also get respect from their peers, as well. This can be a new and affirming experience for them.

• **A positive peer and community environment**. Although the class is just one period of one day in the week, participants can also gather outside of the classroom for recreation or volunteer activities. This helps them create their own safe, positive peer and community environment.

• **Validation of their own experiences**. Class feedback can help participants do a reality check and gain perspective on how their parents' behaviors have affected them. By seeing how other participants have been affected by family situations, participants are better able to understand their own situations.

- **Absolution of blame**. It is very difficult to let go of guilt. Participants must hear often and from many different sources that they are not the cause of their parents' alcoholism or other family problems.

LifeGuides Policies and Procedures

Policies and procedures should reflect the role that schools have, will, and MUST play in early intervention. Schools do not exist in a vacuum. Educators who are interested in the intellectual, emotional, social, and moral development of students will not ignore influences outside the school that affect that development.

The LifeGuides Program does not require that a special portion of the school's policies be devoted to the specific concerns of children from alcoholic and other disrupted family environments. It is highly likely that many aspects of current school policies already legitimize school-based intervention for family problems in the following ways:

Policies that Recognize the Connection Between Family Problems and School Behavior

Many schools have statements to the effect that "when personal, financial, social, or family problems are interfering with a student's performance or behavior, the school will offer pre-assessment services, counseling, or referral to resources in the community."

Policies that Acknowledge the School's Role in Drug Abuse Prevention

Any school that has a firm statement on its role in prevention or intervention for drug use can simply enumerate the issues that put a person at risk for drug use, including parental alcoholism and other family problems. Education, guidance, and support services on these issues, then, can be viewed as fitting in well with drug abuse prevention efforts.

Policies on Student Self-esteem and Depression

Policy-mandated prevention programs that recognize the roles low self-esteem and depression play in school problems or in the development of drug problems also reinforce the position that the Life-Guides Program is compatible with the school's mission.

Policies on the School's Role in Child Protection

Parental alcoholism and other family problems are related to neglect or abuse. Whenever there is suspicion of neglect or abuse, the schools must take action. In taking such action, school personnel should be prepared to deal with the school-related effects of family problems.

Using Student Assistance Procedures

"A Student Assistance Approach is Needed," on page 28, explains the basic steps of student assistance programming. The following paragraphs describe how the first three steps — identification, initial action, and pre-assessment — work to the benefit of prospective LifeGuides Program participants.

Step One: Identifying Troubled Youths

One of the most perplexing aspects of trying to identify young people from disrupted family environments is that they often have very different reactions to stress in the family. The feelings of self-hatred and depression caused by an abusive or neglectful parent will make one child act out in an angry, distracting manner, while a sibling will be quiet, hardworking, and overachieving. In schools, as in most other settings, the disruptive children usually receive the at-

A Student Assistance Approach Is Needed

Because most students from disrupted family environments share a variety of symptoms and problems, it is impossible to deal with one problem area without encountering others. Fortunately, the same basic processes used to help drug users through student assistance programs can be used for children from disrupted family environments. By following the basic tenets of student assistance programming, educators can identify and refer for assistance all young people who would benefit most from these services. In order to help troubled students, educators, parents, and others must work together to accomplish six basic steps of student assistance programming:

■ **Identification.** Identify troubled students as soon as possible, before their problems get worse and destroy any chance for a rewarding experience in school.

■ **Initial action.** Find some way to reach those students and take steps toward an effective, positive process of change.

■ **Pre-assessment.** Help young people examine and sort out their lives to the extent that they can decide what should be done to keep the process of change moving in a positive direction.

■ **Referral to needed services.** Get youth the help they need — within the school or in the community — to face and overcome whatever personal problems are troubling them.

■ **Appropriate use of the continuum of care.** Do as much as possible to ensure that troubled youth take advantage of the opportunities given to them.

■ **Support for change.** Give young people support for changes made so that those changes can become solid and permanent.

Student assistance is a major approach

Student assistance programs are not just a vague, undefined portion of the continuum of care falling somewhere between prevention and treatment. They are based on a flexible, focused early-intervention model that provides clear objectives for implementation and evaluation. They are geared specifically toward identification, screening, referral and follow-up support for students with alcohol/drug or other disruptive personal problems. The basics of student assistance programming are covered in greater detail in two Community Intervention publications, *One Step Ahead: Early-Intervention Strategies for Adolescent Drug Problems* and *Effective Student Assistance Programs* (Muldoon and Crowley, 1986). (See Appendix B for details.)

tention, while the quiet ones tend to go unnoticed. Also, the disruptive children are usually dealt with as the sole source of the problem, rather than as victims of dysfunctional patterns in their families.

Among the most common ways that LifeGuides Program participants are identified are:

- "Holding up the mirror." This is a process of showing films and offering educational sessions about the plight of children living in stressful home environments. After such sessions, the children in need tend to reveal themselves to the person making the presentation. This is one of the most effective ways of getting students to identify themselves. A problem with relying too much on this method, however, is that the high-achieving students tend to self-identify more than the underachievers or students who act out.

- Identification by other LifeGuides participants. Participants will frequently recruit other students who would benefit from the LifeGuides Program.

- Professionals who work with youth. Guidance counselors or other helping professionals often refer to the LifeGuides Program students whose problem behavior seems to be related to family issues.

- Publicity about the Program. Facilitators can advertise the Program in school publications, listing its name, purpose, meeting time, and referral information. This is one of the least effective methods of identification, but it does occasionally bring in a new participant.

- Special intervention programs. Some schools get many referrals from truancy and drop-out prevention programs. A student with 39 absences, for instance, may turn out to be a student kept home by a parent to babysit or to take care of other parental responsibilities.

- Cues from schoolwork. Sometimes students reveal family problems by focusing on them in written assignments. Also, all of the behaviors listed under "Similar Symptoms For Different Problems," on page 15 in the "LifeGuides Overview" section, can help identify children adversely affected by family problems.

- Referrals from "feeder schools." In some school systems, primary, middle, and secondary schools all have services for children from alcoholic or other disrupted family environments. When these children are about to leave one school, they are referred to the student assistance counselor in their new school with the suggestion that the youths continue in the LifeGuides Program. These students make up a solid foundation of experienced participants who help new members understand how to cope with and overcome the problems they are facing.

Identification in Prevention Programs

A wide variety of drug prevention programs are being taught in schools today. These include lessons on problem-solving and decision-making skills; self-control and self-esteem; relaxation and coping strategies for relieving stress and anxiety; and general interpersonal skills. All of these subject areas offer troubled youth opportunities to ask for help, directly or indirectly. When talking about the amount of alcohol use in the country, for instance, a teacher may hear a youth respond, "My dad sure drinks a lot!" When talking about feeling sad or depressed, another child may say, "I get depressed when my parents are fighting."

During discussions of problem areas such as chemical abuse, parental alcoholism, bulimia, and suicidal behavior, facilitators should watch for certain behaviors:

- Extreme negativism about the subject; for example, "Who would ever do anything like that? That kind of person is really out of it!"

- A normally passive or distracted student becoming active or focused during the discussion.

- Frequent requests to leave the room.

- Lingering after the session to ask innocent questions or to shuffle material.

- Frequent, casual mention of familiarity with a particular problem being discussed.

- Changes in attendance patterns when a particular subject is going to be discussed.

Any of these behaviors may indicate that the subject matter is especially relevant to a young person's life.

Some schools are very active in seeking out troubled students. In one Ohio school, counselors sent a form out to all homerooms at the beginning of the year. On the form a number of topics were listed, including:

- Divorce
- Loss
- Sex
- Dating in or out of school
- Suicide
- Dealing with stress
- School problems

Student Assistance Program Records

One issue that school districts must come to terms with is the privacy of student assistance program records. Most policies and procedures concerning student records are concerned primarily with academic issues, ability testing, and disciplinary actions. In many states there are no provisions for the keeping of confidential records by student assistance counselors. The same rules that apply to academic records also apply to any records kept by student assistance counselors. This often means that parents and school personnel not involved in the student assistance program can gain access to the files of counselors. This has caused SAP counselors to keep less than adequate records since they are not sure the information can be protected from inappropriate, untimely review by administrators or parents.

Although student assistance programming is a new and growing field, the activity of early-intervention has been going on for many years in schools. Early-intervention for many problems is an important part of a school's role in the community. Policies concerning student records should reflect this. Student assistance programs should be able to keep confidential records in the same way social service agencies can. Student assistance program records should be protected from scrutiny by administrators or parents. Information contained in them should not go into the students' cumulative files.

The class log: A safe way to record important information

In most school districts, notes such as a class log kept by a facilitator would not be considered part of a student's file. They are the property of the facilitators and can be reviewed only by the facilitators. The Life-Guides Program log, then, can be a useful tool for keeping track of important information on the progress of participants while not risking the inadvertent divulging of sensitive information.

Careful phrasing of notes in participant files

In many school districts, any notes that go into a file with a student's name on it may be considered part of the student's school record and, therefore, available for review by administrators and parents. If facilitators keep files on individual students, notes in those files should not be overly explicit. Such files should be disposed of when participants are no longer in the school or are, for some reason, unlikely to return to the LifeGuides Program.

- Family relationships
- Death
- Friends
- Loneliness
- Other

Participants were asked if they would be interested in having a chance to discuss any of these topics with a group of like-minded peers. Facilitators had 100 responses out of 2,500 students.

Step Two: Initial Action

Some adults may be afraid that by talking to a troubled student they will cause additional emotional turmoil. This fear is not borne out in experience.

Teachers and other professionals cannot stir up anything that is not already there. Children from alcoholic and other high-stress families are already suffering. They already know that something is very wrong. Most of these children are relieved to find they are not alone and that there is help for their problems. This knowledge alone helps them immensely.

Some children with problem behaviors may never openly admit that there is anything amiss in their families. Teachers and LifeGuides class facilitators need not always confront these students, nor assume that they have not made an impression even though they get no sign that a youth has heard and accepted the information given him. It takes a while for this information to sink in, especially if it has had a strong emotional impact. Staff can approach children in a way that does not require an immediate response: "This is something that you might want to do or that might be useful to you later, even if you can't use it now. I just want you to know."

Step Three: Pre-assessment

Using a student assistance approach, pre-assessment counselors will see all students whose academic or behavioral problems have not responded to normal school procedures. Within any group of 100 troubled students, at least 30 of them — and more likely, 50 to 70 of them — will be children from disrupted family environments. They may also be drug users, have eating disorders, and be depressed. Just what problem merits the highest priority for immediate action must be determined on a case-by-case basis. A child of emotionally neglectful parents who is smoking marijuana every day would most likely need to work

on his drug use problem before he could benefit from services for family problems. But no matter what services take priority, the information and experiences available in the LifeGuides Program should eventually be offered to all youths who need them.

No Diagnosis is Needed

It is not the responsibility of a student assistance counselor to diagnose family problems by means of a pre-assessment interview or in the course of the LifeGuides Program. If a student feels his life has been disrupted by the drug abuse or other behaviors of someone close to him, he is, de facto, an appropriate participant for the Program.

It is extremely rare for students to enter the LifeGuides Program simply for the purpose of skipping other classes or joining an "in group." Those who attempt to do so usually do not stick with the program in any event.

Student Assistance Data Collection Procedures

When students are referred to student assistance programs because of serious concerns about their chemical use, it is helpful to gather detailed data on their current achievement and behavior from teachers and other staff members. That data gives student assistance personnel something specific with which to confront resistant youths.

In the LifeGuides classes, which are usually voluntary, it is less common for participants to cover up school-related behavior problems. Nonetheless, the use of data from staff members is still very helpful. There will be participants who feel they need to cover up and deny current problems. There may also be participants who, because they are so shy, will not let facilitators or other class participants know when they are doing well. In these instances, data from other school personnel can be very helpful. Detailed information about data collection instruments and procedures is given in the *Facilitator's Guide for the Insight Class Program* (Muldoon, 1987, pages 40–49) and *One Step Ahead* (Muldoon and Crowley, 1986, pages 71–91).

The LifeGuides Interview is also part of the pre-assessment process. In the interview, the facilitators review with prospective participants how things are going, what effect family problems are having on them, and what needs the LifeGuides Program can best help fill. The facilitator also describes the Program and answers any questions the prospective participant may have.

Guidelines for Assigning Students to a LifeGuides Class

Grade level is the main criterion used for grouping LifeGuides participants, although gender can also pay a role. Here are some suggestions:

Separate Junior and Senior High School Students

LifeGuides classes in the middle schools or junior high schools differ from those in senior high schools. The younger students' communication skills are not as highly developed, and they are less able to sustain a supportive, growth-oriented group process on their own. The junior high classes are more structured, more information is provided, and more formal exercises are used. The class moves more methodically, according to the plans of the facilitators.

In senior high school, participants take more responsibility for the direction of the LifeGuides class. The focus of each session flows from the check-ins and from whatever direction the participants themselves want to give the class. The participants' daily stresses and their coping strategies reflect the greater autonomy and responsibility of these senior high school students. Some of them may have to work to pay for their basic needs; some may have decided to move out of their family homes; and some may have been told to leave by their parents.

Separate Sexes in Some Instances

In junior high school, it is often preferable to separate the boys from the girls. They are at an age when everything is so embarrassing that the boys and girls tend to get silly in front of each other. This is not always the case, but if it recurs in a particular school, separating the sexes may be the best procedure.

It is also helpful to have a man co-facilitate the boys groups, if possible. This provides them with the male role model they may be missing at home and helps to keep a lid on the junior high machismo.

If there are very few boys in the general pool of LifeGuides Program participants, it is best to put them all into one class, along with some girls, so they don't feel too isolated. For instance, there may be fifteen girls who want to be in a LifeGuides class and only three boys. Those three boys should be in the same class so they don't feel completely "out of it" as the only male in a "girls group."

Even in senior high school some facilitators choose to separate young men and women because of the special concerns each group might have. For example, boys with alcoholic fathers may become very confused in their identity as males. Typically, a boy feels a great deal of anger toward his father, but expresses it in aggressive, violent, or destructive ways. He may also find it extremely difficult to separate his anger about his father's drinking from his other feelings for his father.

Girls often have issues related to sexual abuse as well as issues with their mothers. Some facilitators have developed "Women's Support Groups" for daughters of alcoholics and daughters of abusive fathers. Even if the cause of their problems are not exactly the same, the issues are certainly similar enough to provide a common bond.

Class Size

Whenever a class gets too large, above ten or eleven participants, it is time to separate it into two classes. Some facilitators continue to use grade level as a criterion when appropriate and possible. They would attempt, for instance, to create a new class of ninth and tenth graders and another of eleventh and twelfth graders.

The amount of time allotted for a LifeGuides class should be taken into account when deciding on class size. If the school schedule provides for fifty-minute classes, it is best to keep the class size low, perhaps no larger than eight. Otherwise, there will be just too little time to give participants the attention they need. In schools with longer class periods, larger classes can be tried.

Scheduling LifeGuides Classes

How LifeGuides classes are scheduled is highly dependent on the policies and procedures of specific school buildings. Here are some guidelines:

Schedule LifeGuides Classes During the School Day

Schools should do everything possible to ensure that children under stress receive needed services. Scheduling a LifeGuides class after the school day will mean that students who live far from the school, those who want to be involved in extracurricular activities after school and those who feel pressure to assist at home after school will all be reluctant to attend. That scheduling simply adds more stress to their lives.

If LifeGuides classes are scheduled during the school day, there are several options:

• **Classes scheduled at the same period for every meeting.** In large schools with thirty or forty Life-Guides participants, the fixed meeting time can work well. If five different LifeGuides classes meet at five fixed but different times during a Wednesday, for instance, it is likely that many or most participants will be able to pick a time when they are regularly free. In this case, some students will miss class time while others will meet during their study periods. The problem with this method is that a participant could end up missing twenty or more class sessions on one particular academic subject if he or she attends a LifeGuides class throughout the school year.

- **The rotating schedule.** Under this schedule, the class might meet every Wednesday, but the meeting time would be different for each session. This keeps students from missing too much of a single course. A rotating schedule is possible if the facilitators are counselors and do not have to teach regularly scheduled classes. The disadvantages of a rotating schedule are that it might be difficult to keep the same room for the LifeGuides class and it increases the likelihood of participants being confused about when and where to meet. This is a ready-made excuse for those who want to avoid a particular session.

- **Alternating between two class periods**. This is probably the best compromise. Participants will not miss too much of a single academic subject during the year and the schedule is simple enough to avoid confusion.

Try to Use the Same Classroom, Even When a Class Meets at Varying Times

Some facilitators believe that, although participants are not affected by changes in the times of day the class meets, it is important that the meeting room remains the same. Participants become comfortable in a particular environment and may find it difficult to adjust to several different meeting rooms.

Schedule Classes on Tuesdays and Wednesdays

Holidays tend to take place on Mondays, staff training days on Thursdays and Fridays.

Schedule Classes Early in the Day

LifeGuides class participants may be involved in special work-study, vocational-ed, or early-release programs in the afternoons.

Provide Participants with a Printed Calendar of Class Times and Locations

At the beginning of every quarter, participants can be given a sheet detailing the exact meeting times and locations for their particular LifeGuides class.

Students Must Make Up Any Work Missed in Regular Classes

Students must keep pace with their regular classes when they attend a LifeGuides class. This means they must learn what their homework assignments are, when tests are scheduled, and what the class will be working on when they next attend.

Attendance in The LifeGuides Program

Family problems typically run in cycles. No matter what the problem — parental alcoholism, impending divorce, the physical or mental disability of one of the parents — families do not maintain a steady level of function or dysfunction. This variability can lead to problems for the LifeGuides facilitator. Over a period of time conflict among family members will increase to the point where the fighting becomes too much for a young person to tolerate. At that point, the youth may want to join the LifeGuides Program. However, the family will eventually become tired of its fighting and things will quiet down at home. The youth may then want to stop attending the LifeGuides Program. Rather than using the program to grow and prepare themselves for the next series of challenges that come their way, some participants use it primarily for support during crisis situations. This can be very disruptive to the LifeGuides Program process. Without consistent attendance by participants, the program becomes chaotic. If out of a group of twelve participants, six are not showing up regularly because of the cyclical nature of their problems, the program lacks continuity and the necessary sense of trust does not develop.

There is no easy solution to this problem. Since the program is voluntary, facilitators may be reluctant to make hard-and-fast rules about attendance. Nonetheless, some counselors will be very persistent in this matter. If participants miss two sessions in a row, a facilitator will contact them and let them know that the program cannot function with people coming and going, and that the program will not help them and the other participants if they all do not attend consistently. They will then be challenged to make a decision — either commit to regular class attendance or drop out of the program. Those who drop out are encouraged to attend one more class to tell the other participants of their decision.

It is a good idea to ask new participants to commit to at least three class sessions before deciding whether or not to continue in the LifeGuides Program. Facilitators report that participants who stay for at least three sessions tend to become long-term participants.

Obtaining Passes for the LifeGuides Class

Some LifeGuides Program facilitators have all students report to their regular classes first to receive a pass from the classroom teacher. This forces the student to touch base with the classroom teacher and also foils any attempts by students to use the Life-Guides class to avoid a certain teacher. In very large schools, having students report to their regular class first may not be practical if it takes too much time to walk from one classroom to another. It takes away from the time allotted for the LifeGuides class.

Another common method for distributing passes is for the facilitator to put them in teachers' mailboxes the day before a LifeGuides class session.

Rules on Drug Use by Participants

Some schools insist that before students may participate in any support group, they must agree to abstain from all chemicals. Many other schools, however, are more flexible in this area. Rather than making personal drug use an issue before the program begins, facilitators wait to see how students behave in the class, what types of drug-use behaviors they describe, and what problems they are having with alcohol and other drugs. Facilitators make use of any instances of drug use — current or past — to help participants comprehend the risks they face for serious, long-term problems.

Immediate expulsion of the student from the program and reporting of all drug use to an administrator would not be appropriate for every instance of alcohol or drug use. Facilitators should confront the use of alcohol and other drugs and explain the special risks that participants have for chemical dependency.

Any instances of drug use that indicate a clear and immediate risk to a person's health or safety are best reported both to school officials and parents. Usually, LifeGuides facilitators will have established enough rapport with participants to encourage them to talk openly about the problem with their parents. In a few instances, participants will be asked to leave the Life-Guides Program because their drug use is interfering with their ability to profit from the experience. In such cases, facilitators would likely recommend or refer the student directly to an Insight Class or to a social service agency for professional assessment.

Maintaining Cooperation from the Staff

Willing cooperation from school staff is needed if Life-Guides classes are to run smoothly during the school day. It is helpful for facilitators to send memos to the staff to thank them for their cooperation and to encourage further support. Here are examples of simple, to-the-point memos that help keep school staff supportive of the program:

Thanks to the whole staff for allowing students to come to LifeGuides classes this year. And thanks, too, for keeping them in class when they weren't keeping up with assignments. We also appreciate your cooperation in meeting with teachers from treatment centers, parents, and other concerned people. Our LifeGuides Program was 34 students strong this year, thanks to your help.

To Our Colleagues:

Your cooperation, criticism, referrals, and support have made our LifeGuides Program possible again this year. It's heart-warming when our participants talk about the understanding and support they receive from their teachers.

Thank you!

Facilitators' Roles and Responsibilities

There are numerous steps in the development and implementation of a LifeGuides class. "LifeGuides Facilitators' Roles and Responsibilities," on page 36, details some of the most important of these. Foremost among a facilitator's responsibilities is maintaining a healthy pattern of communication and interaction among participants.

Guiding the Class Process

Since the LifeGuides class is most often implemented as an ongoing class rather than a time-limited course, participants have time to become more comfortable with each other. Facilitators can guide this process by teaching participants techniques for communicating clearly and interacting effectively in a group situation. Some useful techniques are described in the "Becoming Aware" material under "Communication and Listening Skills," beginning on page 83. Although the comments there are for the benefit of participants, the information can help facilitators as well. Facilitators should both "practice and preach" effective communication skills in the class.

Need to Avoid Therapy

The LifeGuides class is designed to be just that, a CLASS with a specified curriculum. While its goals have more to do with emotional and social growth and development than with immediate academic achievement, the approach is largely educational.

When the class discusses family relationships, for instance, participants will not delve into the history of those relationships in great detail. The class will focus instead on here-and-now problems and strengths. Rather than talking about the details and history of physical or emotional abuse in a family, the class will focus on how that history is currently affecting the person — in school and elsewhere — and what practical steps the person can take to cope with his or her feelings. When appropriate, the participant will be told of agencies offering therapy to help resolve the painful feelings relating to abuse. The therapy will be left to services outside of the school.

LifeGuides class facilitators need not be unduly concerned about addressing personal and emotional issues. Schools have always played a major role in the emotional lives of young people. The demands for achievement, the constant comparisons between the achievers and the non-achievers, concerns about acceptance, and rejection of peers at school all place tremendous stress on those who are having problems in any of these areas. When educators do not admit that personal issues are of major concern to the school, they are likely to make the students' lives even more stressful.

Tone of the LifeGuides Class

The tone of the LifeGuides class, compared to either the Insight Class or abstinence support groups, will be less often confrontive and more often supportive and nurturing. Confrontation will occasionally be necessary, however. Even those in the most intense pain must be willing to acknowledge it, at least in part, and be willing to take some action to help themselves.

Realistic Expectations of Participants

Of all the support groups and educational classes offered in intervention and prevention programs, those for children from disrupted family environments may be the most difficult to facilitate. This is not because the problems are so complex or the techniques so demanding. Rather, it is because the pain

LifeGuides Facilitators' Roles and Responsibilities

The responsibilities of Life-Guides Program facilitators can be broken down into two general categories: preparing for the Life-Guides Program and coordinating and facilitating a class.

Preparing for the LifeGuides Program

■ Initiate and maintain contact with professionals who have expertise in child abuse, suicide prevention, working with children of alcoholics, and other issues as they arise.

■ If necessary, seek education and training on how to facilitate class discussions, role-plays, and other experiential learning techniques.

■ Review school procedures relevant to the LifeGuides Program.

■ Make the administration and appropriate committees aware when school procedures present problems for the effective functioning of a Life-Guides class.

■ Negotiate procedures on attendance.

■ Design consent forms for parents and for teachers.

■ Negotiate with administrators and other staff for the best times to offer a LifeGuides class.

■ Provide inservice training to staff on the LifeGuides Program: its rationale, procedures, and criteria for referral.

■ Provide inservice training to staff on identification and initial action with troubled students.

■ Describe appropriate classroom methods for working with youth from disrupted family environments.

Coordinating and Facilitating a Class

■ Conduct LifeGuides interviews.

■ Assign participants to specific LifeGuides classes.

■ Assist participants in getting permission from teachers to attend the LifeGuides Program.

■ Assist participants in obtaining permission from parents to attend a LifeGuides class.

■ Make sure consent forms are signed by parents (if required).

■ Be prepared to talk to parents to explain participants' needs for the LifeGuides Program.

■ Arrange for passes for all participants.

■ Keep in contact with the teachers of LifeGuides participants. Be sure each participant is progressing adequately in other classes and that teachers are aware of the appropriateness and effectiveness of the LifeGuides Program for each student.

■ Review all the exercises in Phase I and Phase II prior to beginning a LifeGuides class.

■ Make a general but flexible plan outlining the subject areas that will be focused on first and the specific exercises within each area that will be used.

■ Be prepared to present basic didactic material on the subject area being addressed each week.

■ Assess the progress of each participant.

■ Guide the class process so that it remains healthy and safe for each participant.

■ Make sure that all class activity remains confidential.

Facilitators should Keep their Expectations of Themselves Within Reason

They are expected to:

■ Educate participants about drug use, other family problems, and the effects of those problems on participants.

■ Be honest.

■ Be good listeners.

■ Not be easily manipulated.

Facilitators are not expected to:

■ Cure drug problems.

■ Solve any family problems.

■ Be expert counselors.

■ Never make mistakes.

■ Have all the answers.

■ Entertain the participants.

■ Convince, convert, or win arguments.

■ Provide diagnoses or labels.

of these children can be so deep, their shame so overwhelming, their isolation so complete.

Neither the LifeGuides class facilitators nor other staff members should have high expectations for visible change among participants. Students who are trying to remain drug-free in an aftercare or an abstinence support group will show more visible change than students in a LifeGuides class. When a primary source of a youth's problems is her own use of chemicals, the youth can take responsibility for the behavior and try to change it. But when a major source of stress is another's behavior, the youth, the facilitator and the class have much less direct control, and it is more difficult for the youth to detach and let go of the problems.

Facilitators should be prepared for some difficult young people, especially early in the process. Participants can be depressed, humorless, and very needy. They might whine a lot and are not always fun to be with. They can bring up the same problems again and again, but take little positive action. These are what therapists call "help-rejecting complainers." They may have poor attendance and poor behavior in the LifeGuides and other classes. Many will use inappropriate language, be sexually active, and have drinking problems.

Changes happen gradually, if not imperceptibly. The learning students do may not be readily apparent, but, if a student remains in the class, the facilitators can be sure that the support is helping and some change is taking place.

Have at Least Two Facilitators for Each Class

Having two facilitators provides many advantages.

• One facilitator might have strong presentation skills, while the other might be more group-process oriented or skilled at picking up nonverbal cues.

• One facilitator can be the "live wire" who gets the class into a receptive mood for a presentation, while the other is more tuned into the participants' feelings.

• Having two facilitators allows for emotional support for each facilitator when the class is not going as smoothly as they would want, or when the pain of some of the participants is intense.

• Having two facilitators is useful for keeping track of the data shared in the class and recalling it when needed.

• Two facilitators can offer each other advice about their presenting and processing skills.

• Two facilitators can share the burden of follow-up on the many different issues that arise. Students in a LifeGuides class will bring many problems to class that need to be addressed outside of the class, such as entering counseling or therapy, and requesting foster placement.

• Facilitators can help each other maintain boundaries with especially needy participants. Sometimes the problems of participants will seem so overwhelming that a facilitator will become exhausted from the emotional strain of trying to "save" the youth. A more detached observer, in the form of a co-facilitator, can point out the over-involvement and help the facilitator become more appropriately detached.

The Importance of Experiential Training for Facilitators

It is extremely helpful for LifeGuides class facilitators to go through experiential training on group process. Effective training in this area would include information on the theory of support group processes and actual experience in both leading and participating in a group. An example of such training is Community Intervention's Group Facilitator's Training, which consists of five days of training with several hours each day spent in a group.

Working with a more experienced facilitator in a LifeGuides class, an Insight Class or an abstinence support group is also a good way for a new facilitator to go beyond book learning to grasp, at an emotional level, the nature of this process.

Facilitators who have participated in Alcoholics Anonymous, Al-Anon, or similar self-help groups have had an opportunity to learn about some of the key issues facing the children of alcoholics. Those who are not members of such groups can attend open meetings of AA or Al-Anon.

Have Outside Resources Available

LifeGuides class facilitators are not required to be experts on every problem faced by young people. Before starting a LifeGuides class, however, facilitators must be sensitized to certain issues and know what resources are available locally to help them when they encounter the following problems:

• Child abuse

Key Contacts For Special Problems

BEFORE STARTING A LIFEGUIDES PROGRAM, facilitators should make contact with professionals in the school or community who can consult with them and facilitate referrals when special problems arise. At the very minimum, the following key contacts should be identified:

CHILD ABUSE, in-house contacts

A person who can help clarify possible instances of reportable abuse and determine when to contact community agencies.

Name _____ Phone number _____

Name _____ Phone number _____

CHILD ABUSE, community contacts

Someone who knows the local system and can give advice as to the best way to access the system.

Name _____ Phone number _____

Name _____ Phone number _____

SUICIDE EMERGENCIES, in-house contacts

A person who can help clarify the need for intervention, be available to stay with potentially suicidal youth, and help contact parents and appropriate professionals or agencies.

Name _____ Phone number _____

Name _____ Phone number _____

SUICIDE EMERGENCIES, community contacts

Persons who can offer immediate advice regarding the extent of apparent risk implied by a youth's statements and behavior and/or who can help admit the youth to a secure environment.

Name _____ Phone number _____

Name _____ Phone number _____

- Suicidal adolescents
- Sexual identity problems
- Alcoholic parents
- Eating disorders

Resources should be lined up before the need for them arises, as it is inevitable that anyone who works in a LifeGuides class for any period of time will encounter each of these problems. The issues of child abuse and suicidal adolescents merit special attention. Before starting a LifeGuides class, facilitators should complete the form on page 38, "Key Contacts for Special Problems." The books described in Appendix A, beginning on page 189, offer some basic information on these issues.

Working with Parents

When and how the parents of LifeGuides class participants are contacted depends both on school policies and on the discretion of the facilitators. This differs from most other student assistance program services. An Insight Class facilitator, for instance, may be required to get the parents involved immediately in the assessment and intervention process. Usually the youth in question has broken some rule or law regarding drug use, and the parents' help is requested and sometimes required by the schools or courts.

Children who are under stress because of disrupted home lives have a right to seek help FOR THEMSELVES. Parents of teenagers should not be in a position of saying, "I do not want my daughter to talk to a counselor, even if she thinks that is what she wants."

The Rights of Children

Thirty years ago, many courts and social service agencies considered children's rights to be secondary to parental rights. The courts would take children out of abusive homes only in the most extreme circumstances. No counseling or treatment could be conducted in any manner without parental permission. School personnel might lament the fact that all the children from a particular family were coming to school poorly dressed and that the father was physically abusive, but the general mores of society dictated that "outsiders shouldn't get involved in family problems."

The concept of society's duties to children has changed markedly since that time. Courts now make custody decisions based on what is best for the child. The concept of parental rights remains valid, but the best interests of the child are the major criteria used in deciding how to intervene.

Because what is best for the child often necessitates getting help for family problems, there are now state laws that allow children to get help without their parents' consent. While this is not the basis upon which most children gain access to a LifeGuides class, it is a reminder that children do have rights to some information and assistance regardless of their parents' degree of enthusiasm. There will be times when students gain access to school services when their parents don't want them to. Certainly, in most cases, older students would be given information about counseling for depression related to family problems even if the parents objected.

For the most part, however, interactions with parents will not be based on power but on expressions of concern. These concerns will usually be supported by a report of school-related behaviors that call for intervention.

A Pro-family Approach

Those working with children from disrupted family environments must be advocates for the children. But that does not imply they are AGAINST anybody, especially the parents. LifeGuides class facilitators will want to remain ready, willing, and able to assist parents who ask for help. This may take the form of answering questions about the LifeGuides class, giving support to the spouse of an alcoholic, or providing a list of local services for alcoholism, drug abuse, family problems, financial problems, and other issues.

The LifeGuides Program is a pro-family approach to helping family members cope and grow. The helping process is not a win–lose situation, with the children getting help to the detriment of the parents. It is a win–win situation.

A family is not helped — in any sense of the word — by the children being locked tightly in the role of enablers of alcoholism or victims of verbal or physical abuse. Conversely, a family is not under attack when a young person decides that he must take time for himself, both to study and to have fun, within reasonable limits.

Fear of the consequences of "butting into" a family's privacy often stops school staff from taking action. But experienced LifeGuides facilitators have found that direct confrontation or intervention into a child's family is seldom necessary. Contact with parents begins with an honest concern for the child's welfare.

Parents Need Support

LifeGuides class facilitators find that few participants, when compared to the general population, live with both of their natural parents. Many — in some classes, most — participants come from single-parent homes. Their parents tend to face more financial and emotional stress than adults in two-parent homes. Just as their children do, then, the parents of LifeGuides participants need support as well.

Occasionally, LifeGuides facilitators will want to confront parents about the problems their children are facing and the changes that need to be made in order to help the children. Before confrontation can be effective, the facilitators must show the parents that they are truly concerned about them and their families. The need to give empathy and support to parents is a point facilitators can easily lose sight of when intervening to help children. Frequently, the parents who need help and direction the most will reject any assistance offered. In such cases, empathy and support may not be the only things the parents need, but they are essential.

How Facilitators Approach Parents Will Depend on the Reason for Contacting Them

LifeGuides facilitators and other school personnel may have a variety of reasons for contacting parents. These include:

- To get parental permission for children to attend the class.

- To get further information from the parents.

- To have the parents become partners in a supportive process. Parents should be told if their child is in need of outside services, and they should be encouraged to obtain those services.

- To make the parents aware of the stress their children are under. Parents often then make the connection between that stress and family problems. Usually, the healthiest of the parents will make the connection.

All contacts with parents will begin by discussing a young person's problems. If a child is very depressed, specific, school-related data should be offered. The staff person who contacts the parents could talk to the parent about this and then ask, "Is there anything you know of outside of school that could be related to this problem?"

There will also be situations in which the parents must be called in to discuss an academic or disciplinary problem because the student's performance or behavior is not acceptable. Such discussions will cover a variety of areas, and it is possible that family stress will be mentioned.

Open-ended questions to parents can yield a great deal of information relevant to the LifeGuides process. A facilitator could say: "I'd like to talk to you for a couple of minutes about your daughter. Her teachers have noted that lately she seems quite different and is depressed. What ideas do you have about what's going on with her?"

Another approach might be, "Mr. Johnson, I'm the chemical awareness counselor at the high school. We are seeing certain behaviors with Betty in school. I know that kids often behave at home like they do at school, and I wonder if you are seeing the same things."

The parent, whether or not he or she says so, may start thinking about the connection between family problems and this children's behavior. Sometimes this is the parent's first step in beginning to overcome denial and reaching out for help.

Although open-ended questions or statements are the preferred method of inquiry in the majority of cases, they are not always productive. When parents are very reticent about the child's problem, facilitators can use a series of simple, pointed, closed-ended questions. A facilitator could say, "In my experience, these are some of the typical problems bothering kids when they are having trouble at school. Could it be:

- "He's not getting enough sleep?" (Starting with physical symptoms is the safest approach.)

- "That he is having some problems with his sister or brothers?"

- "That he is working too hard? Too many hours?" Further questions in this area could include:

- "How many hours is he working?"

- "Does he have any problems on the job?" (For instance, youths who work at fast-food restaurants sometimes feel pressure from their peers to give them free food. LifeGuides participants are likely to find such pressure very stressful.)

It is best not to ask if the problem seems to be "trouble with peers." Parents are all too ready to blame their children's friends for the problems. They may use this as their major excuse for not attempting any changes in the home.

One approach to inquiring about the situation at home is to preface those questions with a question about school: "Has your daughter said anything about school? Are there any school problems that she is concerned about?" This line of inquiry shows the parents that the facilitator is willing to take responsibility for any stresses the school may be causing the child. Then, a similarly phrased question can be asked about home: "Is there anything bothering her at home?"

Additional information on interviewing parents can be found in the *Facilitator's Guide for the Insight Class Program,* (Muldoon, 1987, pages 29–30.)

Parents Are Not the Focus of Interventions

Some educators and social service professionals are reluctant to work with children from high-stress families because they think they will have to confront the parents about their drinking, drug use, or other problem behaviors. This is not the case.

The goals of the LifeGuides Program are focused on the children. Certainly, intervening to help the children may eventually lead to some healthy changes in the behavior of other family members, but that is neither the goal of the class nor the responsibility of the facilitators.

Facilitators tend to be more involved with the parents of junior high participants. For these children, emancipation from their parents is both less likely and generally less desirable. Therefore, because the children's well-being will greatly depend on the health of the parents, facilitators are more likely to work closely with the parents and to provide information regarding where to get additional help for their families.

But even with younger participants, facilitators let parents know that the focus of the class is on the children. Parents also need to be reminded that the discussion with the facilitator is completely confidential, as is the class itself.

Getting Parental Consent for a Student's Participation

The problem that worries new LifeGuides class facilitators the most, and experienced facilitators the least, is getting consent from parents for their children to participate. It is rare for parents not to grant permission to attend a LifeGuides class, even for younger children, over whom parents have more control.

Just how consent is handled varies from state to state, district to district. In many districts, parental consent is required in the primary and middle schools, but not in senior high school. In others, parental consent is required for all participants. In all districts reviewed for this publication, the consent of just one of the parents was sufficient.

Some schools require that the parents be notified by the third session, others require that letters be sent to parents before students can enter the class. Still others send letters to all parents at the beginning of the year that list all support groups and special classes requiring parental permission. Parents indicate their consent, or lack of it, should their child wish to enroll in a support group or special class during the school year. When deciding what procedure would work best in a given school, program planners and facilitators need the advice, consent, and backing of the school administration.

When parental consent is required, facilitators will find it necessary to describe the class to parents. Describing the general goals of the class will often suffice. Facilitators simply review the child's problems with self-esteem, depression, concentration, or school performance and suggest the class as a means of addressing these problems.

Even when parents will not sign a release, the facilitators and school counselors do not have to stop working with the child. School counselors can continue to meet with students for brief, regular visits. Perhaps, in addition to offering support to the students, the facilitators can also suggest different ways to approach the parents to obtain permission for participation in the LifeGuides class.

The LifeGuides Interview

The goals of a LifeGuides Interview are to:

- **Assess, in a general fashion, the student's current emotional state and functioning.**The basic questions are, "How are you feeling?" and "How is it going?" The assessment aspects of this session need not be emphasized to the point of gathering minute details. The entire LifeGuides process involves self-assessment. Material will accumulate rapidly once a participant joins the class and begins to let go of his or her defenses.

- **Describe the class and assess the person's level of understanding and commitment to the process.**

- **Initiate the intervention process**. In some cases, the interview may turn out to be crisis intervention if it is necessary to calm the prospective participant and help him or her avoid panic. If there appears to be some immediate threat to the person's well-being, either suicidal tendencies or abuse in the home, immediate action will have to be taken.

Barriers to the Assessment Process

Typical experiences of children from disrupted family environments sometimes impede LifeGuides interviews. For example,

- Many of these youths have developed a distorted perception of reality. If their parents have confused them by denying reality — for example, refusing to admit that events the child witnessed ever occurred — it may have become second nature for them to see things as they are "supposed to be" rather than as they are. Younger participants, especially, use fantasy as a form of denial. Initially, then, information from prospective participants may be a description of how they would like things to be rather than how things are.

- Youths may distrust all adults because of the unreliability of their parents or the other adults in their lives.

- Youths may have been warned by their parents not to talk about family issues, sometimes under threat of severe discipline or violence.

- Youths may feel very loyal toward their parents and consider any discussion of family problems as unethical or at least as an ungrateful thing to do.

- Shame, of course, is a major barrier to honest disclosure of facts and feelings. Most young people feel very embarrassed about the shortcomings of their families.

- Prospective participants may have a realistic fear of prejudice. Perhaps they have revealed information in the past to people who reacted with hostility or disrespect for their parents or their family.

A facilitator can begin the LifeGuides Interview by letting the youth know who he or she is and what the facilitator's role is in the school. This can include mention of any groups or special classes the person facilitates in addition to the LifeGuides Program.

Sometimes it is necessary to meet with youths in several individual sessions before they participate in a LifeGuides class. Experienced facilitators caution, however, that these individual sessions should not go on too long. Some participants and prospective participants are very needy and dependent, and seek the one thing they have been deprived of at home: the full and undivided attention of an adult. Working with the youth for more than one or two individual sessions might reinforce dependency needs. For the most part, it is best to get the person involved in the class as soon as possible.

Interview Guides

At the end of this section is a **LifeGuides Interview Form** which facilitators can adapt to their own needs. This form can serve as a guideline for the type of information facilitators might touch on when first talking to a prospective LifeGuides participant. The

Factors Related to the Impact of Parental Alcoholism

Just how devastating an impact family problems have on a child depends on many different factors. In some homes, the alcoholism of a parent may totally dominate daily life, while in others it maintains a lower profile and leads to less harmful results. Below are some factors researchers (Booz-Allen and Hamilton, 1974) and practitioners point to that determine the extent of the impact parental alcoholism has on a child. Most of these factors apply to many types of family problems as well as parental alcoholism. They include being:

■ From a lower socioeconomic group. Socioeconomic class can affect children in a variety of ways. For the most part, those from financially well-off families have more resources to draw on when a family is under stress.

■ In a family where violence has occurred. Physical violence within the family creates serious problems for children as they grow into adulthood.

■ Six years of age or younger at the onset of parental alcoholism.

■ An only child. Only-children get less support and have fewer reality checks. Children from large families tend to express more positive feeling toward the alcoholic parent while only-children express more ambivalence and confusion.

■ The oldest in the family. Oldest children and only-children tend to be placed in the middle of parental arguments or have to assume the responsibilities of one of the parents.

■ In a family where the non-alcoholic parent or other adults are not supportive. The supportiveness of the non-alcoholic spouse can have a strong positive effect on the children and greatly lessen the impact of alcoholism on them. A "supportive parent" is characterized by:

– Creating and maintaining a positive family environment despite the alcoholic's behavior.

– Providing basic love, affection, nurturing, and support.

– Protecting the children from abuse by the alcoholic parent and from potentially dangerous situations.

– Helping a child understand the parent's drinking and sort out his own feelings.

– Compensating to the extent possible for the negative role model of the alcoholic parent.

– Encouraging children in their growth and development and in the pursuit of their own interests.

Stages of Development

Another way to consider the impact that family problems have had on the child is to look at the stages of development disrupted by these problems. Naiditch (1987) describes three developmental stages a child must go through:

■ Trust: Through Age 5. This is the time during which a child learns that adults can be relied upon to fulfill basic needs, to protect them, and to provide a safe world.

■ Evaluation: Ages 6-12. During this stage, children are learning how to accomplish tasks, develop opinions, and practice their thinking skills. In an alcoholic family system, children are frequently reprimanded for their opinions and rarely given direct positive attention.

■ Transition: Ages 12-18. In this stage, children work through old problems, separate from the parents, and find a place to grow up. Children of alcoholics are often put into a double bind at this time in their lives. The alcoholic may demand to be taken care of even though the child has not been taught the basic skills needed for adulthood.

If the stage in which children develop basic trust is disrupted, the children will be consistently anxious and fearful. And if the disruption happens before they can speak, they will not have a way to label and identify the sources of that fear. If the children are in the transition stage when the family problems become serious, they are more likely to have the basic trust and skills necessary to deal with the problems incurred when they attempt to leave home.

participants need not ever see this form and, in most cases, it is preferable that they do not. The facilitator can fill in the pre-assessment form after the interview. The confidentiality of the information is addressed in "Student Assistance Program Records" on page 30.

Information on the first part of the form — the prospective participant's address, grade, and record of attendance — can be taken from the student's cumulative files before the interview.

In addition, facilitators can have students complete the "Shock Waves — How the Chemical Use of Others Affects Me," form in the *Becoming Aware Participant Guidebook*. It is illuminating to have students fill this form out twice: during the LifeGuides Interview and then again after sessions on the effects of alcoholism on the family. This helps facilitators see if the participant is more open after the first few sessions.

The "Happy, So-So or Sad?" and "How I See Myself" exercises, in the *Taking Care Participant Guidebook,* could also be given before or after the LifeGuides Interview. These two paper-and-pencil exercises help the facilitator and prospective participant gain insights into the young person's current state and self-concept, and they also serve as screens for depression. The facilitator could review the material during or after the interview. Suggestions on the use of these forms are given in "Feelings," on page 135 and in "Self-esteem: Liking Ourselves," on page 144 in the "Taking Care" material.

Checklist of Participants' Needs

As noted before, "Checklist of Participants' Needs" describing the typical needs of participants is given on page 48. Listed under each area of need are related behaviors. When facilitators have accumulated information from a variety of sources, they can use the checklist to determine which needs are the highest priority for each participant. This will help facilitators organize the information in a practical way that is directly relevant to the LifeGuides class process.

The Use of Drawings

Some facilitators report that they have had good success in asking students to draw during the interview. There are several ways to use this technique including the following suggestions.

Exercise: Drawing Trust Clusters

"Trust clusters" are a way for prospective participants to show whom they trust or feel closest to. The students draw a circle in the center of a page and put their name in it. Then they think of the people with whom they interact at home and at school. For each person, they make a circle either close to or far away from the circle with their name, depending on how close or trusting they feel toward that person, and put that person's name in it. After the student draws circles for six or seven people, there will be clusters on the page, giving a pictorial image of his or her current support system.

Discussion

Facilitators can discuss this image by asking students:

• "What are your reactions when you look at your drawing?"

• "This person is close to you. What is it about this person that makes you trust him so much?"

• "Tell me about this person. Why is she way over here?"

• "How would this be different if you had drawn it two months ago? A year ago?"

• "How would you like this to look a year from now?"

A more open-ended approach to the use of drawing is for the facilitator to give prospective participants paper and pencils or colored writing instruments and let them know they can draw while the two of them talk. Sometimes the drawings will provide interesting insights into a student's feelings or current issues. Although this approach is used more often with younger students, however, it can work quite well with any age.

Describing the Class

The class description should not be too detailed lest the prospective participant's attention wander. The facilitator might briefly describe the LifeGuides class in terms such as these:

"After talking with you, it sounds like you're having a pretty hard time trying to work things out for yourself. We have a class for students who are having some trouble getting along at home. The class is for anyone interested in attending the sessions, listening to the information, and participating in the discussions. The goals of the class are to make you

Checklist of Participants' Needs

In this checklist, the most common needs of LifeGuides participants are listed along with traits relevant to each need area. From your experience with this youth, indicate which traits this person has and where more information is still required. Then estimate which of these needs merit priority in the next fews days or weeks.

Need: Protection from harm

____ Not safe at home.

____ Unaware of the dangers in the home.

____ Feels vulnerable to harm at home.

____ Not safe in the neighborhood.

____ Does not know how to take care of self in the neighborhood.

____ Unaware of dangers in the neighborhood.

____ Vulnerable to abuse at school.

____ A target or victim.

____ Does not know where to go when feeling vulnerable or in danger.

____ Unable to protect others in family who are younger or more vulnerable.

____ Expresses unexplained fears.

Need: Rest and relief from tension

____ Overly tense.

____ Exhausted.

____ Frantic.

____ Has no place for daily relaxation.

____ Works far too hard in school and on the job.

Need: To attain and maintain healthy relationships

____ Has few or no close friends.

____ Has few or no friends in school.

____ Has no healthy relationship within the family.

____ Has no healthy relationship with an adult.

____ Has no plans to expand his or her relationships.

____ Is not working on those plans.

Need: Respect from others

____ Receives little or no respect at home.

____ Subject to verbal abuse at home.

____ Verbally abused at school.

____ Verbally abused on the streets.

____ Is not respected by other members of the Life-Guides Program.

Need: To have the right to seek help

____ Needs additional help.

____ Cannot afford the help.

____ Cannot get to the help.

____ Cannot get to the help because of scheduling problems.

____ Parents are not supportive of obtaining help through the school.

____ Parents are not supportive of obtaining help through a community agency.

Need: To know they are not alone

____ Feels very different from others.

____ Isolated from others.

____ Is not aware that other children have gone through the same thing.

____ Is financially different from the other youths he or she knows.

____ House or neighborhood is different from that of his friends.

Need: To have their own perceptions and feelings validated

____ Confused about what he or she sees and feels.

____ Has difficulty remembering events in his or her life.

____ Recall and description of events differs from that of parents'.

____ Has difficulty describing what the family is like.

____ Says things like, "I feel like I'm going crazy," or "I'm really losing my mind."

Need: To gain some perspective on how they have been affected by their parents' problems and behaviors.

____ Unaware that alcoholism is not the norm.

____ Unaware that a family member abuses chemicals or is chemically dependent.

____ Unable to identify certain role-based behaviors in self or in other family members.

____ Does not recognize enabling or codependent behaviors.

Need: To be absolved of blame

____ Indicates he or she is at fault for the alcoholism.
____ Feels at fault for other family problems.
____ Feels at fault for not taking on responsibilities.
____ Responsibilities are far beyond what a person of his or her age should be expected to undertake.

Need: To separate the parents from the parents' behaviors

____ Shows no respect for parents.
____ No awareness of the parents' ability prior to the onset of alcoholism or other problems.
____ Feels parents have no love for him or her at all.
____ Uses many disparaging terms such as, "drunken bum" and "slob."

Need: To feel hope

____ Feels life is out of control and will always be that way.
____ Feels locked into the family system.
____ Does not believe the chemical abuser can ever change.
____ Does not feel he or she can change.

Need: To take care of themselves

____ Manifests signs of codependency.
____ Feels the need to take care of the rest of the family.
____ Has no fun activities.
____ Doesn't take time for own needs and responsibilities.

Need: To have a safe outlet for dealing with their anger

____ Unaware of anger.
____ Unaware of sources of the anger.
____ Gets in trouble with authority figures.
____ Fights with friends.
____ Is very depressed (anger turned inward).
____ Says many negative things about him or herself.
____ Anger disrupts relationships with friends, co-workers, boss, or teachers.

Need: To understand own risks for chemical dependency and other drug use problems

____ Uses chemicals.
____ Uses chemicals heavily.
____ Uses chemicals to escape.
____ Uses chemicals to mask pain.
____ Is unaware of the risks he or she runs for long-term, serious drug problems.

Need: Positive self-esteem

____ Says many negative things about him- or herself.
____ Feels less intelligent.
____ Feels less good-looking.
____ Feels less likable.
____ Feels less competent.

Need: To be able to cope with daily life

____ Has many stresses in his or her life.
List: _____
_____
_____
_____

____ Is aware of those stresses.
____ What ones has he/she mentioned?
____ What ones has he/she not mentioned? (These may be worst.)
____ What can be done immediately?

feel better about yourself, make you feel more in control of your life, help you learn to have more fun, and do better in school."

The following details should also be covered:

• Dates the class starts and finishes.

• How often the class meets.

• How passes from scheduled classes are handled.

• What goes on in the class. Facilitators can describe the material the class is currently working on. The facilitator might say that they typically start the class with a short warm-up exercise and a presentation by the facilitators, and then open the class up for discussion.

• Number of participants in the class and age of participants.

• Confidentiality issues. Facilitators must emphasis the absolute need for confidentiality (See "Reminders on Confidentiality" in the next section on page 54, for more information.)

• Participation required. Facilitators should let participants know that they do not have to say anything if they do not want to. They will be able to pass on any exercise. It is all right simply to come and listen. A facilitator can also acknowledge that most people feel some fear about joining such a class. The facilitator should ask what concerns or fears the prospective participant has and then address those fears.

• The importance of regular attendance. If participants need to miss a class, they should talk to a facilitator the day before.

• The benefits of participation. Facilitators might repeat what other participants have said about the class and describe some concrete results that participants have experienced. Some prospective participants will have already heard positive comments about the class.

Facilitators can reduce the fears of a new or prospective participant by describing the concerns current participants have or had when they began the class. In this way, most fears of prospective participants will be addressed. The facilitator might scatter phrases like these throughout the discussion:

• "We have had many kids who come here and feel quite alone, like they're the only ones who have problems."

• "Lots of our kids get very confused. Sometimes their parents say one thing and then do another. Sometimes both parents deny that events even took place."

• "I notice you're blaming yourself for your family's problems. That comes up a lot in the LifeGuides class."

• "You seem to feel so responsible for your parents. I've seen that a lot."

• "Our kids tend to be very concerned about losing their parents through drinking, divorce, an accident, or getting sick."

• "Many young people like you can be awfully angry at their parents, because they break promises, because they don't act like they love you, or because you don't get enough help from them when you need it."

• "Sometimes our participants have had experiences that they really don't want to talk about in the class because they're too painful. That's **OK**. Sometimes they will talk to me, and sometimes they will talk to counselors I can refer them to."

• "Many of the kids in our class tell me they've been frightened at one time or another because their parents were fighting or acting wild."

Telling the Parents About the LifeGuides Program

Part of the interview may involve helping youths consider how to approach their parents when asking for their consent to attend the class, if such consent is necessary. Prospective participants may have many feelings around this issue. They may feel very guilty, fearful, vengeful, or resentful when asking for their parents' permission.

Facilitators can suggest that the parents call and talk to them if there are any questions.

LifeGuides Interview Form

DATE: _____

NAME: _____

ADDRESS: _____

STUDENT ID #: _____

AGE: _____ Sex: M _____ F _____

PARENT'S NAME(S): _____

SCHOOL: _____ GRADE: _____

REFERRED BY: _____

A. School

1. How are things going in school?

    a. Classwork _____

    _____

    b. Teachers _____

    _____

    c. Friends _____

    _____

2. Number of days tardy: _____

    Number of days absent: _____

3. Discipline Reports: Number: _____

    Reason(s) _____

    Suspensions: Number: _____

    Reason(s) _____

4. How do your personal or family problems affect you at school?

    _____

B. Family

1. Who do you live with? _____

_____

2. Parents: Married _____

    Divorced _____   When? _____

    Separated _____   When? _____

    Remarried _____   When? _____

3. Siblings: Names, ages. _____

_____

4. What's your family like? _____

_____

5. What does your family do for fun? _____

_____

6. What are your family rules? About curfew? Friends? Fighting? _____

C. Friends

1. Who are your best friends? _____

_____

2. What do you do for fun? _____

_____

3. Do you bring your friends home? _____

_____

4. Have you ever told your friends about problems you have at home? _____

_____

D. Legal

1. Have you ever been picked up by the police? _____

_____

2. Have you ever tried drugs/alcohol?

    a. How often? _____

    b. When? _____

    c. Where? _____

    d. From whom did you get the drugs/alcohol? _____

E. Goals

1. What are your strengths or assets? _____

_____

_____

2. What do you like most about yourself? _____

_____

_____

3. What would you like to change about yourself? _____

_____

_____

4. What do you want to learn in class? _____

_____

_____

Opening Exercises

Check-ins and Warm-ups

Check-ins and warm-ups are those short and simple activities conducted at the beginning of each class session to loosen up the class, increase trust, check in on previous assignments and commitments, and review basic needs.

The opening exercises serve all purposes at once. Even if the main goal is simply to get the class loosened up for a planned presentation and exercise, the facilitators are always probing and looking for issues that might be higher priority than those planned for the day's discussion.

After the opening exercises, the facilitators will have to decide whether to take a class in the planned direction or to follow a lead uncovered by the warm-up. Usually this will not be difficult, since participants will indicate pretty clearly whether an issue is of great importance to them.

Check-ins and warm-ups will vary according to:

- How general or specific the facilitators want the exercises to be. If they want to steer the class toward thoughts or feelings related to a planned presentation, they may choose a related exercise.
- How cohesive and open the class has become. In a new class in which members are still guarded, less demanding warm-ups will be less threatening to participants.
- The age of the participants. The younger participants will usually be given more structured but slightly less demanding exercises than older participants.

Use Exercises From Any Part of the Curriculum

This section describes a variety of exercises that can be used to open a LifeGuides class. But other exercises presented throughout this book can also be ef-fective opening exercises. Before starting a Life-Guides class, therefore, facilitators should become familiar with all the exercises presented. Short exercises from any subject area might be just what participants need on a particular day. In addition, the affirmations and positive feedback games found in "Self-esteem: Liking Ourselves," beginning on page 143 in the "Taking Care" materials, can be used for any or all LifeGuides class sessions.

Should Facilitators Participate in the Exercises?

While it is sometimes helpful for facilitators to demonstrate an exercise, it is not necessary for them to respond to all questions asked of participants or to take part in most exercises. This would take too much valuable class time and dilute the focus, which should be on the needs of the participants.

Facilitators will want to occasionally model responses for the participants, demonstrating risk taking, self-revelation, and effective communication. This might be at the beginning of the year, when many members are just developing effective communication skills, as well as later in the year when the class is about to embark on a new subject area or try a particularly challenging exercise. Such facilitator participation should be brief and to the point.

Facilitators can also help participants by revealing how they tend to feel in certain situations and how they reacted to problems when they were the same age as the participants. Again, such self-revelation should not turn into long, drawn-out life stories, but be brief anecdotes.

The LifeGuides "Becoming Aware" curriculum has a special session on communication for the participants, "Communication and Listening Skills" pages 83–88. Facilitators will find this information useful as well and should review it for their own purposes before beginning the class.

Reminders on Confidentiality

Children from disrupted family environments usually have a great deal of shame about what is going on at home and in the other areas of their lives. It is difficult for them to share this information and to talk about their feelings of shame. They must be totally confident that nothing said in the LifeGuides class will be repeated outside the class.

Since confidentiality is so important, the facilitator may want to start each of the first three or four classes with a statement like this:

"Remember that everything said here is confidential. That means you can't talk about what any other member of the class has said. That includes statements even as seemingly innocent as: 'Gee, you should've heard what Bob said in LifeGuides class today! I can't tell you exactly what he said, but it blew me away.' Even that is breaking confidentiality. A vague sentence like that does a couple of things. It gets other people outside the class wondering just what is going on in Bob's life. People may ask Bob, 'Say, what's happening? I hear you're having a hard time, guy.'

"It also starts the 'twenty questions' game: 'I bet I already know what it was about. It was about his dad, wasn't it.'

"No."

"Then it had to be about his mom, right?"

"Well.....Maybe."

"Probably about her moving out of the house, right?"

Participants can also be told that, although any issue may be raised, not every issue can be discussed in the class. For example, if a participant mentions that she was once sexually abused, the facilitators and the class participants must acknowledge that statement and give her plenty of strokes for bringing it up. Unless this is done, the LifeGuides class will simply be reinforcing the "no-talk rule" dysfunctional families often have regarding a major family problem such as alcoholism or sexual abuse. However, since it is not appropriate for the LifeGuides class to delve into specific, personal details about the behaviors of the family members of participants, the facilitators should intervene and let the participant know that they will discuss that problem in more detail outside of the LifeGuides class. The person can still express her **feelings** about the problem, what she is going to

do to protect herself, and what she will do to address the emotional impact it has had on her.

Facilitators report that they seldom have a problem with participants revealing detailed information about sensitive issues. For example, when describing incidents of sexual abuse participants tend to use generalities such as, "He's such a pervert!" or "He's really disgusting!"

When Facilitators Must Break Confidentiality

Whenever a participant is clearly in danger because of suicidal intentions, abuse from someone else, or high levels of drug use, facilitators must take action to ensure the safety of the youth. This will involve telling someone outside of the class, such as the parents, the police, or a child protection agency. Adults are duty-bound to break confidentiality in such cases. Facilitators should let participants know this at the beginning of the year so participants don't feel betrayed if the situation arises.

Negotiating *How* the Information will be Shared with Someone Outside the Class

Facilitators can reassure participants that, if the facilitators decide they must break confidentiality for the protection of a participant, the participant will be told. In most cases, facilitators will be able to negotiate with the participant just how the necessary information will be reported to someone outside the class. For instance, if a participant has revealed that he is engaging in a clearly dangerous form of drug abuse, the facilitators can let him know that they cannot keep such vital information from his parents. The participant could be given the option of telling his parents himself, possibly by calling them from a telephone in a school office. The facilitators could also invite the parents to school and, with the participant present, discuss the issue of drug abuse.

The facilitators, then, will let participants know when they have to break confidentiality and will negotiate just **how** it will be done. They **must not**, however, negotiate whether they will share the information. This information must be reported to someone outside the class if a participant is in danger.

Exercise: Thumbs Up on Confidentiality

Some facilitators stress the importance of confidentiality by giving several examples and asking participants to judge if confidentiality has been broken. If participants believe that the person speaking in the example was breaking confidentiality, they turn their thumbs down. If they believe the person maintained confidentiality, they put their thumbs up. Facilitators will find it helpful to start out with an obvious example. This gets participants involved quickly, since they are less hesitant to respond.

Below are some examples facilitators can use. After each of the following situations, facilitators ask "Is the person breaking confidentiality?"

- "Hey, Mary, I noticed that Joey was out in the parking lot last period. Doesn't he go to the LifeGuides class with you?" "Yea, but he hasn't been coming much lately." (This is a breach of confidentiality. Participants decide who they want to tell about their participation in a LifeGuides class. Other participants should not decide this for them.)

- A LifeGuides class participant speaking to a friend not in the class: "Today when I was in the LifeGuides class I really started to feel lonely. I was thinking back to when I was a little girl and my dad used to go out to the bar. I was thinking how lonely I was." (This is keeping confidentiality because it is all right to talk about feelings that come up during the class.)

- Parent: "Did you go to your meeting today?" Child: "Sure." Parent: "Well, what did you talk about?" Child: "Today we talked about how Mary went to a party over the weekend. She got drunk and her parents found out. But her parents were drunk too. She said that sometimes she gets drunk with her parents." (An obvious breach of confidentiality.)

- Parent: "What happened in your LifeGuides class today?" Child: "Today we talked about how important it is for me to learn to have fun. I found out that when I have fun, it helps me feel better about myself. I've got to try harder to find things I like to do." (This is not a breach of confidentiality. The conversation did not reveal any specific information given by another participant.)

Opening Ritual: Why We are Here

Many self-help groups and school-based support groups use some ritual to start off a meeting. The LifeGuides class can also use some basic reading to remind participants of why they joined the class and what they hope to accomplish in it.

In each of the partiicipant guidebooks there is a short statement on "Why We Are Here." The statement, which describes three basic ground rules for the class and some key goals, can be read by a participant at the beginning of each class session. The

facilitators and participants may want to discuss and make changes to the statement.

Reading From a Daily Meditation Guide

There are a variety of daily meditation booklets available. These booklets typically provide a daily reading coupled with some key issue to meditate on. Several of these guides are listed in Appendix A, on page 189.

The facilitators can choose a booklet and ask one of the group participants to give the daily reading. Other class members can make brief comments about the reading.

Have Participants Choose the Reading

One problem with reading from a meditation guide is that there is a specific reading for each date of the year. If the reading for the date of the class meeting is totally irrelevant to anything the class has been focusing on, or to anything participants have shown the slightest interest in, this ritual can fall flat.

To make the weekly reading more meaningful, a participant can be assigned to look through one or more books during the week to choose the meditation for the next session. The participant will use his or her own criteria for picking a particular reading.

Work on Assignments, Commitments, Goals

Some or all of the participants may be working on specific personal goals. Facilitators can start the class by asking those who are working on specific programs, or who had specific assignments, to describe what and how they did.

If the entire class was given an assignment to complete during the week, facilitators may go around the group and ask each participant to report briefly on what they did.

Who Wants Time?

Facilitators can go around the circle of participants and ask them to tell the class how things are going for them and whether they want time. Facilitators could provide some simple structure for this, such as "clockwise, starting on the right."

Asking for time at the beginning of class should not be a prerequisite for raising important issues during the session. A person may not have anything important to discuss at the beginning of the class, but finds that the class has touched on some feelings that she would like to bring up.

There are two types of participants who will likely ask for time:

- **Those who like to live in crisis** and who like to define their problems in terms of crisis. These participants will usually have a problem to present: an argument with their parents, a struggle at school, a fight with a boyfriend or girlfriend. Often, these crises are meant to distract rather than focus. With some experience, LifeGuides facilitators will be able to spot "emergencies" that are raised in order to distract the class from a subject a participant finds threatening. It is not uncommon that just as the issue of participant drug use is about to be discussed complaints about parental behavior rise tremendously.

- **The more assertive participants** will ask for time, while the less assertive, shy, and retiring types will not.

Facilitators who want to use the "Who-wants-time?" approach should consider requests for time as guidelines for pacing the class, not an absolute agenda. Facilitators may also want to check in with any participants who haven't asked for time or spoken for a while.

When participants ask for time, they can also say, quite briefly, what they want the time for. For example, "I need some time to talk about a fight I had with my parents," or "I wanted to talk about some hassles with my boyfriend." The facilitators will have to determine what issues seem to be a priority. Depression and threats of running away — e.g., "I've got to get out of this house!" — will have to be addressed in some fashion. Lower priority will usually be given to complaints about family rules or restrictions, e.g., "I'm really angry at my mother because she won't let me go to the concert tomorrow night."

Acknowledge the Joy

Care must be taken not to overlook participants who are feeling very positive about themselves. During an opening go-round, a participant might say, "I feel just great today! Things are finally going right!" These participants should not be considered a low priority for class time just because they do not need immediate support while others appear to be in pain or turmoil. Rather, it is very important to recognize the students who are feeling well and ask them to talk about it. These participants can usually explain quickly why they are feeling so good. The class can acknowledge and share the joy with that person before moving on to other issues.

What's Happened Since the Last Session

Questions or directives to share briefly what happened since the last session are probably the most frequently used check-in technique in the LifeGuides process. Here are a variety of statements facilitators can use to check in with participants:

- "Briefly share individual highs and lows since the last meeting."
- "Share something significant that happened this week."
- "Share something important that you discovered about yourself this week."
- "What risks did you take this week, and what were the results?"
- "Describe a conflict you witnessed this week."
- "Name one thing you did to help a person this week."
- "Share a new behavior you tried this week and tell how it worked."
- "How did you take care of yourself? What did you do for yourself that was healthy?"

Exercise: What Participants are Experiencing in the Present Moment

Here are some simple ways facilitators can get at participants' current moods and outlooks:

- Ask them to name the main feeling they are experiencing right then. Some facilitators make it a rule that physical symptoms cannot be used ("I'm tired, I feel sick"), because they are more like complaints than self-revelation. The terms "fine," "all right," and "OK" should also be avoided. Facilitators can ask participants to use the "Feeling List," which is at the end of each of the three participant guidebooks.

- Ask them to describe their current situation and mood in terms of a weather report. Facilitators could give examples of how to use meteorological terms to describe feelings: "Well, I have a lot of work today, but I'm not feeling too bad, so I guess I'm 'fair-to-partly cloudy.'" Or, "I feel great, so I expect sunshine and high 70's all day."

- Observe two minutes of silence, and then ask participants to share what is going on inside of them.
- Ask them to name one thing that is really bothering them.

Exercise:
Who and How Do You Trust?

The subject of trust can come up almost any time during the LifeGuides class process. Participants' trust levels will determine how they behave in the class, how they accept support, and how they face the challenges of growth. Facilitators can use the following questions as opening exercises for almost any session or whenever the subject of trust arises:

- "What does the word 'trust' mean to you? Give examples."
- "On a scale of one to ten, do you think you are, in general, very trusting or not at all trusting?"
- "Who do you trust most in the world?"
- "Who do you trust least?"
- "In general, do you trust people of the same sex or people of the opposite sex?"
- "Who in your family do you trust?"
- "Who in the school do you trust?"
- "Who don't you trust?"
- "We can trust different people in different ways. For instance, you may trust many people not to harm you, but fewer people to be honest with you. Tell us, then, not only whom you trust, but in what ways you trust them."
- "How does your trust level affect the way you behave at home? In the classroom? With your friends in this class?"
- "Draw 'trust clusters.' " (See page 47 in the "LifeGuides Interview.")

The LifeGuides class can take a more introspective turn by examining the origins of the trust levels revealed by each participant. Facilitators can ask participants:

- "What about your life makes you as trusting or distrusting as you are?"
- "Did you use to trust much more than you do today?"
- "Tell us about a time in your life when you were most trusting."
- "Tell us what makes you more trusting and what makes you less trusting."

- "How does your trust level affect the way you behave at home? In the classroom? With your friends in this class?"

Exercise:
The Great Graduated Trust Experiment

In this exercise, participants are asked to respond to a series of increasingly more revealing and risky questions, found in the *Becoming Aware Participant Guidebook*. The questions are posed to the class one at a time, with each member of the class responding to the question before the class moves on to the next one. The primary purpose of the exercise is not to learn the information given in response to the questions, but to determine the limits of trust in the class and the reasons for those limits. It is very important for facilitators to let participants know it is all right to decline to respond and appropriate to have limits on self-revelation. The facilitator can say:

"We are going to go around the circle, responding to simple questions. When we have all answered the first question, I will pose another. Each question asks you to reveal a little bit more about yourself. The list of questions was made up by kids like you who were in a support group. The questions will get a little more difficult for some of you to answer. That's OK. We don't expect you to answer all of them."

When facilitators ask for clarification about why a participant doesn't want to respond to a question, the first response may be, "Cause it's none of your business!" That kind of statement can still be revealing. If the participant responds with anger, fear, or hurt, the facilitator can reflect that in a gentle, non-confrontive manner:

- "That sounds like a subject you have a lot of feelings about."
- "Talking about _____ can be hard. Does anyone else feel that way?"
- "Why do we find it hard to talk about ___?"
- "Let's keep track of the things we find kind of risky or scary to talk about." (A facilitator can list them on the board.)

The exercise can stop after half or more of the participants have declined to answer certain questions. Facilitators can then note the areas participants have declined to talk about and say:

Calculating the Risks

If I really wanted to hurt your feelings, what would I say?

Do you have a pet peeve, something about the world or people that bothers you? If so, what?

What is one of your greatest fears?

What is your favorite instrument (to play or to listen to)?

Name something you are good at.

What is your favorite pet or would be if you could have any pet you wanted?

What makes you respect authority?

If you could change anything about your body, what would it be?

What do you believe comes after death?

What one thing are you struggling with the most right now?

What is one of your strongest defenses (sarcasm, violence, silence, etc.)

What is your favorite pigout food?

What is one goal you have for the future?

What is your favorite color?

If you could change one thing about your closest friend, what would it be?

What is your favorite game, hobby, or pastime?

What really gets you angry?

What upsets you most about your parents/guardians?

If someone wanted to make your day (cheer you up), what should they say?

Name something that not many people know about you (old habits, sleep with Teddy bear, etc.).

- "It looks like ___ are risky topics for us. Later on we'll be talking about ___. We'll see that a lot of kids like you have problems in that area."

- "It isn't just that these are topics that are hard to talk about. Being with a group of people can be a problem too. There are things we'd say to our close friends that we wouldn't say in the class. Why is that?"

Exercise:
Calculating the Risks

This exercise is less threatening than the "Graduated Trust Experiment." Participants are given copies of "Calculating the Risks" on page 58. This contains the same items as the list read to participants during the previous exercise, but they are in random order. The class can break into pairs or threes and rank the items from less risky to more risky. The exercise can be processed in the same way as the "Graduated Trust Experiment."

Exercise:
Gratitude Reminder

Facilitators can have participants spend three minutes writing down what they are grateful for, and then go around the class and ask participants to read their lists. Facilitators can write down what participants say on a flipchart or a blackboard. The class can examine their pool of items and comment on any commonality or uniqueness among the items.

Participants can take their personal lists home so they can read them first thing every morning. They can also add to the list and report back to the next class about any additions they have made.

LifeGuides Audiotape Series

Relaxation, stress management, and instilling hope are all critical issues for LifeGuides participants. In addition to the LifeGuides Program, participants would benefit from daily meditations or reminders to help them work in these areas. The LifeGuides Audiotape series (available in 1990) is described in the "Taking Care" sessions on stress reduction (page 151. These tapes could be described and made available to participants earlier in the curriculum if the facilitators so desire.

Introducing a New Participant to the Class

Although many participants will be enrolled in a LifeGuides Program from the beginning of the school year, the enrollment will usually remain open. The LifeGuides Program is offered, in part, to students who are having trouble coping with the stresses in their lives. Just when the stress will become most acute cannot be predicted or controlled.

Facilitators can have the other participants do most of the work when bringing a new participant into the LifeGuides Program. They can ask participants to tell the new participant who they are, what year they are in at school, how they got into the class, and why they are there. This process also provides facilitators with an opportunity to see how participants are coming along. Participants' reasons for being in class may have changed significantly from those they offered when they first began the LifeGuides Program.

If facilitators find that this approach takes too much time, they can have participants simply react to a list of statements relevant to why they are in the class. Facilitators can ask:

- "Who was referred by a teacher?"

- "Who came because someone else in the class suggested it to them?"

- "Who came partly because of troubles in school?"

- "Who was having some troubles at home?"

- "Who knows someone who drinks too much?"

This gives a new person some idea of who is in the class without going through every participant's personal story.

Another way of having the new participant learn about the others is to have each person give one example of what they have gotten out of the class so far. Responses may range from the humorous and superficial, "I get to skip social studies when I come here," to the more meaningful, "I have more friends now," and "I feel better about myself."

Facilitators can also ask if any participant wants to explain the "class tools" to the new participant. (See page 70 in the "Becoming Aware" section.) Once a participant starts to do this, other participants will usually add their own comments.

When Issues of Personal Safety Arise

During any of the daily check-ins and warm-ups, participants may give some sign that they felt threatened during the week. This can happen even if all the appropriate child protection services have been notified and put into action. These are limited and slow-moving bureaucracies. Children need to assume responsibility for their own safety.

Review the Section on Personal Safety

Before beginning the LifeGuides Program, facilitators should review the section in "Becoming Aware" on personal safety, beginning on page 75. This provides some exercises for helping participants become more street-wise and safety conscious. It also provides guidelines on what to do when an issue of personal safety arises.

Weekly Facilitator Tasks

After each LifeGuides Program session, facilitators should take the time to assess the class process and to fill in a class log (see "Sample Class Log," page 68).

The following general guidelines can help facilitators assess current dynamics and relationships in the class.

- Who is participating, not participating, monopolizing?
- Is the class staying on the subject or going off on tangents?
- Should the class wander more or tighten up?
- Are there cliques forming?
- Who is interrupting others or talking over others?

Some form of go-round exercise can also be used to assess the class process. Facilitators can ask each person or the class as a whole:

- "How was our group meeting today?"
- "Do you feel people listened?"
- "Did everyone speak?"
- "Was it helpful?"

Asking the class to assess its own process should not be attempted until after several sessions. In the earlier stages of the process and with the younger participants, students will probably attack the class in some way because of their fears, rather than assess the process. Some of the participants will simply not have the skills to offer useful comments on the process until they have been in the class for a while.

Planning a LifeGuides Class

This section provides an overview of the Life-Guides curriculum resources as well as some ideas about how to plan a LifeGuides class. To do this, facilitators and program planners must take into account the needs of participants, the skills and interests of the facilitators, and the locally defined accepted role of the schools in prevention and early-intervention.

Facilitators and program planners should review the LifeGuides Program curriculum well in advance of the first session. The LifeGuides Curriculum Resources, on pages 1–4, lists the suggested films, lectures, and exercises under each subject area in the three LifeGuides phases. By reviewing this overview, facilitators will be able to choose the subject areas and exercises they believe need emphasis.

Planners and facilitators must make two key decisions: (1) whether to make the class available to all children from disrupted family environments, or to design it primarily for children of alcoholics; and (2) whether to take an open-ended approach, in which participants can continue to attend as long as they feel the need, or to design a focused, time-limited curriculum.

Focus on Children of Alcoholics Only?

As was mentioned in the introduction, the LifeGuides Program has its roots in the "Concerned Persons Groups" offered by schools and social service agencies to the children of alcoholics. The LifeGuides curriculum, as described here, has a strong emphasis on problems related to parental alcoholism, but it also describes how other problems, particularly divorce and abuse, affect children.

Those who choose to offer the program only or primarily to children of alcoholics will have no problem making the curriculum specific to that issue. They *will* have trouble, however, turning down youths affected by different family problems who could so readily benefit from a LifeGuides class.

Those who would like to offer the program to students affected by any kind of disruptive family problem can also, of course, do so using the curriculum. The exercises are appropriate for all these youths. Even exercises on chemical dependency are appropriate, since all participants are at least as likely — and probably much more likely — than the general population to find drug-use problems among friends and family other than their parents.

The more reading facilitators do, in a wide range of problem areas, the better prepared they will be to challenge and offer support in various kinds of situations. Facilitators would do well to look over some of the literature described in Appendix A, page 189.

Open-ended Process or a Focused, Time-limited Curriculum

If planners and facilitators see the LifeGuides Program as a means of *both* imparting information and offering ongoing support, they will most likely use an open-ended approach. Participants can stay for an entire year, or even longer if they feel the need. The focus will not only be on learning important information, but also on changing attitudes and behaviors that prevent participants from growing socially, emotionally, and academically.

A LifeGuides class does not have to be open-ended. It can focus primarily on imparting information and be offered for eight to twelve sessions per quarter.

When the number of sessions offered is limited, the class will stray from the prepared curriculum less often. Facilitators will handle participant crises or problems by assisting students in getting counseling within the school or the community. In a time-limited class, participants can be required to complete the class once they sign up for it.

Facilitators who have only used the open-ended approach may believe the information-oriented, structured approach is too academic, methodical, and limited to do any good. But this belief discounts the tremendous empowerment information alone can provide when it is the right information about the major problems in a youth's life. All of the issues on the Checklist of Participants' Needs (page 48) can be addressed in important ways in a structured, information-oriented LifeGuides class.

The Three LifeGuides Phases

The three phases of the LifeGuides Program are **Phase I, Becoming Aware; Phase II, Taking Care**; and **Phase III, Moving On.** All three phases, of course, contribute to building the self-esteem of participants and providing them with support to cope with the stresses in their lives. There are, however, differences in the kinds of goals focused on. Here is a description of the general goals for each phase:

Phase I: Becoming Aware

The goals of the Becoming Aware portion of the Life-Guides Program are:

- To help participants review how their lives have been going in the months preceding the start of a LifeGuides class.

- To give participants some skills to make their participation in a LifeGuides class more productive.

- To provide them with basic knowledge about how families work and what families do for people.

- To show participants what happens to families when a parent is impaired by alcoholism or some other problem.

Phase II: Taking Care

The main goals of the Taking Care portion of the curriculum are to help participants:

- Become aware of the defenses they may be using that prevent them from recognizing the problems they face and taking action to cope with or alleviate the problem.

- Cope with life as they presently find it.

- Begin, even in the smallest way, to take steps to change those attitudes and behaviors that keep them stuck with their problems.

- Learn how their feelings have been affected by their experiences, at home, in school and elsewhere.

- Become aware of how they feel about themselves and about their lives in general.

- Understand what their feelings are and how to express them in a healthy, productive manner

Phase III: Moving On

Moving On is the growth part of the curriculum. It contains exercises similar to the many "Life Skills" prevention curricula currently available. The information and exercises are, however, tailored to meet the needs of the children from disrupted family environments. The goals of the Moving On portion of the curriculum are:

- To deepen participants' understanding of their families, of their roles in their own families, and how those roles affect their behavior in the rest of their lives.

- To review the concept of co-dependency and consider how co-dependent behavior may be detracting from participants' growth and development.

- To help participants learn how to start and maintain satisfying personal relationships.

- To help participants learn how to be appropriately assertive.

- To help participants learn and be able to use problem-solving and decision-making techniques.

- To help participants learn to have fun and to enjoy themselves in a healthy, fulfilling way.

The Three LifeGuides Phases are not Meant to be Rigid Prescriptions Regarding What Subject Matter a Class Should be Working On

The general sequence described by the three phases parallels the pattern commonly used by experienced facilitators of Concerned Persons Groups and other support services for children from disrupted family environments. The general flow of the sessions will start with subject matter from **Becoming Aware,** move on to **Taking Care,** and end with material from **Moving On.** The facilitators will frequently want to draw on background information and exercises from phases they are not currently focusing on.

The participant guidebooks have material related to some, but not all, of the exercises given in the curriculum, allowing those using an open-ended approach more flexibility. The class will usually be focusing on the material for a particular phase and will be using the guidebook for that phase. However, the class can also try many exercises from other phases that do not require any guidebook material.

Facilitators Should Keep Their Own Copies of the Participant Guidebooks

Within each subject area the *Facilitator's Guide* describes the content of the related exercises and the procedures for carrying them out. The guide does not usually duplicate the layout of and every detail of the exercises as they appear in the participant guidebooks. Facilitators can easily borrow a participant's personal guidebook when explaining an exercise, but it is best for the facilitators to keep their own copies of the three participant guidebooks. In addition to using these when explaining an exercise, facilitators can make special notes in them recording how they have customized the exercises to suit their own purposes.

General Content of the Subject Areas

Material on each subject area of the three phases of the curriculum contains background information and a brief description of some of the relevant key issues; general goals to be accomplished for that subject area; affirmations to help participants gain a positive attitude and take an active approach to dealing with the issues raised; and a series of relevant exercises.

Background Information

Much of the background information is contained in the introductory comments that precede the goals for each subject area. Some background information is also placed among the exercises. This would include all information not specifically labeled "Exercise."

With the exception of the information on the process of addiction, the introductory material is seldom longer than one or two pages. This information is usually addressed to the facilitators, not to participants. Facilitators will decide how much information they want to offer to participants at any one time and will phrase it to fit each particular group of students. The approach will vary, of course, depending on whether the class is all boys in junior high school, a mixed class of senior high school students, and so forth. The written directions for most exercises are addressed directly to the participants.

Goals

The list of goals in each subject area are general guidelines for focus rather than prescribed learner outcomes. The facilitators can peruse the list of goals and decide which would be most pertinent to a particular class at a given time. The class logs for each session include a place for facilitators to list the goal or goals focused on for that session.

Using the "Affirmations"

Each subject area in the LifeGuides Program curriculum contains "affirmations" relevant to that particular subject area. Facilitators can make use of those affirmations as follows:

• Go around the class and have each participant read at least one affirmation. Allow 10 to 15 seconds of silence after each affirmation has been read.

• Whenever a participant seems to be falling into negative or irrational thinking, have him or her repeat, several times in succession, an appropriate affirmation from the list.

• Have participants use the affirmations as homework. They are to repeat them every day during the week until the next session.

Exercises

There are many exercises to choose from in planning a LifeGuides class. Facilitators will not be able to use all of them in a year. Sometimes, the discussion following opening exercises will carry a class through most of the sessions in the quarter. The material in the rest of this *Facilitator's Guide* should not be looked at as a huge number of tasks that a class must accomplish, but rather as a compendium of resources to draw on when needed.

Facilitators will use their own judgment in deciding which methods to use and the direction of the class for a period of time. As mentioned, the Checklist of Participant Needs can be used to guide the decision-making process. Facilitators can refer to the checklist to review the needs of each participant, as well as to keep track of common themes for the class as a whole.

Those facilitators who have two or more LifeGuides classes during the week can try different approaches with different classes. This gives the facilitator a chance to see what material works best in various situations and provides variety to those who work constantly with youth from disrupted family environments.

Example of a Structured LifeGuides Class

On pages 65–67 is an example of a tightly planned and structured LifeGuides class, based on the premise that the class will be held for thirty-two weeks during a school year. The curriculum presumes that most of the participants are new to the process. They need, first of all, some solid information about how to participate effectively in a group situation and about how families are affected by alcoholism and other disruptive problems. In this curriculum, then, the three phases are emphasized as follows:

- Phase I: Fifteen sessions
- Phase II: Ten sessions
- Phase III: Six sessions
- Year-end wrap up and preparing for summer vacation: One session

The emphasis is on providing basic information about chemical dependency and related family problems, as well as on examining closely how those problems have affected a person's self-concept and outlook on life.

Within such a weighting of emphasis among the three phases, there are still many options. The example provided simply demonstrates how a curriculum compatible with that plan might look.

Use of the Class Log

A class log helps facilitators remember what exercises were done, how they worked, and how participants reacted. This information will help them decide how to structure the next session or revamp the curriculum for the coming year. A format for the class log is provided on page 68. Such a log helps facilitators keep track of what material was presented, what exercises were tried, how participants reacted, and what needs of the participants appear to be most pressing.

It is very important for facilitators to note any large or small success that occurs during the LifeGuides class. Observable change in the feelings, attitudes, or behavior of participants is not always easily apparent to school staff, facilitators, or the participants themselves. If a careful record is kept, positive changes can be noted and reinforced.

Sample LifeGuides Program Curriculum

(The asterisks indicate subject matter or exercises that have related material in the participant guidebooks.)

Phase I: Becoming Aware

Start-up at the Beginning of the Year

Session 1:

Facilitators' Introductions

Exercise: Reviewing Class Tools

Exercise: Which Words Describe You Best? *

Session 2:

Exercise: More About Me. *

Exercise: Summer Vacation Review *

Exercise: Filling Out the DaySavers Card *

Personal Safety

Session 3:

Exercise: Personal Safety Review *

Exercise: Reviewing the Week

Contingency Plan for Weekends, Holidays, and Summer Vacation

Communication and Listening Skills

Session 4:

Breaking the Sound Barrier: Blocks to Clear Communication

Family Problems Lead to Poor Communication

Exercise: Communication Problems In the Family

Session 5:

Blocks to Communication in a LifeGuides Class

Characteristics of Useful Feedback *

Typical Clarifying Responses

What's a "Normal" Family?

Session 6:

Exercise: The All-American Family Quiz *

Exercise: Day-to-day — Family Routines *

Session 7:

Exercise: Playing by the Rules *

Exercise: Family Circles and Family X's — What Kids Need From Families *

Session 8:

Exercise: Family Photographs

Exercise: Drawing the Family Table

Drug and Alcohol Use: What's Normal, What's Not?

Session 9:

Exercise: What's Normal, What's Not? *

Mood Swings

Session 10:

Stage One: Experimentation — Learning How Chemicals Affect Moods

Stage Two: Social/Recreational Use — Seeking the Mood Swing

Alcoholism and Drug Dependence: When Use Goes Out of Control.

Session 11:

Exercise: True/False Quiz on Alcoholism and Drug Addiction *

Session 12:

Exercise: Dear Miss Helpful *

Stage Three: Harmful Involvement

Stage Four: Chemical Dependency — The Relationship Becomes Primary

Chemical Dependency is a Disease

Exercise: Signals Worth Watching *

Shock Waves: How Alcoholism Affects the Family

Session 13:

Review of the Progression of Chemical Dependency

How the Family is Affected

Family Rules Change

Exercise: Special Rules for Special Problems *

Session 14:

Exercise: Shock Waves — How the Chemical Use of Another Affects Me *

Typical Reactions to Alcoholism in the Family

Exercise: How Families React to Other Serious Problems

Something to Think About: Participants' Risks for Future Problems

Session 15:

Many Opportunities to Point Out Participants' Risks for Drug Problems

Exercise: Six Signs of Risks for Serious Problems *

Risks for Problems in Relationships

Phase II: Taking Care

Denial: Dance of Deception

Session 16:

Move Slowly in Confronting Denial

Reading: "Don't be Fooled by Me." *

Exercise: Masks Over Masks

Taking Off the Masks *

Session 17:

Exercise: A Few Fast Moves *

Exercise: A Few Fast Family Moves *

Enabling: The Helping that Hurts

Session 18:

Exercise: Enabling is Hard Work

Exercise: Enabling — Helping That Hurts *

Feelings: Where They Come From — Where They Take Us

Session 19:

The Use of Expressive Techniques That Will Help Reveal Emotions

Exercise: The Feeling Cube

Exercise: Feeling-level Reactions to Family Stories

Session 20:

Exercise: Happy, So-So or Sad *

Anger and Conflicting Feelings

Session 21:

Helping Participants Recognize, Accept, and Deal with their Anger *

Exercise: Accepting contradictory feelings

Self-esteem: Liking Ourselves

Session 22:

Exercise: Extra Work on Affirmations *

Tasks and Challenges Improve
Participants' Self-esteem

Exercise: Short and Simple Positive
Feedback Games

Session 23:

Exercise: How I See Myself *

Exercise: The Guilt Disposal

Coping with Daily Challenges

Session 24:

Exercise: Ten Up, Ten Down *

Exercise: My Life, Right Now *

Session 25:

Exercise: Pack Up Your Sorrows

Exercise: Inventory of Stress-Reducers *

Exercise: The 60-Second Tension Check

Phase III: Moving On

Family Roles: Rigid and Restricting or Guidelines for Growth?

Session 26:

Exercise: The Family Circle

Family Talk As It Might be Given in a Life-
Guides Class

Codependency and Co-dependent Behaviors: Too Close for Comfort?

Session 27:

Exercise: Too Close for Comfort — the Codependency Inventory *

The Pitfalls of Codependency *

Interpersonal Skills: Finding Fulfillment in Relationships.

Session 28:

Exercise: What Keeps You From Making More
Friends? *

Exercise: Initiating Conversation

Assertiveness Skills: Standing Up for Yourself

Session 29:

Exercise: What's Assertive, What's Not? *

Exercise: Examples of Non-assertive, Assertive,
and Aggressive Behaviors *

Taking Care of Business: Problem-solving, Decision-making and Goal-setting

Session 30:

Exercise: Stop That Stinkin' Thinkin' *

Basic Steps in Problem-solving and
Decision-making *

Exercise: Case Examples for Problem-solving

Taking Care of Ourselves, Having Fun

Session 31:

Trying New Activities

Exercise: What Keeps Me From Having Fun? *

Exercise: How to be a Kid Again *

Session 32:

Review of Plan for Summer Vacation

Keep in mind that this proposed curriculum was
for students who are new to the process. For a class
made up of students who have already had experience
in support groups or the LifeGuides Program, the
weighting could be reversed as follows:

– **Phase I**: Six Sessions.

– **Phase II**: Ten Sessions.

– **Phase III**: Fifteen Sessions.

SAMPLE
Class Log for Sessions on Personal Safety

Date: _____

Facilitators: _____

Opening Go-Rounds Used: _____

Objectives emphasized:

____ To make sure that participants are aware of any threats to their physical safety that may arise in their homes, on the streets, or at school.

____ To assess how they currently deal with potentially dangerous situations.

____ To get them to realize that they must depend on their own good judgment for their personal safety.

____ To help them be aware of all options and services available to them when they feel threatened.

____ To have them develop contingency plans for specific potentially dangerous situations.

____ To encourage participants to plan for a number of common situations that threaten their health or safety.

____ To encourage participants to begin the networking process that will provide them with personal and professional resources in emergency situations.

____ Others: _____

_____

Subjects Discussed: _____

_____

Major Exercise Used: _____

_____

Films or other Audio-Visual Aids Used: _____

_____

Comments on Process: _____

_____

Note any Successes that Happened in Class or Were Described by Participants: _____

_____

ATTENDANCE AND COMMENTS ON PARTICIPANTS ON NEXT PAGE

In Attendance:

Name: _____   Name: _____

Name: _____   Name: _____

Name: _____   Name: _____

Name: _____   Name: _____

Name: _____   Name: _____

Name: _____   Name: _____

Comments:

Phase I: Becoming Aware

Start-up at the Beginning of the Year

It is not unusual for past participants to ask that the LifeGuides Program start immediately when school begins in the fall. Facilitators should not feel undue pressure to give in to these requests, however. Postponing the first session of the LifeGuides Program for several weeks gives participants time to become focused on their classes, accustomed to their schedules, and settled into school social life. It also gives the LifeGuides Program facilitators a chance to touch base with experienced participants, contact participants from other special classes and support groups — former junior high students moving into senior high, for instance — and meet with prospective new participants.

Keep A List of All Prospective Participants. Whenever a student asks when the program will start, a facilitator can respond, "If you're interested, let me get your name and I'll contact you when we're ready. Also, if you know other people who are interested, have them tell me and I'll get them on the list." In this way, participants help build the initial core group for the program. When the facilitators are ready to begin the LifeGuides Program, they can use the list to check participants' current schedules and then choose the best time for the class.

Another reason for postponing the commencement of the LifeGuides class is to allow time to build staff support for the program. This usually involves a number of staff training programs on the problems of typical LifeGuides participants, along with a description of how the program works. One of the best things to include in such in-service training is a description of participants who have made demonstrable, positive changes while in the class. Support from the staff will lead to an increase in appropriate referrals to the class.

Goals for the Start-up Sessions

The goals for sessions in this subject area include:

- To start developing a cohesive group of participants.
- To establish ground rules, guidelines, and expectations for the year.
- To review the experiences participants had over the summer.
- To review plans, goals, and commitments made by experienced participants prior to summer vacation.
- To see how well lessons learned in the previous year held through the summer.
- To ensure that participants have sufficient support to cope with their daily lives and deal with emergencies.

Review of material for the experienced participants in the class may mean that new participants will be exposed to issues for the first time. Reviewing this material and raising issues for discussion will start new participants thinking about the issues and sets the stage for discussions when they come up later in the year.

Affirmations on Sharing and Trusting

The following affirmations can be read in the class before or after all sessions related to starting up and building cohesiveness. They can also be assigned for reading during the week. The affirmations are found in the *Becoming Aware Participant Guidebook:*

- I have come here to share my experiences, feelings, and observations with others.
- By sharing, I will learn and those around me will learn.
- I can learn to trust the people in my class.

- I will try my best to make myself worthy of the trust of others.
- I believe that this class, the facilitators, and the other participants will help me feel better about myself and my life.

The "Why We Are Here" reading, in the *Becoming Aware Participant Guidebook,* can be introduced to the class at this point. Each session, a different participant can be asked to read the statement.

Overview

- Opening exercises
- Facilitators' introductions
- Exercise: Reviewing Class Tools
- Exercise: Which Words Describe You Best?
- Exercise: Fun Ways to Get Acquainted
- Exercise: Brief Life History
- Exercise: Lists of Interests and Traits
- Exercise: Group by Birth Order
- Exercise: More About Me
- Exercise: Summer Vacation Review
- Exercise: Current Connections
- Exercise: Filling Out the DaySavers Card

Opening Exercises

Before the class, the facilitators can review "Opening Exercises: Check-ins and Warm-ups," beginning on page 53, and decide if any of them suit the needs of the participants, the facilitators, or the process at this time.

Problems with Stock Responses. In the beginning of the year, especially with junior high school students, the responses to opening exercises are very short and very non-revealing: "Fine" or "I don't know" can come up all the time. That's when the "Feeling Checklist," in the *Becoming Aware Participant Guidebook,* can help. Facilitators can say, "Look at the feeling checklist. Which one best fits how you feel?"

Facilitators' Introductions

The facilitators should take several minutes to introduce themselves at the beginning of the first session. The content of the introductions would be basically the same as that described for facilitator introductions during the LifeGuides Interview (page 45). After the facilitators introduce themselves, they can ask par-ticipants what they know about the LifeGuides Program or support groups. Some questions to ask are:

- "What have you heard about the LifeGuides class?" (Junior high students are likely to try to please the facilitators by saying positive things. Responses from senior high students will be more frank.)
- "Have you ever known anyone who went to a support group or special program like this?"
- "Have you ever been to a support group or special program before?"

Exercise: Reviewing Class Tools

Class rules are really class tools. The guidelines used to keep the class safe, positive, and productive do not restrict as much as they empower.

Participants can help review the class tools. Facilitators can ask participants to describe the class tools from a previous year or to list what they believe the tools should be. Facilitators will, of course, be sure that the following points are covered:

- Confidentiality. (See page 54 in "Opening Exercises," for details on confidentiality.)
- One person speaks at a time.
- Every person receives respect.
- There are no put-downs.
- Participants have the right to pass on an exercise if they feel too threatened by it. (This does not mean facilitators or other participants cannot put some pressure on those who are reluctant to take reasonable risks in the class. Facilitators can encourage participants to overcome their fears, but when a participant is clearly unwilling or unable to respond, that person's decision must be respected.)
- No smoking or eating in class.
- Drug use: The issue of drug use is handled as it is with all students. Students are expected to be drug free. If participants reveal drug use, it will be addressed in class. (See page 34 for more discussion on this issue). All use of alcohol and other drugs that indicates a serious health or safety risk must, of course, be reported.
- Scheduling and make-up time. (Explain the specific procedures to be used for passes, homework missed, and so forth. See pages 32 in "LifeGuides Policies and Procedures," for a review of how some of these issues are typically handled.)

Facilitators should give participants time to review these tools, letting them look at the list as it grows and think about it for a while. Facilitators should also give them permission to add to the list.

Some participants will give too many responses. A person with a need to control the situation in order to feel safe may want to add five or ten details. Usually those details will have been assumed under other rules. In that case, facilitators and participants can let the person know that his or her concerns are already covered under the present class tools.

Exercise:
Which Words Describe You Best?

In this exercise facilitators have participants circle six words from the "Adjective Checklist," in the *Becoming Aware Participant Guidebook,* to describe themselves. Each participant then shares with the class the adjectives he or she circled. While it is too soon in the class process to have members provide much feedback to each other, some mild feedback could be attempted with this exercise. Facilitators could ask participants, "Which other adjectives do you think would apply to Jan?" Most often, relatively positive or innocuous adjectives will be chosen.

Observations and Discussion. Some process questions facilitators might use are:

- "How difficult was it for you to check this list?"
- "Were you more comfortable with the positive or with the negative adjectives?"
- "Count how many negatives and how many positives you checked."
- "What did you learn from this exercise? Can you make an 'I learned —' sentence?"

Exercise:
Fun Ways to Get Acquainted

Some simple and fun ways for participants to get acquainted include having participants break into pairs and tell each other:

- How they would describe themselves in terms of an animal; an object.
- Their favorite color.
- The game they most like to play.
- The celebrity they most wish to be like, and why.
- The traits they most admire in that celebrity.

These statements can be written on a chalkboard or flipchart. The partners of the dyads are to listen closely,

taking notes if they wish. At the end of four minutes, they switch roles. At the end of another four minutes the class comes together and each partner introduces the other partner.

Discussion
In this and in the following exercises involving introductions, facilitators can ask process questions and make comments such as:

- "Well, we all seem to like..."
- "How did it feel to share that information?"
- "Was it hard or easy for you to share?"
- "Was it hard to remember the information your partner was telling you?"
- "What, of all the things your partner told you, surprised you most?"

Since the getting-acquainted exercises are usually fun for participants, they are effective even if there are no new participants and people are already acquainted. Participants who already know each other will perform the exercises even more willingly and provide further insights about themselves to their classmates.

Exercise:
Brief Life History

After class breaks into pairs, the partners tell each other a simple, short history: Where they were born, how old they are, what classes they are taking, how they feel about being in the school, and how they feel about being in the LifeGuides class and what they hope to get out of it. Then each partner introduces the other partner to the class.

Although these questions may not seem to be very revealing, this kind of information is not readily shared on a daily basis. The exercise helps build cohesion among class participants.

Exercise:
List of Interests and Traits

Facilitators can list all or some of the following categories on newsprint or a chalkboard, leaving enough space under each category for participants to add information. Every participant will review the sheets, write their first name and the appropriate response for each category in the list:

- Favorite songs.
- Most admired person.
- Favorite movie.

- Best subject in school.
- Best book ever read. (This should not be used, of course, in a class with a participant who cannot read or who has very poor reading skills.)
- Birth order in the family.
- Number of brothers and sisters.
- Favorite sport to play.
- Favorite sport to watch.
- Favorite game to play.

Exercise:
Group by Birth Order

In a class of nine to twelve participants, it may be possible to form three groups — youngest, oldest, and middle children. In a smaller class, participants can divide into two groups — those who are the oldest in their families and those who are not the oldest.

Discussion

In their subgroups, participants can talk about what they like about their particular birth order and what they think people who fall into the other categories are like. They can describe the positive aspects of their ordinal position and the positive aspects of other ordinal positions, and then they can discuss the negative aspects of both as well. This exercise typically leads to banter about what it is like to live with other people.

Observations

This exercise often provides interesting information about family dynamics. A participant may say, for instance, "I hate being the oldest because my mother expects me to pass messages to my father when she's mad at him"; or, "My older brother's never around. When he is, he and my dad just get into fights."

Facilitators need not point out the implications of such statements, but they can note their observations in the class log for that session and keep them in mind for future reference.

Exercise:
More About Me

In a class that has been meeting for a longer period of time, more meaningful questions can be posed. The statements in "More About Me," in the *Becoming Aware Participant Guidebook,* place greater pressure on participants to reveal important information about themselves. Participants can take ten minutes to fill out the form during the class.

The class can break into pairs or small groups and go through the questions. Participants can pair off by shared interests. For instance, facilitators might say, "Find someone who plays a sport that you like to play," or "Find someone who has the same birth order as you." Of course, the facilitators could use a straightforward method, such as having the class pair off by twos starting on a facilitator's right and going around the circle.

The facilitators can ask participants to answer twelve of the questions. This allows participants to stay away from issues they do not presently want to discuss in class.

Another approach to discussing the list is to have participants pull numbers out of a hat and respond to the numbered question that corresponds to the number they have drawn. This type of structure would probably work best with junior high school students.

Discussion

After the exercise, facilitators can share their observations and ask for comments about how people felt when doing the exercises:
- "How did you feel doing this?"
- "What did you like about it?"
- "What didn't you like?"
- "How did it affect your trust level in the class?"
- "Did you learn something about yourself?"
- "Did you learn something about each other?"

Exercise:
Summer Vacation Review

Since junior high students are more dependent on their parents for vacation activities, this exercise may be more relevant to them than to senior high students.

The first sessions of the LifeGuides class in the fall of the school year often focus largely on processing the events that took place over the summer and dealing with the difficulties in transition from the relatively unstructured summer vacation to the more regulated school environment.

Children from disrupted family environments often have difficulty with free time, but summer can be especially difficult. Many of them have problems being at home, have trouble having fun, and have trouble planning. Even though they might acknowledge that they need structure in their lives, some participants become accustomed over the summer vacation to the lack of restrictions on them when parents neglect their responsibilities to provide guidance. Others may have spent too much time at home and return to school feeling oppressed by the family environment.

Summer is also the time when many young people drink the most. Children from alcoholic and other disrupted family environments, who are at higher risk than others for heavy drinking and drug use, are likely to run into drug-use problems over the summer.

Facilitators can begin the exercise by asking participants to fill out the "Summer Vacation Review," in their *Becoming Aware Participant Guidebook*.

Discussion

Working in pairs, small groups, or as a class, participants can discuss each item on the form. Some summary questions for facilitators to consider are:

• "Did you do enough this summer? Too much?"
• "Did you do the activities you really enjoy?"
• "If you were bored, why?"

Participants' written responses will help identify the barriers they encounter to having fun and feeling safe. This information can be an important planning tool if participants save their responses and review them at the end of the school year as a pre-summer exercise. Participants can use the information to develop contingency plans for their safety, make personal growth goals for the vacation period, and plan fun activities for themselves.

Exercise:
Current Connections

This exercise helps remind participants of all the viable sources of support available to them. Working as pairs, three's, or the class as a whole, participants can answer the following questions:

• "Who did you spend the most time with last week?"
• "Who did you share a feeling with?"
• "Was there someone you wanted to be with but couldn't?"
• "Who are your closest friends?"
• "Who do you talk to when you have a problem?"
• "Who do you have fun with?"

Exercise:
Trust Clusters

If most participants haven't already done it, the "Trust Clusters" exercise in the "LifeGuides Interview," on page 47, can be tried in class or assigned for homework.

Exercise:
Filling Out the DaySavers Card

Not everyone needs to be a lifesaver. Usually, just helping someone get through a day is good enough — which is what the DaySavers Card is all about.

Participants can be encouraged to keep a list of people to call when they are in a crisis or otherwise in need of support. The list can be kept in the form of a "DaySavers Card," which facilitators can make up following the format on page 74.

Facilitators can pass these cards out at the beginning of the year and have participants fill them in. In later sessions, facilitators can ask participants to take their cards out and share who is on their list. They can also be asked to take a minute or so to see if they want to revise their lists. This enables facilitators to see if participants are carrying their cards with them and helps participants review all the possible sources of support. Participants should consider a range of people to put on the DaySavers Card, including:

• Other LifeGuides Program members.
• An Al-Anon or AlaTeen group or sponsor.
• Any school personnel they feel comfortable with.
• Any counselor, administrator, coach, youth leader, or family doctor they feel comfortable with.
• Siblings, aunts, and uncles who are capable of offering protection, support, or assistance.

If the facilitators are fairly certain participants will not feel intruded upon, they can ask participants to share their phone numbers with each other in class. Otherwise, completing the DaySavers Card can be a homework assignment. Participants should be asked to be sure they have the numbers of several friends, relatives, and at least one professional whom they feel comfortable calling in an emergency.

Facilitators should decide whether to give their home phone numbers to participants. Unless this has already been done successfully, it is probably best not to. Instead, facilitators can make sure students have the number of the school office, and then leave instructions for the office to try to accommodate LifeGuides participants by contacting one of the facilitators if possible. The facilitator can then contact the participant.

Format for the DaySavers Card

DaySavers

LifeGuides class members:

_____

_____

_____

_____

_____

An Al-Anon group or sponsor:

_____

_____

_____

Siblings, aunts, and uncles:

DaySavers

LifeGuides class members:

_____

_____

_____

_____

_____

_____

_____

_____

Any school personnel you are comfortable with:

School Office Number: _____

Any counselor, administrator, or family doctor you feel comfortable with:

_____

_____

_____

_____

_____

Personal Safety

All children should know how to take care of themselves. Even parents in the safest neighborhoods must teach their children to be street-wise so they will not fall prey to those seeking to exploit or harm them.

Children from disrupted family environments may need even more assistance in this area. They must know what to do when their own homes are no longer safe.

Children from alcoholic and other disrupted family environments are at risk not only in their homes, but in the streets and schools as well. They are perhaps at greater risk of being victimized or involved in physical confrontations than are other children because of their low self-esteem, the lack of parental guidance concerning personal safety, and their misdirected anger. The activities described in this section can be particularly beneficial if issues of personal safety seem especially important to a particular class. Before conducting these exercises, facilitators should review their own attitudes toward the dangers young people face today. Here are what one author (Hechinger, 1984) calls "false beliefs" about personal safety and children:

- Talking about dangers will scare children.
- To put fear in children is all bad.
- What they don't know can't hurt them.
- Nothing bad can happen in our neighborhood.
- Self-protection is based on physical skill and athletic ability.
- Having a bad experience will make a child tougher and stronger.

Facilitators should look for signs of these misconceptions in their own behavior, as well as in participants' statements and behaviors.

Facilators should be careful about confronting "enabling" behaviors. "Enabling" refers to all the words and actions people employ to help alcoholics and other people with problem behaviors avoid the consequences of their actions.

Chemical dependency professionals who are facilitating a LifeGuides class must be cautious about their attitudes toward enabling behaviors. Certainly, if a drunken adult asks a person to bring him a drink, taking that drink to him can be considered enabling. However, if the consequence of not taking the drink to the adult is to risk abuse, to do so is an appropriate survival technique. Participants who are not living in safe environments cannot be expected to cease their enabling behaviors unless they feel safe in doing so. Facilitators cannot aggressively confront them on enabling without also taking into consideration the potential risks involved in stopping the enabling behavior.

Goals for Sessions on Personal Safety

The goals for sessions in this subject area include:

- To make sure that participants are aware of any threats to their physical safety that may arise in their homes, on the streets, or at school.
- To assess how they currently deal with potentially dangerous situations.
- To help them realize they must depend on their own good judgment for their personal safety.
- To help them be aware of all options and services available to them when they feel threatened.
- To help them develop contingency plans for specific potentially dangerous situations.
- To encourage participants to plan for a number of common situations that could threaten their health or safety.
- To encourage participants to begin the networking process that will provide them with personal and professional resources in emergency situations.

Affirmations on Personal Safety

The following affirmations and rational thoughts about safety can be read in the class before or after sessions on personal safety. They are found in the *Becoming Aware Participant Guidebook* and can also be assigned for reading during the week.

- I have a right to be safe in my own home, on the streets, at school, and at work.
- I want to feel safe and secure in my home, on the streets, at school, and at work.
- I WILL be safe and secure in my home, on the streets, at school, and at work.
- I have a right to take care of myself even when those who should take care of me don't.
- I am a competent person and can trust my own judgment. If I think a situation is unsafe, I'm probably right.
- It is not my fault if I am not protected.
- I deserve care, concern, and protection.
- I have a right to seek the help of anyone I trust when I feel threatened.
- I will not let the need to protect anyone's secrets keep me from getting the help I need.

Overview

- Exercise: Negative Thoughts That Prevent Effective Action
- Exercise: Personal Safety Review
- Exercise: Reviewing the Week
- Exercise: Case Examples on Personal Safety
- Vulnerability to Sexual Abuse
- Exercise: Affirmations on Touch and the Right to privacy
- Safety Tips
- Exercise: Safety on the Streets
- Suicide Prevention
- Contingency Planning for Weekends, Holidays and Summer Vacation

Exercise:
Negative Thoughts That Prevent Effective Action

Facilitators can read the following statements, or write them on the chalkboard, explaining to participants that these beliefs may be keeping them from getting help when they need it:

- "Feeling ashamed to admit to problems at home or elsewhere."
- "Fear of reprisal from parents, bullies, or strangers."

- "Being locked into a role or view of self that keeps you from taking action."
- "Believing that 'I deserve what I get.'"
- "Believing and accepting that it is normal to feel vulnerable and afraid at home, at school, or on the streets."
- "Believing that you must live in a state of risk and fear in order to keep your house together or to protect someone younger than you."

Discussion

Facilitators can ask:

- "Which of these beliefs, attitudes, or feelings apply to you?"
- "Have there been times in your life when you have felt this way, even if you don't right now?"
- "Can you give an example of when one of these beliefs, attitudes, or feelings caused you some trouble?"
- "What can you do to remind yourself that these are irrational beliefs that can get you into trouble?"

Exercise:
Personal Safety Review

Facilitators can have participants fill out and discuss the "Personal Safety Review," in the *Becoming Aware Participant Guidebook*. The significance of the answers to these questions depends, of course, on the age and demonstrated competence of the participant. Facilitators can say: "How safe we feel in a place depends on the place and situation, how much we know about it, how much we trust those around us, and how self-confident we feel. Take a few minutes now to fill out the 'Personal Safety Review' in your guidebook."

Participants can discuss their responses in pairs, in small groups, or with the entire class.

Discussion

Facilitators can ask participants:

- "Where do you feel safest?"
- "Are there any similarities among the places you feel safest?"
- "Are there any places where you *feel* safe when, perhaps, you are not?"
- "Where do you feel least safe? Any similarities there?"
- "What makes a place safe for you?"
- "What do you do about those places where you feel unsafe? Ask each other's opinions on that."
- "What can we do to feel safer?"

Exercise:
Reviewing the Week

Facilitators can ask participants:

- "How safe did you feel in your home this week? At school? On the streets?"
- "What events took place that made you fear for your own safety?"
- "How did you feel at the time?"
- "What options did you consider?"
- "What did you actually do?"
- "How did it turn out?"
- "How did you feel about yourself?"
- "Do you feel safe now?"
- "How will you handle a similar situation in the future?"

Discussion

The steps below can be gone through in class whenever an issue of personal safety arises.

Identify the problem or threat. Facilitators should ask some simple questions such as, "Do you feel safe now? Are you afraid to go home? Where would you go if you didn't go home? Who would you call?" Basically, the facilitators want to see if the person has an adequate support system.

Try to determine why a young person has revealed certain information. Some participants will have little concern about their ability to keep themselves safe. Rather, they are simply sharing the information because it is something that affects them emotionally and they want another person to know about it. Others will be in need of information and assistance.

Sometimes youths will describe situations in which they are clearly in danger but not aware of it. They may describe vague feelings of unease but have no ability to articulate exactly what the problem is. The other participants can help them identify the source and degree of danger.

Clarify the need for change. Facilitators need to let the endangered participants know that they do not have to accept the status quo and live in such fear. They can take charge of the situation and work to devise a specific, practical plan that can be implemented immediately.

The class setting helps this process. Other participants can provide practical tips on how they take care of themselves. They can also be available for support during the week if the person is afraid.

When going through these steps, facilitators should note any problem that the individual or class has in making decisions. Perhaps an exercise in decision-making would be helpful. (See "Problem-solving, Decision-making and Goal-setting" in the *Moving On Participant Guidebook.*)

Exercise:
Case Examples on Personal Safety

The facilitators can read or have one of the participants read the following case examples to the class.

"Thirteen-year-old Tom is home watching television on a Saturday night. He can hear his father arguing with his mother in the next room. Then Tom hears a plate crash, and his mother runs out of the living room and goes upstairs. His father throws the kitchen table over and starts yelling, 'I'm sick and tired of the lazy idiots in this family! This house is a mess! I want this place cleaned up now, and if it's not, there is going to be hell to pay!'

"Tom knows that, when his father has gotten like this in the past, he has sometimes become violent with his mother and Tom. Tom is the only child at home."

"Fourteen-year-old Sally is in her first year of high school. On her way to the cafeteria, two senior girls stop her and tell her to give them her lunch money. They also say that they are going to expect to get 50 cents from her every day or else 'there will be trouble.' "

"Fifteen-year-old Lewis and his two younger sisters are with their father, visiting relatives. After a night of drinking, his dad, who is clearly quite drunk, says 'Let's go home.' He starts to go to the car. He drops his keys several times, and falls when he bends down to pick them up. Everyone else at the party is laughing at his act."

"Sixteen-year-old Sarah has just walked in the door after school. She finds her two-year-old sister and five-year-old brother crying in the living room. The mother is drunk, screaming at the children, slamming a pot against the table telling them how angry she is because the kids have made a mess. She is verbally abusing them, saying that they are 'no good stupid little brats!' Sarah's brother starts to cry, and her mother sticks her face into his and tells him she will smash him if he doesn't stop."

Discussion

After each example facilitators should ask:

- "If that person lived in this community, what should he or she do?"
- "What would be the worst thing for that person to do?"
- "What would be the consequences of that course of action?"
- "What would prevent that person from doing something positive?"
- "What personal attitudes and feelings would help a person in this situation?"
- "What Makes You More Vulnerable"? Facilitators can have the participants consider how vulnerable the young people in the examples would be if they were feeling sad, depressed, or unloved. Participants can review all of the previous situations with that question in mind and consider how each situation is made much worse by low self-esteem and sadness.

Vulnerability to Sexual Abuse

Adults working with children from disrupted family environments find a high incidence of reports of sexual abuse by support group participants. The subject of sexual abuse and related intervention is extremely broad and complex. In addition to making contact with local people skilled in this area, facilitators would do well to make use of the resources on physical and sexual abuse recommended in Appendix A, on page 189.

Facilitators should tell participants that low self-concept, lack of assertiveness, and feelings of isolation and loneliness can make young people particularly vulnerable to sexual abuse. The facilitators can summarize the following findings of a researcher in this field (Finkelhor, 1984):

Work with children who have been molested suggests that the abuse could have been prevented in many cases if they had had prior instruction. Lack of knowledge and uncertainty about what to do can play a role in a child's victimization. Afterward, children often say:

- They were confused and mislead by the offender's insistence that the sexual activity was proper and normal.
- They did not know they had a right to refuse.
- They did not believe they would be defended by other adults (including parents) if they refused or complained.
- They were thrown off their guard when the adult behaved in away that they had never been led to expect.

Simply by raising this issue, the facilitators will be letting participants know that they are willing to listen to and assist children who have been victims.

Exercise:
Affirmations on Touch and the Right to Privacy

The following general guidelines on touch and rights to privacy are listed in the *Becoming Aware Participant Guidebook*. Participants can read them in the class or at home during the week.

- I will be hugged, touched, or kissed only if I trust the person and feel comfortable.
- I will let people know when I do not want to be hugged, touched, or kissed.
- If someone touches me in a way I am not comfortable with, I will tell them not to do that.
- If someone wants to touch me in a way that I am uncomfortable with or afraid of, I will leave immediately.
- If I am touched in a way that makes me feel uncomfortable or scared, I will tell an adult whom I trust.

Discussion

Facilitators can ask participants to consider the following issues when they read the affirmations on touch:

- "Can you say each one of these statements confidently?"
- "Are there some that you are not sure you will really do?"
- "What would keep you from doing any of the behaviors stated in the affirmations?"

Safety Tips

Although facilitators can go over the following suggestions on safety in a single class session, there is a need to give safety information to participants several times during the year, and facilitators should look for opportune times to do so. When participants describe their lives outside of the class, facilitators can look for signs of unsafe behavior and mention specific safety guidelines. Facilitators can judge for themselves which rules are most important for their communities and which may not be necessary. Determining which safety tips to emphasize will also depend on the age of participants. Here are some safety tips for facilitators to suggest to participants:

- "Walk to school, recreational events, and other activities with a group."

- "Don't hang around an empty school building or stay in the school yard when all your friends have left."

- "If you feel threatened by someone outside after school, go back into the building and find a counselor, teacher, maintenance person, or office worker to help you."

- "Walk in the middle of the sidewalk; avoid bushes and doorways."

- "Avoid empty lots, vacant buildings, and alleys."

- "Notice and try to remember any places on your school-to-home route that you could go to if you needed to get away from someone you felt threatened by. Stores, post offices, police stations, recreation centers, and service stations could serve as temporary places of safety."

- "Always carry at least fifty cents in change to make phone calls in an emergency. Notice and try to remember the locations of public telephones along your school-to-home route."

- "Don't show off with money or valuable possessions. Keep them out of sight if possible."

- "Don't wear obviously valuable jewelry, like gold chains, at school or out on the streets."

- "Don't make a habit of talking about money or other valuables you or your parents have at home. Even if you are telling a friend you trust, that person may tell someone less trustworthy."

- "When you go out after school, at night, or on weekends, let your parents or some other adult know where you will be and when you expect to get back. If possible, give them a phone number where you can be reached."

- "If you have a feeling that something is going to happen, trust your intuition. This can occur on the streets, at parties, in hallways, etc."

- "Do not hitchhike."

- "Do not ask for or accept a ride home from a person you have just met."

- "Do not invite people into your house unless you know them very well."

- "Do not drive after you have been drinking."

- "Do not ride with anyone else who has been drinking."

- "Make an agreement with your parents that, if you find yourself in a situation where you either have to ride with a person who has been drinking or you yourself have been drinking and must drive, you will call them for a ride."

- "If you are likely to end up having to ride with a parent who has been drinking, make an agreement with another relative or a friend that you will call them for

assistance the next time you feel endangered riding with your parent."

Discussion

The issue of calling someone for a ride after a participant has been drinking, or has been at a party where other people have been drinking, must be handled with some care. Participants are not to get the idea that they have permission to drink as long as they don't drive drunk. When schools have urged parents and students to adopt the policy of calling for a ride home, they also tell parents that it is extremely important to talk to their children about their drinking on the morning after the event has taken place. They also should level appropriate consequences.

With some LifeGuides participants, there may be no adult in the home who will confront participants about their drinking. In that case, all the LifeGuides facilitator can do is take opportunities to do so in class.

Exercise: Safety on the Streets

Facilitators can read the following scenarios to the class:

"You have just gotten your allowance and are going to a movie. On the way, two boys you have never seen before ask you for money and threaten to harm you if you don't give it to them. What do you do?"

Here are some appropriate responses the class might come up with or be told about:

- Give up the money.
- Get a description.
- Call police immediately.
- Call parents immediately.

Facilitators can then ask participants, "What would you do in the same situation if you knew the two boys but they say, 'Don't tell anybody or you'll be in serious trouble'?"

"What would you do if you were riding on a bus and a stranger sits down beside you and tries to talk you into coming to a party with him. He is very insistent and won't take no for an answer."

Some of the options are:

- Go to another seat.
- Blend in with the crowd by standing up.
- Tell the driver.
- Sit near the driver.

"It is 6:00 at night in the winter. Your mother said she would come and pick you up after work but did not. Your place of work is not in a very safe neighborhood. You cannot reach her by phone. What do you do?"

"Suppose you are in a fast-food restaurant and a nineteen-year-old man comes and sits down with you. What would you do?"

Discussion

In discussing the street-safety incidents, participants are likely to reveal some dangerous attitudes or behaviors. For instance, it is not unlikely that many older boys will say they would take a swing at anybody who confronted them on the streets, whether or not that person has a weapon. That kind of "macho" attitude should be confronted and discussed in the classroom. The facilitators can say:

- "Why do you feel you have to fight that person even if he has an advantage over you?"
- "What do you lose by giving up your money?"

In some situations participants might rightly say that, if they give up their money, they will be marked as a victim and be targeted again and again. In those cases, the facilitators must work hard to give the participants ideas on how to avoid the situation altogether. In most situations, the incident would involve a stranger, and there is not much likelihood that the stranger would seek the same victim again.

Suicide Prevention

Occasionally, discussions of feelings or a participant's current situation will indicate that a young person is very depressed and perhaps suicidal. Some of the signs facilitators should look for during the weekly check-ins are listed in "Things to Do If You Suspect a Youth is at Risk for Suicide," on page 81.

The Role of Peers in Suicide Prevention

It is very important for participants to know what to do if another young person tells them he or she is considering suicide. It is well known that young people who are considering suicide are more likely to tell another young person than an adult. Often, this is accompanied by a demand for a promise not to tell anybody else. The facilitators can discuss the issue with the LifeGuides participants. They should be told that suicidal intention is a secret they cannot afford to keep and that they should tell a facilitator or other adult immediately if they know of anyone who has talked about committing suicide.

Contingency Planning for Weekends, Holidays, and Summer Vacation

An important part of every class is making sure that all participants have useful plans for the weekend. These are plans that will help them find some peace and quiet, and deal with any emergency situations that arise in the home or elsewhere. To help them assess their current situations, participants can be asked:

- "What is your favorite room in the house? What do you like about it?"
- "Where do you most like to be? To spend the most time?"
- "Where do you like to go to have fun?"
- "Where do you like to go to think and be in peace?"

A participant's inability to come up with positive answers to any of these questions is an indication that the class has plenty of work to do to prepare the youth for time away from school.

Coping with Emergency Situations During Weekends or Vacations

Whether preparing for the weekend, for a visit to a parent's for the holidays, or for a summer vacation, each participant should know:

- The phone numbers of grandparents, foster parents, a social worker, or other people whom they can call if conditions become threatening.
- Where they go can if the situation at home deteriorates in a dangerous way.

Participants' plans can vary greatly, depending on what services are available in each situation. The Christmas holidays are tremendously stressful for children of alcoholics. At this time of year, not only are expectations for love and fun high, the possibility of disruption due to drinking problems is also high. Beginning at least two class sessions before the Christmas holidays, facilitators can ask:

- "How are people feeling about the upcoming holidays?"
- "What has happened during past holidays?"
- "What can you do to prevent that from happening again?"

In one LifeGuides program, a girl was planning to go back to her mother's for the holidays. That was a bad decision since every time she went back there her mother got drunk and started fights. One of the program participants who drove a car gave the girl her telephone

Things To Do If You Suspect A Youth Is At Risk For Suicide

If you believe a person you know is considering suicide, keep in mind the following DOs and DON'Ts.

Don't!

- Be afraid to believe your eyes and ears when you start picking up signs that a person may be suicidal.

- Argue or debate with the person about the ethics, fairness, or morality of committing suicide.

- Pass judgment on the person, take offense, act appalled, or act disappointed in the person.

- Ignore the signs or stop working with the person merely because he or she appears to be manipulative, whiny, extremely immature, or attention-seeking. People actually kill themselves in order to get attention.

- Make promises that aren't in your power to keep or give false assurances that everything will be all right.

- Assume that a recent attempt which passed without serious consequences means the crisis is over.

- Abandon the person because the pain is too oppressive and burdensome. If it feels that way, get another trusted person in on the situation as soon as possible.

- Try to handle it alone. At least seek consultation. Preferably, also seek support.

- Above all, don't be afraid to talk about it. Don't be frightened about putting ideas into the person's head. No one commits suicide because someone asks them about it. In fact, you will often find that a youth is very relieved to have someone mention the issue so it can be discussed openly.

Do!

- Listen closely to the person. Keep the person talking and listen closely to what he or she is saying. Encourage the expression of painful feelings. Encouraging the person to express thoughts and feelings and to ask questions will lower anxiety.

- Stay calm and stay available. Don't panic. Stay with the suicidal person. If the person has called you on the phone, use another phone to call for help. Keep that person on the line. If you have to hang up, make sure the person gives you a phone number where he or she can be called back.

- Get help from a trained professional as soon as possible. Call a suicide prevention center or a hospital with a psychiatric service for advice. If your school has a crisis team that handles potentially suicidal youth, contact them immediately. (Right now, **before** you encounter a suicide crisis, find out whom you can contact if and when a crisis arises: a student assistance counselor, administrators, agency psychologist, etc. Don't wait for a crisis to occur. Be prepared.)

- Find out what's going on in the person's life. This means, first of all, identifying all current stresses. Encourage the person to relate how he or she came to decide on suicide. Reconstruct events and identify problems.

- Let the person know you recognize and empathize with the pain. Do not attempt to minimize the problems by telling the person to be grateful or trying to point out how lucky he or she is.

- Make sure that the individual knows the possible consequences of his or her actions. For instance, does the person know that death is permanent, that people won't be relieved to have him or her gone, or that there is no way he or she can observe or enjoy the reactions of others?

Continued on next page

Continued from previous page

■ Help the person consider alternatives. Some suicidal people think they have to be perfect or life isn't worth living. Help them identify alternatives to this perfection-or-death viewpoint.

■ Explore the future, looking for signs of hope. Encourage the person to envision different scenarios of how the future could be.

■ Encourage delaying suicidal plans.

■ Ask the person to turn the means of suicide over to **you.** If the person has pills or a gun in his or her possession, get them away from the person if you can.

■ Get significant others involved. Parents or others who live with the person.

■ Even if you have already made general agreements about the privacy of individual or group counseling sessions, you may break that confidence in the case of suicidal adolescents. Life-threatening situations are not included in agreements about the confidentiality of counseling, especially with minors. This applies even if you did not make such an exception explicit beforehand.

■ Arrange for someone to stay with the person. If you have to leave a person in order to find help, try to get someone who is willing to stay with the person while you are gone. Get an adult, if possible. Having another adolescent stay with the person may be very stressful for both young people.

■ Assist the person in getting professional help from a counselor, psychologist, social worker, psychiatrist, etc. Make sure that the person gets somewhere. Go with the person to the appropriate office or agency.

number and told her to call. "If you get over there and it gets to be a horror show, call me and I'll come get you."

In another program, a ninth grader and his younger brother had to go to his father's girlfriend's house for the holidays. They hated to do that. They didn't know any of their father's girlfriend's relatives and were not particularly interested in spending time with them. In class, they made a decision to go to their father's house early, before his girlfriend was due to arrive, and open presents. That way they would have some special time alone with their father and still go wherever he wanted them to go later in the day.

Communication and Listening Skills

Sessions in this subject area provide tools to help facilitators and participants improve communication skills throughout the year.

Participants need constant assistance in order to develop effective communication skills. Although the information and exercises in this section can be presented early in the school year, the material merely lays a foundation for learning that will take place as the class progresses. Facilitators should always be ready to assist participants who are struggling to communicate. They can also look for ongoing opportunities to model some of the techniques described here.

Goals for Sessions on Communication and Listening Skills

Goals for sessions in this subject area include:

- To help participants be aware of the patterns of communication they use in the LifeGuides class.
- To help participants gain insights as to how they have developed these patterns of communication.
- To give the participants some tools for improving their communication patterns in the class, at home, and elsewhere.

Affirmations on Communication and Respectful Listening

These affirmations can be used as warm-ups for each session in this subject area, or participants can recite the affirmations daily during the week. The affirmations are listed in the *Becoming Aware Participant Guidebook*.

- I will listen carefully to what other people say to me.
- I will say what I think and how I feel.

- I have a right to be listened to.
- I owe other people respect and will show this respect by listening carefully.
- Other people owe me respect and should show that respect by listening to me.
- I will not stereotype others.
- I will not presume I already know what someone else is saying.
- I will help other people who are having trouble communicating their ideas and thoughts to me.

Overview

- Exercise: Where'd My Message Go?
- Breaking the Sound Barrier: Blocks to Clear Communication
- Family Problems Lead to Poor Communication
- Exercise: Communication Problems in the Family
- Blocks to Communication in a LifeGuides Class
- Exercise: Demonstration Role-Play
- Characteristics of Useful Feedback
- Typical Clarifying Responses
- Active Listening
- Exercise: Experience, Behaviors, and Feelings

Exercise:
Where'd My Message Go?

This is a fun exercise for both junior and senior high students. It is a way to show them how messages get distorted and lost if they are filtered through other people. The facilitator can introduce the exercise as follows:

"Direct communication is very important. If I want Jan to know something, it's better for me to tell her directly than to have someone else tell her. Sometimes, in families and among friends, we pass messages through others. We do this because we are mad at the person, too shy to talk to the person, or just unable to meet with the person.

"We're going to do a little exercise to see how hard it is to keep a message straight when it's filtered through others. I'm going to whisper a message to ____ here on my right. She is going to whisper to ____, and so on until the message gets back to ____, on my left. Let's see what happens."

The facilitator should then whisper the following message: "Tell ____ [the last person in the message chain] to meet me at the basketball game. I'll be wearing a red hat and be waiting by the clock. He should buy the tickets ahead of time."

Almost invariably, the message will become grossly distorted by the time it gets around to the last person. (If it doesn't, the class should be commended for remarkable attentiveness and retention.)

Discussion

Facilitators can ask:

- "How hard was it for you to remember the message?"
- "Could you tell who distorted the message?" (Usually, this is impossible.)
- "This was a factual message. Would it be easier or harder if there was some emotional content like, 'Tell Bob I'm really angry at him. Tell him to meet me after school so we can talk it out.' "
- "Have you ever had a message get lost like this? When?"

Breaking the Sound Barrier — Blocks to Clear Communication

The following barriers to communication can be presented as a lecture. The facilitators could also break this material down into brief one- or two-minute lectures and introduce each of the barriers at the beginning of the first four or five LifeGuides class sessions. This can be part of an ongoing training process to help the class get up-to-speed at the beginning of the year.

Discussion

The general barriers to communication are usually not too threatening to discuss. After each individual barrier is presented, facilicators can ask:

- "Have you seen this kind of problem in communication?"

- "Give me another example from outside this class of this kind of problem."
- "Tell of a time when you have used this kind of communication."
- "How can we avoid this problem in the classroom?"

Discussions about communication problems can be very revealing of participants' family dynamics and ways of socializing. Facilitators should be sure to note important information in the class log for future reference. Here are the barriers:

We Often Round Off Messages

People tend to "round off" messages by grouping the content they hear into general categories. To do this, they exaggerate some differences and lose track of others. For instance, a speaker may say: "Some Vietnam veterans became addicted to heroin while they were overseas. This, combined with the lack of recognition they received when they returned home, has put a great deal of pressure on them. Some have not been able to cope and have been in need of psychological services. They have also found it difficult to keep a job." A listener who rounds off the message may say, "Vietnam vets are a bunch of lazy dope addicts who don't care to work."

We Hear Our Old "Tapes" Rather Than What is Being Said

Some words or conflicts trip off old messages from the past. Tom's parents may have told him that wanting to play basketball rather than going to work after school is the sign of a selfish child. The concept of selfishness may begin to dominate the way he looks at all of his wants and needs. In class, comments such as, "Tom, I don't think you're listening very closely to what Karen is saying," may be heard by Tom as meaning, "You are a very self-centered person and don't even care about what Karen is saying."

A student who has been told consistently by a teacher that "this work is garbage. If you can't do better than this, you might as well drop the course" will not be ready to hear constructive criticism. Another teacher may tell her, "I see that you're having a lot of trouble with this material." The student may "turn off" the speaker and start to walk away. The speaker may go on to say, "I think I see just where your problem is. If you will come to my office during your free time tomorrow, I can help you." The student may not stay around long enough to hear the entire message.

We Expect to Hear What We Heard Before

At the beginning of every class for the first few weeks, facilitators might say, "Let's start on my left and have everyone say what they did this week." If the following week the facilitator says, "Let's start on my right and have everyone say what they did this week," it is very likely that the person on the left will start talking.

We Presume the Speaker Agrees with Us

A girl may be on a bus driving through a poor neighborhood and say, "Boy, the housing here sure is lousy." She may mean to say that she feels sorry for kids who are having such a hard time. The person sitting next to her may hold prejudices against poor people and presume that she means, "These are sure sloppy, lazy people in this neighborhood."

A boy may have a low self-concept and say to himself, "I'm just dumb! I can't get any of this material!" If a person says to him, "I'm amazed you did so poorly on the test," he may presume the person is saying that he must be really stupid. But in fact, the person may mean she is surprised that he did so poorly because she thinks he is so smart.

We Make Everything Black or White

This has to do not only with the way we hear and speak, but with our view of the world. We may believe we are either beautiful or ugly, popular or complete outcasts, totally happy or totally depressed. It is easier to put people into categories than to look for varying degrees of good and bad, effective or ineffective, attentive or inattentive. If a group of girls are talking about the problems they have had with guys, each girl might get the general message that "Guys are just no good. You can't trust them and they only use you." In fact, each person may not have had such black-and-white experiences, but when they think they hear the group saying, "Guys are no good," they start to see their own experiences as proof of that statement.

This is also an example of the effect that group pressure has on communication. If people in a group are talking about someone who is not there and the talk drifts in a negative direction, it is much more likely that the talk will continue in the negative direction rather than turn to a positive direction.

Family Problems Lead to Poor Communication

Children from disrupted family environments face major barriers to healthy communication in their lives. The following barriers can be presented by facilitators, followed by the discussion questions given in the previous section.

The No-Talk Rule

This rule means that members of the family do not talk about family problems to anyone. This includes outsiders and each other. This need to talk *around* the problems creates very indirect patterns of communication.

Value Judgments

Communication is often very emotional and judgmental rather than specific and to the point. A child is more likely to hear, "You idiot! You never do anything right!" than, "Tom, you left your bike in the driveway again. I have asked you not to do that."

Low Self-esteem and Its Effect on Communication

People who do not have positive self-esteem will be indirect in expressing their opinions and feelings, and more likely to presume that other people are stating or implying negative things about them.

Rigid Family Roles

Later in the LifeGuides class, participants will hear about the various roles that people fall into within their own families (see "Role Exploration," beginning on page 153 in the "Moving On" section). These roles include being a Super Kid, a Rebel, or the Joker. The people who fall into the position of being the rebel in their families often get blamed for everything. This is a way of stereotyping. If a family rebel comes in with a bad mark on his report card, he might be told, "You lazy, no-good bum. You're not like your sister. You never study and you never do your work. You're going to end up a failure." In homes where individuals are not locked into roles, there will be fewer presumptions made and more efforts to clarify situations. Children might be told, "You're having trouble with this one class. Do you know why that is? Is it the subject matter, the teacher, or your job which keeps you working all the time?"

Exercise:
Communication Problems in the Family

After presenting this information, facilitators can have the class break into pairs or smaller groups to discuss the following:

- "Have you observed any of these problems in communication at home?"
- "Give an example of each, if you can."
- "How do those ways of communicating or not communicating make you feel?"

• "Can you think of examples of how the way you communicate at home affects the way you communicate outside of your home?"

Blocks to Communication in a LifeGuides Class

Common blocks to clear communication in a LifeGuides class include:

• Being an authority.

• Ignoring what the person says.

• Giving the person reassurance before truly understanding the situation and how the person feels about it.

• Analyzing the person.

• Labeling the person.

• Being judgmental.

• Giving advice or trying to fix the person.

• Using cliches instead of giving real feelings and real responses. Sometimes people will automatically say, "I know how you feel, that's a bummer" and other phrases without really meaning much by them.

• Bringing all discussions back to oneself. One technique that people sometimes use to divert attention to themselves is to say, "Yeah I know what you mean. I had an experience just like that. Last night...."

• Quoting recovery jargon. This can be very frustrating to people. All of the sayings used by the self-help groups contain much truth and wisdom. They must be used sparingly, however. For instance, if a person is saying how terrible she feels about something in her life, it is not sufficient and often not even helpful to say things like, "Let go and let God," "You're trying to run his program," or "Just take it one day at time."

Exercise:
Demonstration Role-Play

The facilitators can demonstrate all of these barriers to clear communication in a simple conversation. One facilitator starts off with a simple question, and then each participant responds in turn with some statement incorporating the barriers. This can be a humorous demonstration. For instance:

"Boy, this job I have is hard!"

"No it isn't. All tough bosses are the same. You just butter them up and you'll get along OK." (The authority knows the problem without asking.)

"But I got fired today!"

"Look, tomorrow, when you go to work, tell the boss how smart he is. You'll do just fine." (Ignoring and giving useless reassurance.)

"Man, you're not even listening to me!"

"Bob, you've always had a problem believing people care about you. You probably have trouble with your father that makes it hard to get along with other men." (Analyzing)

Etc....

Participants will find it even more humorous if the facilitators use current school or class data to build the role-play. The humor helps diffuse any shame that participants might feel about what they consider their own blunders in communication. And by focusing on themselves, facilitators demonstrate their willingness not to take themselves too seriously.

The participants can be challenged to carry on their own conversation. A simple starting phrase should suffice. For instance: "Judy, tell Jan that you're worried about taking a driving license exam. Jan, you start out with the first barrier, being an authority. Use all the barriers you can."

Discussion

Facilitators can say:

• "Which one of these barriers have you fallen into so far in the class?"

• "If you are willing, share that with the class" (or your partner or small group).

• "Which ones have you observed?"

• "What can we do to avoid them?"

Discussion of communication problems should not be shaming. Facilitators can give the message that, although these blocks to communication do slow down the class, they are normal. Everybody uses them at one time or another.

Characteristics of Useful Feedback

Useful feedback is possible only when facilitators and participants pay close attention to what others say, how they say it, what they mean, and how they feel. The following aspects of useful feedback can be re-phrased in a variety of ways, and examples can be offered or solicited. Useful feedback:

• **Is specific rather than general.** To be told that one is deluded is not as effective as being told, "You say you don't have a problem with chemicals, but just yesterday you named five different major problems in your life that you admitted were related to chemicals."

- **Is focused on behavior rather than on the person.** It is preferable for a person to be told that he talked more than anyone else in the meeting than to be told that he is a loud-mouth.

- **Takes into account the needs of the receiver of the feedback.** Feedback can be destructive when it serves only the needs of the giver and fails to consider the needs of the person on the receiving end. It is given to help, not to hurt.

- **Involves the amount of information the receiver can use,** rather than the amount of information a person wants to give.

- **Is directed toward behavior that the receiver can do something about.**

- **Involves the sharing of ideas and information,** rather than giving advice.

- **Is timely.** Feedback on something someone did three or four sessions ago is not as useful as feedback on immediate behavior.

- **Is solicited rather than imposed.** Although this is not always possible in the LifeGuides class process, feedback is most useful when the receiver has indicated a desire to learn more about himself or herself.

- **Focuses on the feelings of the speaker,** who has observed or felt the effects of the behavior.

- **Allows both the giver and the receiver an opportunity to check out the information with the class.**

Discussion

Facilitators can open this discussion by saying, "In your *Becoming Aware Participant Guidebook* is a list of the characteristics of useful feedback. Let's look at that now."

- "Can anyone give me an example of the first characteristic of useful feedback?"

- "The second?"

- "Can anyone give me examples of feedback that break any one of these rules?"

Facilitators can tell participants to use the feedback list to see how well they're doing in the class, as well as to review their own ways of talking — in class, at home, and with their friends.

Typical Clarifying Responses

Facilitators should tell participants that one of the most effective ways to overcome communication barriers is for participants to repeat what they think was said. When someone in class says something that may have several meanings, the facilitators or other participants can say, "What I think you are saying is…" and then summarize the message. The person or the rest of class can help clarify the message.

There are also responses to another's statements that help to clarify not only what a person is saying or means to say, but what that person wants to accomplish as a result. Some responses simply provide validation, letting the person know that he or she is OK; that it's all right to feel a certain way. These responses include:

- If that had happened to me I would have felt…

- I sure have felt like that sometimes.

- I can understand why you'd feel that way.

- How did you feel when (he said that, you did that, that happened)?

- It sounds like you're saying…; what you seem to be saying to me…; when I listen to you I feel…

- Give me some examples of what you mean by that.

- I think a lot of us would have acted the same way.

- I am having trouble understanding what Tom is saying. Can anyone else help me out?

- What do you want from the class?

- How can I help you right now?

Active Listening

Participants will need to be taught active listening. Facilitators can tell them to look directly at the person speaking, allow the person to speak uninterrupted, repeat what they hear the person saying, and be aware of any nonverbal behaviors. Participants should listen for **experiences, behaviors,** and **feelings.** Facilitators can give them some examples of each:

"Experiences are what happens to a person. When a participant says, 'I was sent to the principal's office today,' he is talking about an experience."

"Behaviors are actions a person does or fails to do. If a group member says, 'I am in a lot of trouble because I am not getting to school on time,' he is talking about his behavior."

"Feelings are caused by or associated with experiences or behaviors. If a participant says, 'I am really worried because I am not making it to school on time,' he is talking about a feeling related to his own *behavior*. If he says, 'I am scared to death of what the principal will do to me,' he is talking about a feeling related to an *experience*."

Facilitators can expect youth in the LifeGuides class to talk freely about things that have happened to them, but not about what they do and not what they feel about those experiences. Facilitators and participants must listen closely to find out how experiences, behaviors, and feelings are related. For instance, if a participant mentions a feeling, they need to find out what experiences and behaviors may be connected with it. If a participant mentions a behavior, facilitators should try to find out what experiences and emotions were connected with it.

Exercise:
Experience, Behaviors, Feelings

Facilitators can ask each participant to describe some event that happened to them during the week. When they describe the event, they should specify the experience, behaviors, and feelings. The event need not be one that had great emotional impact. The purpose of this exercise is to teach participants to listen closely to each other and probe for missing pieces of the puzzles presented to them.

What's a "Normal" Family?

The concept of a "normal" family can be both confusing and mystifying to children from disrupted family environments. Participants' images of what a family should be might have come from watching the warm, funny, loving, caring, and unflappable parents on television sitcoms. The ideal family is usually portrayed as a two-parent family living in a single-family dwelling.

The families of a great many LifeGuides Program participants will share few or none of these characteristics. Experienced facilitators report that a majority of youths who join LifeGuides classes or similar programs seldom live with both their natural parents and frequently have only one adult in the home.

When participants realize that their families are not like the overly-idealized ones they have seen on TV, they feel inferior. They also tend to focus on irrelevant details as the sources of their pain rather than on the more important issues. They may decide, for instance, they feel inferior to others because their family has such an old car. They may believe that having a good-looking car will make them more respected by others.

Goals for Sessions on "Normal" Families

Goals for sessions in this subject area include:

- To help participants realize that the "ideal" family is primarily a Hollywood fabrication.
- To help them understand that, in many respects, they are not as different from other youths as they may think.
- To help them understand what a family should provide even though families are seldom perfect.
- To provide them with some simple ways of looking at their experiences at home.
- To help them decide what needs they have that their families cannot meet and which of those are so important that they should be met elsewhere.

Affirmations on Families

The following affirmations can be read in the class before or after sessions in this subject area. They are are found in *Becoming Aware Participant Guidebook* and can also be assigned for reading during the week.

- My family does not have to be perfect.
- I do not have to be a perfect kid in a perfect family.
- I can get my needs met from my family even if there are problems there.
- I can be happy in my family even if the family is facing some problems.
- I do not have to count on or expect my family to meet every need that families meet for other kids.
- I can find other ways to have my needs met when my family cannot meet them.

Overview

- Exercise: The All-American Family Quiz
- A Day in the Life of a Perfect Family:
- Exercise: Role-play on the Perfect Family
- Exercise: The Perfect American Family One-Act Play
- Exercise: Day-To-Day — Family Routines
- Exercise: Playing by the Rules
- Exercise: Family Circles and Family X's — What Kids Need From Families
- Exercise: Family Photographs
- Exercise: Drawing the Family Table
- Exercise: The Family Diagram.
- The Family Mobile

Exercise:
The All-American Family Quiz

Participants may have many misconceptions of what "normal" means. "The All-American Family Quiz," in the *Becoming Aware Participant Handbook*, is a simple,

The All-American Family Quiz

The purpose of this "quiz" is to help you understand what you think a "family" is or should be. Take a few minutes to indicate your beliefs and opinions about families.

1. What percentage of kids live in single-parent homes? (22%. See page 10. Local statistics can be much higher)

____ 1-5%	____ 21-25%
____ 6-10	____ 26-30%
____ 11-15%	____ 31-35%
____ 16-20%	____ 36-40%

2. What percentage of kids under 16 whose mothers were married have had their parents get divorced? (38% for white youths, 75% for black youths. See page 10. Local statistics may be available to facilitators.)

____ 1-10%	____ 41-50%
____ 11-20%	____ 51-60%
____ 21-30%	____ 61-70%
____ 31-40%	____ 71-80%

3. What is the rate of alcoholism and alcohol abuse in our society? (10%; 4% alcohol abusers; 6% alcoholic - Williams, 1987. Local statistics can be much higher than this.)

____ 1-10%	____ 41-50%
____ 11-20%	____ 51-60%
____ 21-30%	____ 61-70%
____ 31-40%	____ 71-80%

4. What percentage of kids live in homes troubled by drinking or drug use? (About 20-25%. See page 10. Local statistics can often be much higher.)

____ 1-10%	____ 41-50%
____ 11-20%	____ 51-60%
____ 21-30%	____ 61-70%
____ 31-40%	____ 71-80%

5. What percentage of families do **not** own their own home? (36.7% —U.S. Bureau of Census, 1987, Page 440. Local statistics can often be higher.)

____ 1-10%	____ 41-50%
____ 11-20%	____ 51-60%
____ 21-30%	____ 61-70%
____ 31-40%	____ 71-80%

multiple-choice test that can serve as a reality-testing device. Most of the questions are answered by some general facts, but attitudes and opinions are usually expressed during this exercise as well.

Facilitators can give the quiz in two ways: Read the questions aloud in class, or have the participants complete the "The All-American Family Quiz" in the *Becoming Aware Participant Guidebook*. If the facilitators choose to read the questions in the class, they could say:

"I am going to ask a few questions about the typical American family. Then I'm going to read some possible answers. Raise your hand when you think I've read the correct answer."

Facilitators can read any or all questions. If the participants are using their guidebooks to take the quiz, they can answer all questions. Some of their responses can be discussed immediately, some in later sessions. (The participants' version, of course, does not have the answers or the citations.)

Discussion

Facilitators can say:

• "Obviously, not every family lives like the ones we see on television."

• "What answer surprised you the most? The least?"

• "These answers describe the averages around the country. Do you think things are different around here?" (This gives participants a chance to talk about families without necessarily describing their own.)

• "How would you describe the 'ideal' family on television?"

• "What do you like about that ideal?"

• "What is realistic about it?"

• "What is unreal or unlikely about it?"

Another way to conduct the exercise is to have participants discuss the questions in pairs or small groups. After the participants have had a chance to try and agree on the answers, facilitators should ask each pair or small group for their conclusions and their reasons for reaching those conclusions. The data participants draw on can be very revealing of their daily experiences.

The facilitators may know that there is a high rate of divorce in the families of participants in a particular LifeGuides class. If the facilitators believe it would be safe to discuss that issue, they could ask participants to estimate or guess what the statistics would be for their particular class. Facilitators can then give the actual percentages for that class. Throughout this discussion, the facilitators should not, of course, name the participants whose families fall into the various categories

The statistical *Abrastics of the United States: 1988* (U.S. Bureau of Census, 1987) offers an abundance of reference material applicable to Black and Hispanic groups. This volume is available in the references section of most libraries..

A Day in the Life of a Perfect Family

The following two exercises give participants a chance to de-mystify the idea of the perfect, All-American family. The role-play or one-act play should be performed with much exaggeration. The exercises tend to work well with a class that has at least two extroverts who are willing to ham it up when they play their roles. Facilitators can also carry it off if they feel comfortable doing so. If all participants are somewhat reserved or the participants are not yet comfortable with each other, the role-play and one-act play should be skipped.

Exercise: Role-Play on the Perfect Family

On page 92 are descriptions of four roles for the "perfect family" role play. The facilitators can tell participants that they need volunteers to play the members of a perfect family: mom, dad, a sixteen-year-old son, and a fourteen-year-old daughter. (If they wish, one of the facilitators can take on a role.)

When the volunteers have been selected, they are each given a copy of their own role along with a description of the setting. After they have looked their roles over for four or five minutes, the facilitator will set the stage by saying: "The perfect family is sitting around the breakfast table while mom cooks pancakes. They are just about to start their busy day when dad mentions a certain problem. They have to solve their problems in the way that a perfect family should."

Discussion

Since the participants who acted in the role-play took the risks, they should be given an opportunity to comment first. Facilitators should thank all participants for participating and say:

• "How did you feel in your roles?"

• "What was real and not real?"

• "Even though some of this is exaggerated, there may be things we like about this perfect family. Is there anything you liked?"

• "Have you seen some of those things in your own home?"

• "Is there anything you didn't like?" (Look for indications that participants distrust the characters; that the characters weren't honest with their feelings.)

Roles for the "Perfect Family" Role-Play

The setting: The family is sitting around the breakfast table. There are two problems to solve. Dad's car has a broken window, and Dad wants to find out how it happened. Once you discuss how it happened, you must decide how everyone will get where they must go today. Since Dad can't use his car, Mom must drive everybody everywhere. In handling the time conflicts, the family shows humor, love, and concern for others.

- -

Your role: Mom. You are the perfect mom. You cook the best, most nutritious but still tasty pancakes for your children. (You learned how at the PTA committee meeting for "Caring, Concerned, Competent Moms.")

You can clean the house, look beautiful, drive the kids anywhere they want to go in the new station wagon.

Your are **always** cheerful.

In discussing how to get everybody where they have to go today, you will mention all the things you wanted to do, but will GLADLY CANCEL for the sake of your family. You had planned to go to a meeting of your Garden Club, to volunteer at the hospital, and to a meeting of a special task force on drug abuse.

- -

Your role: Dad. You are a doctor and you coach a soccer team. You are fair, honest, direct, loving, humorous and are ALWAYS SMILING. You love your children AND NEVER GET MAD AT THEM.

You will compliment Mom on her pancakes and compliment everyone else in the family for something (how they look, how they behave at breakfast, what they've accomplished, etc).

- You must find out who broke your car's window but not get at all mad.

- You must negotiate and compromise CHEERFULLY when trying to figure out a way for Mom to drive you all the places you have to go: your office in the morning, the hospital at noon, home from the hospital at dinner time, and out to coach a soccer game at night.

- -

Your role: Chet (16 years old). You are captain of both the debate team and the football team, and you volunteer down at the nursing home after school. You help little children on the block, especially a little poor child in a wheelchair. Last night, you broke the window on your dad's car when you were teaching the child how to hit a baseball. He hit it better than you expected and it went through the window.

You will compliment Mom on her pancakes and compliment everyone else in the family for something (how they look, how they behave at breakfast, what they've accomplished, etc.).

- Talk about your accomplishments, busy day and all the things you must do.

- Admit that you broke the window, explain how it happened, then explain how you will take care of getting it fixed.

- You must negotiate and compromise CHEERFULLY when trying to figure out a way for Mom to drive you all the places you have to go: Home from football practice, then out to a youth group meeting at the church.

- -

Your role: Ellie (14 years old). You are practically perfect. You help Mom clean the house, do the dishes, get A's in school, and are head of your own club, "Future Perfect Moms of America."

- You will compliment Mom on her pancakes and compliment everyone else in the family for something (how they look, how they behave at breakfast, what they've accomplished, etc.).

- Talk about your accomplishments, busy day and all the things you must do.

- You must negotiate and compromise CHEERFULLY when trying to figure out a way for Mom to drive you all the places you have to go: to ballet practice after school and Girl Scouts in the evening.

Exercise:
The Perfect American Family One-Act Play

The one-act play can be done as a reading. It can also be assigned to several participants to prepare for the class. Such assignments can be good for self-esteem. Participants have an opportunity to do something for the class and to be praised for their efforts.

Characters: Father (Chuck), mother (Donna), 16-year-old son (Chet), 14-year-old daughter, (Ellie).

It is morning and the family is getting ready for the day.

Mother is dressed in her chiffon skirt and is making breakfast for the family. The father is not there yet. Chet and Ellie are eating.

Ellie: "Gee, Mom, those were great pancakes! May I have more, please?"

Mom: "Oh sure, Ellie. That's a recipe I learned from the PTA Loving Mothers Healthy Cooking Class. It has all the best nutrients!"

Chet: "Boy, Mom, I really appreciate that! I have to go volunteer down at the nursing home after football practice today. I better not eat too many, though, because Dad will want some too."

Mom: "Oh, Chet, you're such a good boy!" *(Mother pats Chet on the head.)*

Dad enters. He always smiles: "Hi honey!" *(Gives wife a peck on the cheek. Then, looking at Chet and Ellie:* "How're my two little jewels today?"

Chet: "Great, Dad!"

Ellie: "Super!" *(Ellie hops up and gives Dad a hug.)*

Dad: "Boy, these pancakes look great! I'm going to need all the energy I can get! After I finish seeing all of the lovable little children in my doctor's office, I'm going to have to go and coach the Little League team tonight."

They eat silently for about 30 seconds.

Dad: "Say, kids, I noticed that somebody hit a baseball through the window of my car last night. Do any of you know anything about it?"

Chet and Ellie look quickly at each other, then stare down in embarrassment.

Dad: "Well?"

Ellie: "Well, uhh . . ."

Chet interrupts: "Well, Dad, you see, you know that little boy down the street in the wheelchair? Well, I canceled my date with Jeannie — you know, the captain of the cheerleaders — so I could help him

have some fun playing baseball. Well, seems like the little guy could hit the ball harder than I figured, and he sent it right through the car window. But don't worry, I already talked to Mr. Morton about a job at the grocery store so I can help pay for it."

Mom: "Oh, Chet, you're so thoughtful."

Dad: "Well, I don't condone smashing car windows with baseballs, but it looks like you had a good reason. Call me at my office today and we'll talk about it some more. Got to go!"

Family leaves, each one giving Mom a peck on the cheek.

Discussion

Discussion questions from the role-play on the perfect family can be adapted for processing the one-act play.

Exercise:
Day-to-Day — Family Routines

Participants can use the sheets provided in their *Becoming Aware Participant Guidebook* to give general descriptions of their families. This is to be a fairly concrete view, not an analysis of strengths or dysfunction in the family. It is primarily a way for the participants to share a little more about themselves.

Discussion

Family routines provide insight into how much order, structure, and support a youth is getting from the family.

Any one of these statements can lead to long class discussions. Whether or not the family eats together, for instance, can become a major family issue. Sometimes the reasons resulting in a family conflict are relatively minor. The teenagers of the family may simply want to rush on to other, and what they consider more interesting, activities. The parents, on the other hand, may want to keep them settled for a given period of time during dinner in order to maintain some semblance of family unity.

In other instances, problems in this area can point to more serious issues. The family may be avoiding a major family secret — such as, one of the parents is having an affair or has asked for a divorce — by never being together. Perhaps a family who used to have fun talking at dinnertime no longer shares any formal meals whatsoever because the pressure is so intense. The loss of this ritual may be symptomatic of the disintegration of the family as a whole. On the other hand, a rigid adherence to full attendance at family meals is a sign of a desperate attempt to force a family to be together when most members would rather avoid each other.

Some questions facilitators can ask include:

- "What do you like about your family's routines?"
- "What don't you like?"
- "How are the routines different from what they were a year ago? Two years ago? When you were seven years old?"
- "When did they change?"
- "Why do you think they changed?"

Exercise:
Playing by the Rules

Facilitators can use this exercise to learn more about the structure and order participants get from their families. Facilitators can say:

"Every family has some rules. Sometimes the rules are very simple and clear: you must be home by certain times on weeknights and weekends; someone must do the dishes on Monday and Wednesday night; someone must take out the garbage on certain days; someone must wash dishes."

"It is not just the rules themselves that are important, but how the rules are made and enforced."

"In your *Becoming Aware Participant Guidebook* is an exercise called 'Playing by the Rules'. Look at that now and fill in your family rules."

"At the bottom of the page under 'True or False on Family Rules,' put a check by the statements that apply to your family."

Discussion

Facilitators can say:

- "Which of these rules do you like?"
- "Which don't you like?"
- "Which do you think are pretty normal?"
- "Do you have some that are unusual?"
- "Are these rules spelled out clearly?"
- "Do you have some rules that are unspoken but very important?"

In a healthy home:

- Rules are clear. For rules to work well, they must be clear to everyone and must be applied consistently. In a healthy family, most rules are clearly directly by the parents. The children don't have to guess what they are.

- The rules are consistent. The parents do not change the rules every time they have a change of mood.
- There are boundaries between family members. If a family member is having trouble, other family members are concerned. They don't feel that they have failed, however, every time another member of the family fails or is in trouble.
- Personal space and physical boundaries are clear. People are allowed privacy in their rooms, in bathrooms, and in their personal relationships.
- Roles are age-appropriate. The parents do the parenting and the children are allowed to be children. Children do not have to do the work of adults.
- The adults are in charge. They set the rules for behavior, curfews, and other discipline issues. One of the most important rules is often unspoken but quite clear: who gets to make the rules. In some families, parents will set some of the rules and then leave others for negotiation. For example, they might say the kids have to help with the dishes, but who does what and which nights can be negotiated.

Most families have rules on communication. Rules on what can and cannot be said will become very strict, however, when the adults start having problems, such as alcohol or drug abuse. More information on how the rules can change when a family member uses drugs or alcohol can be found further on in this section beginning on page 109, "Shock Waves — How Alcoholism Affects the Family."

Rules about anger are often very strict. In some families, it is not all right to express anger. When people cannot express anger directly, they must express it indirectly. Instead of saying, "I'm angry that you messed up the living room and didn't clean it up," a mother might say, "Gee, Joan, I feel so sad that I have to make you stay in tonight as a consequence for messing up the living room. I'm really sorry that can't go out with your friends."

Exercise:
Family Circles and Family Xs — What Kids Need From Families

This exercise can provide insights into relevant aspects of a participant's family situation without getting overly intrusive or revealing. Facilitators can introduce the exercise this way:

"Families can do many things for us when we are growing up. There's a list of some of these in your *Becoming Aware Participant Guidebook* under the heading, 'Family Circles and Family Xs: What Kids Need from Families.' We're going to look at that list right now. For each need that is listed on the left, put an X somewhere on the line to its right to indicate how important it is for *families* to take care of that need."

Facilitators can then ask participants to indicate how well each of those needs **IS CURRENTLY BEING MET** in their own families by putting a **circle** on each line to indicate their degree of satisfaction. A mark to the far left side means, "I am satisfied. This need is met very well by my family." A mark to the far right side means, "I am very unsatisfied. This need is not being met at all."

A note on confidentiality. Facilitators can explain to participants that the form does not specifically list "Satisfied" and "Unsatisfied" to protect confidentiality. Should someone see the booklet without the participant's permission, the meanings of the circles on each line would not be immediately clear.

Discussion

In discussing participants' responses to the needs, facilitators can ask:

- "How much do we agree on which are the most important needs for families to meet?"
- "What additional needs did anyone write in? Does anyone else want to add those to their lists?"
- "How close are your circles to your Xs?"
- "Let's look at some that are close together."
- "Let's look at some that are far apart."
- "Do you think needs that are usually met in families can be met other places as well? What are you doing now to get some needs met that aren't getting met at home?"
- "Has that helped?"

Facilitators can point out that it is often futile to expect too much from a person who is alcoholic, depressed, or distracted by the trauma of divorce. The information in "Detachment," on page 165 of the "Moving On" section of this book, could be introduced briefly at this point.

Exercise:
Family Photographs

Participants can bring in photos of their families or individual family members. If they have a picture of all family members together, facilitators can say:

- "Tell us who is in your family and point to them."
- "They look happy in this picture. When was this taken?"

- "Where was this taken?"
- "How were you feeling that day?"
- "Is that typical?"
- "Who is closest to your father in this picture? Is that typical?"
- "How do you feel when you look at this photograph?"

Exercise:
Drawing the Family Table

The facilitator can have the participants sketch an outline of a dinner table as seen from above and ask them to put a circle at the table for everyone in the family; then put the person's name in the circle.

The family dinner table can tell a lot about what is going on at home. Perhaps mother is not there for some reason, or mother is at home but never at the table because she's fixing the dinner. Perhaps there is anger between one of the parents and one of the children, but it is not directed at the others, and so forth.

Discussion

The facilitators can ask:

- "What's a typical dinner like at your house? Where do you sit?"
- "Draw the lines of communication. Who talks to whom most of the time?" (Colored pencils or crayons can be used. If the communication is generally angry, red can be used;, if it's usually sad or depressing, blue; if it's normal, use pencil; if it's happy, yellow.)
- "Tell us what your lines mean. Give an example of the kinds of things that are said."

Exercise:
The Family Diagram

In this paper-and-pencil exercise, the participants diagram relationships in their families. Using circles to represent family members, the participants can start with mother and father (even if they are separated or divorced) and then draw the children in relation to them. Those who are close to each other will be drawn that way, those who are further apart will be farther away from the other circles.

The use of color can help to clarify communication patterns in the family. As with the family dinner table exercise, red can be used to express angry communication, blue for sad, plain pencil for normal communication, and yellow for happy interactions. Any number of colors can be used to describe a single relationship.

If drinking or drug use is a problem with any member of the family, any chosen symbol (A, D, etc.) can be put in the circle representing that person to denote the problems.

Facilitators can model the exercise by diagraming their own families, revealing as much as they are comfortable with.

The Family Mobile

The family mobile can be introduced in a brief two-minute discussion. The family mobile is a simple, graphic way to introduce participants to the concept of family systems. It will be used here to describe the effects of alcoholism on the family.

Construct a simple family mobile with cutouts of each family member and experiment with the balance of the mobile to decide what setup works best. Using mobile cutouts the facilitators can say the following:

"Although families are made up of individuals, they also work as systems. By systems I mean that there are clear patterns in the way family members interact; there are rules that guide the way all members interact with each other; and the behavior of each person in the system affects all others in that system."

The facilitator can now lift up the family mobile and make the following points:

"This mobile of a family will show you what I mean. In this family [the facilitator can now point to each component of the mobile as he or she talks] this is the mother, the father, an older brother, a sister who is the middle child, and the youngest child here. If the little sister were to get hit by a car and have her arm broken [the facilitator can flick the little sister card with a finger], it sends shock waves throughout the entire family. The other members of the family are frightened by the accident; they have to change their schedules to help each other out for the first several days, while the younger girl is in the hospital; the mother may be angry at the father for not watching the little girl more closely, and so on.

"If the older brother were to run away from home [the facilitator can remove the older brother from the mobile], the entire system gets thrown off balance. The mother may be anxious and worried, the father may be angry, the younger children may be weighed down by their own fears."

Facilitators can then clip the older brother back to the mobile so that it is in balance.

"Parents are especially important to the delicate balance of a family. If the father is upset [facilitator can shake the father card] the entire mobile will move dramatically.

"Later on, when we are talking about the effects of alcoholism and other family problems, we'll see how the entire system is affected when just one member has serious problems."

Drug and Alcohol Use: What's Normal, What's Not?

As noted before, the information and exercises related to the use of alcohol and other drugs are appropriate for all LifeGuides Program participants. These youth are at least as likely — and probably much more likely — than the general population to find drug-use problems among friends and family members. In addition, presenting some basic knowledge about alcoholism and other forms of chemical dependency is important for any program that intends, as one of its goals, to help prevent drug use, abuse, and dependency among students.

Before considering the effects of alcohol and drug use on themselves or their families, participants should review the basics of chemical dependency. The Mood-Swing Graph presented in this session (page 100) serves as the main conceptual model for chemical abuse dependency in the LifeGuides process. By focusing on the effects that drug use has on feelings, participants will develop a greater capacity to understand their own myriad and conflicting feelings.

In presenting the Mood-Swing Graph, facilitators are not to imply that they presume that any participants, their parents, or other relatives are going or have gone through this progression and are chemically dependent.

This section includes background information on the first two stages in the process of alcohol and drug use — experimentation and social/recreational use. Stages three and four — harmful involvement and chemical dependency — are discussed in the next section. During sessions on this subject area, facilitators should watch carefully for information that can be of use in later sessions. When material about alcoholism and drug abuse is presented, participants will start to make many revealing statements. They might manifest signs of denial, enabling, or an inability to separate themselves from their parents' or someone else's problems related to drinking or drug use. Participants cannot absorb all of the information in this subject area at one time. If they are introduced briefly to the concept of enabling during this session, they will be able to see how enabling fits into the overall cycle of addiction. A review of their own enabling behaviors can be left until later.

The class log can be an invaluable tool here. After each session related to chemical dependency and its effects on the family, the facilitators should record signs of denial, enabling, or lack of detachment revealed by participants. These can be used as examples in later sessions. If the facilitators prefer, the specific examples manifested by participants could be adjusted slightly or disguised so participants don't feel singled out or embarrassed by the facilitators' observations.

Goals for Sessions on Drug and Alcohol Use

By considering the information in this subject area and participating in the exercises, participants will:

- Examine what prejudices or misconceptions they may have about alcohol and drug use.
- Look at the way alcohol and other drugs are used in their families.
- Understand the role that feelings play in drug use and addiction.

Affirmations on Learning About Alcohol and Drug Use

The following affirmations can be read in the class before or after sessions on drug use. They can also be assigned for reading during the week. These affirmations are found in the *Becoming Aware Participant Guidebook.*

- The more I learn about alcohol and drug use, the more I will be able to understand myself and my life.

• Knowledge empowers me to make better decisions about my own use of alcohol and other drugs.

• Ignorance can cause me confusion, fear, and anxiety. Knowledge will help me understand my life, the problems I face, and what I can and can't do to make my life better.

Overview

• Using Films and Audiovisual materials: "Friday Night: Five"

• Exercise: What's Normal, What's Not

• Mood Swings

• Stage One: Experimentation — Learning How Chemicals Affect Moods

• Stage Two: Social/Recreational Use — Seeking the Mood Swing

Using Films and Audiovisual Materials

There are many films available that describe the progression of alcoholism and its effects on families and children. These films can be especially helpful in classes for junior high school students. Appendix B, on page 193, includes recommendations for some specific films as well as suggestions on how to fit these films into discussions on the progression of chemical dependency. "Friday Night: Five," described in Appendix B, could be used in a session in this subject area. It portrays a variety of adult drinking patterns and gives participants an opportunity to consider what they consider normal and what they consider problem drinking or alcoholism.

Exercise: What's Normal, What's Not

Children from alcoholic families as well as many children from families disrupted by other parental problems have a distorted view of what normal alcohol use is. Some children may think that drunkenness is the norm, that it is just what adults do when they drink. Others may feel so hostile to any type of alcohol use that they don't think anyone should drink at all. In this exercise, found in the *Becoming Aware Participant Guidebook*, participants will look at several situations and decide what they think is normal ("OK") and what is not ("definitely not OK"). The participants should review to each item on the list and put an "X" in the appropriate column to indicate what they think about each example. When they have done that, they can also put an "F" to indicate how they think their fathers would rate each behavior and an "M" to indicate how their mothers would rate the behavior.

Discussion

The facilitators first process the participant responses on a chalkboard or flipchart. They can draw fifteen lines, one for each question, and then chart the Xs indicating each participant's response. The facilitators can look for:

• General trend of each participant's responses.

• General trends of the response by the class as a whole.

• Comparison of the participants' responses to those of the facilitators.

Questions 2 and 6 and questions 3 and 9 offer an opportunity to see if participants make any distinctions between the use of alcohol by girls and boys. In questions 2 and 3, it is a boy who is drinking; 6 and 9 describe almost identical behavior except that a girl is used in the example.

Journaling Assignment

The participants can give their parents a copy of the "Drug and Alcohol Use: What's Normal, What's not?" form, and ask each of them to fill it out. Participants can also write down the feelings they had about asking their parents to do it, how their parents responded to being asked, and their parents' actual responses to the situations on the form.

Discussion on Discrepancies Between the Participants' and their Mothers' and Fathers' Responses

The class can review the discrepancies between the participants' responses and those of each of their parents. They can also look at the discrepancies between the parents' responses as predicted by the participants. Some questions to ask are:

• "What behaviors are your parents and you in agreement about?"

• "What behaviors do you disagree about the most?"

• "Talk about the discrepancies. How do they come up?"

• "What behaviors do you think your mothers and fathers would disagree about?"

• "What kind of problems do these disagreements cause in your family?"

The facilitators can look for sources of family conflict and possible sources of miscommunication. The facilitators can also ask:

• "Have you ever asked your parents how the felt about such behaviors?"

• "How do you know they would respond the way you think they would?"

Discussion around this exercise is an opportunity for the facilitators to reinforce the no-use rule for participants and for adolescents in general.

Mood Swings

Facilitators can introduce the Mood-Swing Graph as follows:

"Some people have called alcoholism a disease of the feelings. Alcoholics use alcohol to control their feelings, to keep from feeling miserable or to feel good enough just to get through the day. Alcoholics are not the only ones who use chemicals to control their feelings. Many people do. Chemical use — including the use of alcohol, marijuana, uppers, downers — is closely related to how we all feel. Conversely, how we feel is closely related to how we use chemicals."

Here, a facilitator can draw a Mood-Swing Graph on a chalkboard or flipchart. The Mood-Swing Graph helps describe the full range of human feelings, from pain to euphoria. Facilitators should use examples from the participants' daily lives to demonstrate how they can experience a range of feelings in one day. For example:

"Has anyone ever started off the day feeling great and then felt terrible by the end of the first class in school? How many times during a close basketball game do you think you go from feeling great to feeling terrible? What happens to your mood when you're talking to your best friend, or boyfriend, and then turn around to see a police officer walking straight toward you looking angry?"

If material does not readily come to mind, and if participants are not responding quickly to requests for examples of regular mood swings, the following example may be given:

"Marsha wakes up in the morning and gets ready for school. She is having an 'ugly day.' She thinks she looks just terrible, and when looking in the mirror, her sad expression makes her think she is totally unlovable. She is over here on the pain side of the Mood-Swing Graph. Then, on the bus, she sees two of her best friends. They are glad to see her. They start joking and having fun. Her mood swings to the Feeling Good side of the Mood-Swing Graph. By the time she gets to her first class, English, she is feeling OK. In math class, she receives a D grade, and she swings way down to the Feeling Awful spectrum of feelings. By lunch time, she has gotten over her despair and is pretty much back to normal. However, at lunch time, she learns that she has been made captain of the debate team and is feeling great."

[Facilitator should draw a line to the Euphoria end of the Mood-Swing graph.]

Facilitators can use the example to point out:

• A person's mood can go from normal to feeling good naturally.
• A person's feelings naturally return to normal.
• A normal person's mood can go from normal to feeling bad.

Facilitators can say: "A normal person's feelings will naturally return from feeling bad to feeling normal. Not all of us are right in the middle of the chart. Some may be down in the pain side most of the time. If you are here, here, or here [make an "x" progressively toward the pain end of the spectrum], that means you need something to take you in this direction [make an arrow pointing up]."

Discussion

Facilitators can say:

• "Give an example of how your moods swung back and forth some day this week."
• "People do lots of things to help them feel better when they want to. What things do you do?"

Participants' responses can reveal those who really don't have much they like to do. If participants offer vague or unrealistic examples, facilitators can challenge them gently by asking:

• "How often do you do that?"
• "Does it really help?'

The facilitators can note important information on the class log for reference in later sessions.

Stage One: Experimentation — Learning How Chemicals Affect Moods

In presenting the information about experimentation, facilitators can begin by saying:

"Somewhere along the line, just about everybody will come into contact with mood-altering chemicals. Maybe their parents will give them some at a party, maybe they take it from their parents' cabinet when they're very young, or maybe they don't have a drink until they leave high school, start working, go to college, or go into the Armed Services. Whether they seek chemicals or not, whether they are alcoholic or not, whether they want to or not, most people will try alcohol or other drugs. And

Mood-Swing Graph

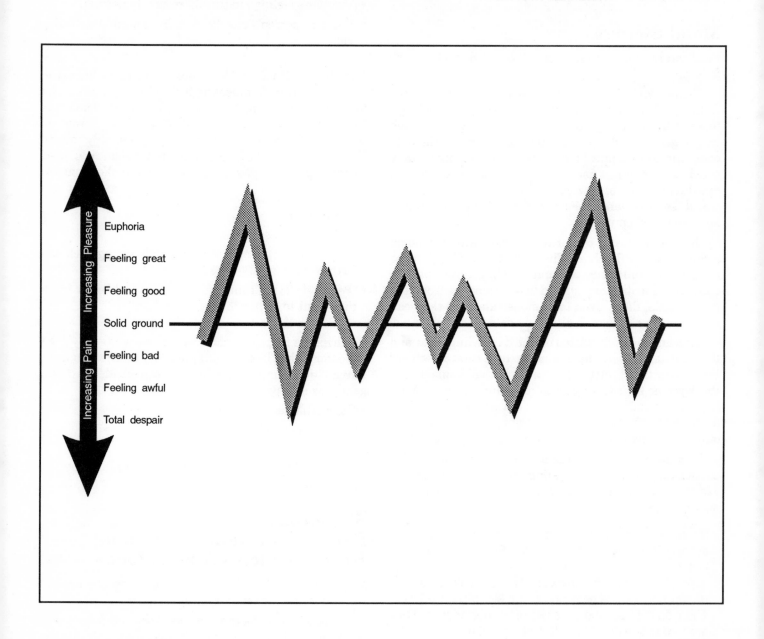

when they do, they are likely to experience a mood swing.

"Most people who try chemicals, especially alcohol, find out that:

• "It makes them feel good.

• "They can control how good they want to feel with it.

• "They will return to normal after they use it."

Facilitators may want to add:

"Some drugs cannot be easily controlled. Drugs like LSD, PCP, and crack are not predictable, and they can cause serious physical and psychological reactions. People have frequently gone through severe emotional crises because of PCP or LSD. Alcohol, on the other hand, is more predictable in its effects. Curiously, that is one reason why alcohol, while at first seeming like a less dangerous drug, is really more dangerous in terms of how addicting it is. Even when people experiment with many different drugs, they tend to stick with the drugs they can control to some extent and the drugs that have predictable effects. Alcohol works every time.

"At first there are usually very few harmful consequences. Users begin to build a trusting relationship with chemicals. People actually do develop relationships with chemicals. They call them their friends, their buddies, their lovers. They can learn to control the degree of the mood swing by regulating the quantity of the chemical intake. Regulating the quantity gives people the illusion of control in their lives.

"Again, if they are over here [the bottom of the graph], they feel less control over their lives and feel more pain. People who discover that they can control and relieve pain by using chemicals tend to use greater quantities over time, and they tend to be at risk for addiction."

Stage Two: Social/Recreational Use —Seeking the Mood Swing

Facilitators can explain to participants that in Stage Two, people use drugs or alcohol regularly, but not so much that they have to change their life style and not so much that use interferes with their lives. An adult in this stage:

• Uses only on certain occasions and avoids high-risk times and places.

• Associates use with fun, relaxation, and good times.

• Is in control of use; use is not in control of the person.

• Anticipates and plans use.

• Obeys laws and follows social rules regarding time, place, drug of choice, and friends.

• May suffer from physical pain such as hangover from occasional overuse, but suffers little emotional pain.

• Can control the amount of use and his or her mood. Learns that a certain amount of the drug has a certain effect.

• Behaves appropriately.

• On rare occasions (usually a special event) may "misuse" (use too much).

The adult also learns that if too much is used, he or she swings back a little bit too far down. But, as time goes by, he or she will drift back to normal. In summary, he or she has learned that some drugs have a predictable effect, that using drugs can be fun, and that they are reliable and can still be controlled.

Facilitators can stress that Stage Two offers too great a risk for any young person. Seeking a mood swing can be a very dangerous game for people who are vulnerable. Facilitators can then say:

"Later on in this class, we will talk about factors that put you at risk for drug problems. One factor is starting drug use at an early age. Researchers have found that the earlier people start to use chemicals on a regular basis, the more likely it is that they will have serious chemical-use problems in the future. Young people seeking a mood swing are like moths that circle around a flame. Moths tend to go closer and closer, and finally they get burned."

Discussion

Facilitators can read the list of characteristics of social or recreational use, pausing after each to ask participants for give an example of use that has that characteristic and of use that does not have that characteristic. For instance, facilitators can say:

"One of the characteristics of social/recreational use is that the person uses the chemicals only on certain occasions and avoids high-risk times and places. Give me an example of adult alcohol use that has that characteristic."

Some examples would be a person of legal age drinking at a party. An example of a high-risk time would be a person stopping to have several drinks on the way home from work and then driving home.

Facilitators should look for signs that the participants believe social/recreational use is acceptable for junior and senior high school students. For instance, they may say, "Well, if I'm at a party and I know someone can give me a ride home, I can have a drink." Facilitators should use that opportunity to point out that drug use at an early age is, in itself, a risk. The younger that people are when they start to use drugs, the more likely they are to develop problems in the future.

Alcoholism and Drug Dependence

When Use Goes Out of Control

In the discussions on experimentation and social use of alcohol and other drugs, participants had an opportunity to consider what they think is acceptable and unacceptable drug use. Discussions and exercises in this next subject area focus on the clearly pathological patterns of use. There are many young people who cannot differentiate even severe forms of chemical dependency from "normal" or social use. Although most participants will have some notion of when use becomes a serious problem, they will have many misconceptions about what causes addiction and what can be done to address the problem.

Goals for Sessions on Alcohol and Drug Dependence

By considering the information under this subject area and taking part in the exercises, participants will:

- Understand the important role that feelings play in the progression of chemical dependency.
- See that alcoholism and drug abuse arise out of the users' needs and feelings, not from anything their children do.
- Learn that they cannot cause, control, or cure another person's chemical dependency.
- Understand the basic processes of use, abuse, and dependency.

Affirmations on Learning About Alcoholism

The following affirmations can be read in class before or after sessions on drug dependence and at other times as well. They can also be assigned for reading during the week. These affirmations can be found in the *Becoming Aware Participant Guidebook*.

- I am not the cause of another person's alcohol and drug use.
- I can never be blamed for the problems caused by another person's drug use.
- I will not try to control or cure another person's drug use since that can only cause me frustration and pain.
- I will not blame anyone for being an addict.
- I will hold people accountable for their actions, not for their disease.

Overview

- Audiovisual Resource: "The Invisible Line"
- Exercise: True/False Quiz on Alcoholism and Drug Addiction
- Exercise: Dear Miss Helpful
- Stage Three: Harmful Involvement
- Stage Four: Chemical Dependency — The Relationship Becomes Primary
- Chemical Dependency is a Disease
- Exercise: Signals Worth Watching
- Journaling

Audiovisual Resource

The film, "The Invisible Line," described in Appendix B, on page 198, shows the growing drug problem of a teenage boy.

Exercise:
True/False Quiz on Alcoholism and Drug Addiction

This exercise covers some of the most common misconceptions about alcoholism and drug addiction. Participants can be told to look at the "True/False Quiz on Alcoholism and Drug Addiction," in their *Becoming Aware Participant Guidebook.* They can be given five or ten minutes to fill out the quiz, alone or in small groups. These same questions can be asked again after information under this subject area has been presented if facilitators want an indication of how much of the information participants understood. The questions on the quiz are:

• You can't be an alcoholic if you just drink beer. (False: People can get just as drunk on beer as they do on mixed drinks. The alcohol content in a can of beer is approximately equal to the alcohol content in a mixed drink.)

• No one can help an alcoholic. Only an alcoholic can help himself. (False: Alcoholics have sought treatment when their spouses, children, and others have encouraged them to do so.)

• Alcoholism is the most common drug problem in the country. (True: There are far more users of alcohol than of any other drug; far more people are addicted to alcohol than to marijuana, cocaine, or heroin.)

• Alcoholics are usually skid-row bums. (False: Alcoholism crosses all lines in a community. Doctors, lawyers, ministers, and priests can all be alcoholic.)

• Very few women are alcoholics. Almost all are men. (False: A third of all alcoholics and alcohol abusers are women.)(Williams, 1987)

• Most alcoholics could stop drinking if they just used their willpower and really decided to stop. (False: Alcoholism is a physical disease. Willpower alone will not work. Medical treatment and Alcoholics Anonymous are the ways that many alcoholics find sobriety after they have tried to do it on willpower alone.)

• Very few alcoholics have jobs. (False: Millions of alcoholics are able to drink heavily and still maintain a job. It is the family who feels the effects of the alcoholism most strongly, usually long before the effects are seen on the job.)

• There is nothing you can do for an alcoholic until he or she hits bottom. They have to realize for themselves that they need help. (False: Experts have found that, when alcoholics are confronted with the effects of their drinking on others and when people stop "enabling"

alcoholics to continue drinking, they will seek and accept treatment for their problem much sooner.)

• Alcoholics drink because they really love the taste of alcohol. (False: Alcoholics drink because it makes them feel good and because they have developed a disease that makes it almost impossible for them to stop on their own once they start to drink. The taste has very little to do with it.)

• Unlike heroin, alcohol is psychologically but not physically addicting. (False: Alcohol is definitely physically addicting.)

• Alcoholics become addicted when there is too much pressure on them. Being nervous about their jobs or about their families can cause them to become alcoholics. (False: Alcoholics become addicted because of their relationship with alcohol. It makes them feel good. There is also an inherited predisposition that makes some drinkers become alcoholic.)

• Because an alcoholic has a disease, he is not responsible for his behavior when drunk. (False: Alcoholics have learned that when they drink, they have serious behavioral problems. They know, before they start drinking, that there will be serious consequences if they do drink.

Discussions and Observations

The facilitators can go through the list of questions and ask participants why they believe each question is true or false. Participants can be asked to give any supporting data or observations they have. Then the facilitators can give the correct answer along with some explanation.

Exercise:
Dear Miss Helpful

This exercise can be used as an opener to help participants focus on the relevant issues in drug and alcohol use. It can also be used at the end of sessions on harmful use and dependency to help participants review some of the most important information.

Facilitators can ask participants to break up into pairs or small groups. Within each group a participant can be selected to read the letter "Dear Miss Helpful," in the *Becoming Aware Participant Guidebook.* The task of the participants is to write a response from Miss Helpful.

Whether reading or listening to the letter, participants may see themselves in the problem presented. The writer of the letter blames herself for her brother's drinking problems, tries to figure out what caused the problem, and attempts to control or even cure her brother's problems by various activities.

Facilitators can introduce the exercise by saying: "Almost every newspaper has a column on personal advice. Perhaps you've read 'Dear Abby' or 'Ann Landers' or one of the several other advice columns. In this next exercise, you will have an opportunity to be an advice columnist. One of you will read this letter to the rest of you [or to your partner, or to the entire class]. Then you will have ten minutes to discuss the problem and offer advice to the letter writer."

Dear Ms. Helpful:

I have a problem with my brother. He and I used to be real close, but we're not anymore. He would always play with me, bring me to his baseball games, and let me hang around when his friends visited. But it's not that way anymore.

I think, maybe, that it's because he's a senior in high school now and has so much work to do. But, anyway, he is not the same guy I used to know.

When he comes home from school now he goes straight to his room, plays records, and smokes cigarettes. (And sometimes other things!)

I think it could be my fault. I was always asking him for advice and help. He seemed like he liked to do it but, maybe, he just got tired of me.

He doesn't bring his friend, Nick, here anymore. Nick was a great guy. Instead, he hangs around these two other guys, and all they talk about is drinking and doing drugs at parties.

I never know what he's going to be like when he comes home. Yesterday, when he came home, he was real high, he was hugging me and wrestling with me and tickling me. But it wasn't like before. He seemed just somewhere else, even when he was laughing and playing with me.

I've tried everything. I've cleaned his room so that he would feel better when he comes home and be in a good mood. Sometimes when his creepy friends have called I've told them he wasn't home. I even found his dope and threw it out. He didn't yell at me like I was afraid he would. He probably figured our mom had found it.

Ms. Helpful, if you have any advice or any tricks to help me make my brother better again, I would really like to hear from you. Please answer my letter soon.

Sincerely,
One Worried Kid

Discussion

Facilitators can ask:

- "Have you ever known anyone like One Worried Kid?"
- "Have you ever been in this kind of situation? When? Who was the person you were concerned about?"
- "What does One Worried Kid think is the cause of her brother's changes in behavior?" (Problems with being a senior, her pestering of her brother for help, etc.)
- "What does she try to do to fix the situation?" (Clean his room, keep his drug-using friends away, throw away his drugs.)
- "Do you think this will work?"
- "What did you tell her to do?"

Stage Three: Harmful Involvement

Facilitators can begin this discussion by reminding participants that in the experimental stage, drinkers or drug users try to fit chemicals into their lives. Harmful abuse comes when they start to try to plan their lives around chemical use. Then facilitators can present the following list of behaviors related to the third stage:

- The user begins to experience periodic loss of control over chemical use and can no longer predict the outcome once chemical use begins.
- The person becomes more ingenious about getting, keeping, using, and hiding drugs.
- The person experiences conflicts in values.
- There is a change in attitude about the worth of formerly enjoyable activities at work or at home.
- Some family activities are dropped.
- The person shows a preoccupation with chemical use. The person will talk about drinks during the day, saying things like, "I can't wait 'til closing time so we can get to the bar. This has been a miserable day."
- The person will withdraw from old friends and adopt new friends who like to drink more or participate only in activities where drinking is involved.
- Friends and loved ones are mistreated.
- Lying and other forms of dishonesty increase. A person will lie to family members about where he is going, or will lie to his boss about why he wasn't at his desk or work station at a particular time. If the person is getting into trouble because of poor work performance, he may blame the problems on others. If money to buy alcohol or other drugs becomes scarce, the person may steal from others.

- Sometimes the value change is hard to recognize because friends have shifted. Shifting to friends with different values hides the value conflict.
- Harmful consequences increase.
- The person may be arrested for DWI or disorderly conduct while under the influence of chemicals.
- The emotional pain increases. Sometimes there is great pain after chemically induced pleasure wears off, e.g., an alcohol hangover or "crashing" after using speed.
- Frequency of drug use increases.
- Stronger chemicals are needed.
- The rules expand: Instead of just using after work, a person will have three cocktails during the lunch hour.
- New ways of using the chemicals are tried.
- Combinations of chemicals are tried.
- Defenses increase. All the defenses mentioned become more frequent and more rigid. Self-delusion becomes more pronounced. The person not only uses the defenses to deceive others, but also comes to deceive himself. He or she often becomes unaware of the seriousness of this condition. Projection of self-hatred onto others may also begin to occur. For example, a man who feels he is worthless and unlovable will accuse his wife of not loving him: "You don't care about me; you don't care about what happens to me! You never did care about me or what I did!"

Discussion

At this point, the facilitators can ask the class:

- "Have any of you seen some of these signs in a person you know?"
- "Without naming that person, can you give examples of some of these things that I've just mentioned?" (The facilitators can reiterate some of the signs, such as loss of control, acting in conflict with personal values, mistreating friends, etc.)
- "Have you been affected by anyone at this stage of chemical dependency?"

Stage Four: Chemical Dependency — The Relationship Becomes Primary

One of the most important points for facilitators to make in this section is, that even though use may start off as experimental or symptomatic, it can take on a life of its own and eventually spin out of the person's control. Participants need to understand that regular, frequent chemical use can turn into an overwhelming urge to recreate the experience of becoming high or intoxicated. This urge can replace all other human needs and become primary and automatic. Facilitators can present the following list of characteristics of Stage Four:

- Use increase
- Person continues to use in spite of repeated negative consequences.
- There are changes in patterns of use. Instead of drinking slowly, users will rush the high. Instead of snorting cocaine, they will smoke it.
- There is a loss of control. Chemical users are no longer able to determine what will happen once they start (how much and how long they will continue to use, how they will behave under the influence).
- There is a loss of choice. They are no longer able to determine when they will use.
- Emotional pain increases.
- Tolerance increases. It takes more alcohol or other drugs to get them high.
- They use just to feel normal.
- They use to medicate pain.
- They develop a close, personal relationship with chemicals.
- Self-worth becomes dependent on the chemical. They only go to parties and talk to others if they are high. They only feel like good hosts when they are able to get their guests drunk.
- Rules fall by the wayside. People who previously got drunk only on weekends start breaking that rule and get drunk every night, or before they go to work or to school.
- Attempts to quit fail.
- Defenses increase.
- Blackouts occur more frequently.
- Physical addiction worsens. People get the shakes when they are not high or start to feel nauseated when they cannot get more heroin, for example.
- People make geographic escapes. An alcoholic may move to another state in the hope that a new job and new locale will make it easier to stop drinking, or easier to get by with excessive drinking.
- Users lose the desire to live; there is a complete spiritual bankruptcy.
- Work-related problems may not become obvious until the latest stages of chemical dependency. A person whose self-worth is closely tied to achievement on the job may do everything possible to keep his work-re-

lated life in order, even if the family life is deteriorating rapidly.

Discussion

At this point, the facilitator can ask the class:

- "Have any of you seen some of these signs in a person you know?"

- "Without naming that person, can you give examples of some of these things that I've just mentioned?" (The facilitator can reiterate some of the signs, such as continued use in spite of consequences, changes in patterns of use, rules about use changing, etc.)

- "Have you been affected by anyone at this stage of chemical dependence?"

Chemical Dependency is a Disease

The disease concept of alcoholism helps those who live with an alcoholic detach from that person's behavior. Once they see that alcoholism is a medically accepted illness, they can look at the alcoholic's behavior as alcohol-driven rather than caused by a lack of love or by something that the participant has done. Alcoholism is described as:

- **A primary disease.** Satisfying the addiction becomes the only goal in life. Further, while drinking or drug use may have been related to other problems at one time, it would not go away if those other problems were to cease immediately. At this stage, the chemical use must be addressed as a problem in its own right.

- **A progressive disease.** People do not stay at the same level of chemical use once they get into the harmful phases. The level will increase. And when people quit for a while and then start again, they start at the level where they left off. For example, a person may have smoked four or five cigarettes a day as a freshman, worked up to two packs a day by his junior year, and then quit. If he starts smoking again, he will be up to two packs a day within a short time. It's the same with an alcoholic's drinking.

- **A chronic disease.** People who are addicted may stop their use, but they are never again able to use normally. Many alcoholics think that, after a few years of sobriety, they will be able to drink normally. Sometimes they do drink normally for one, two, or three weeks, or even six months. But in virtually all cases, they get to the point where drinking once again causes them severe consequences.

- **A Fatal disease.** Continued use by an addict eventually leads to death: Increased tolerance heightens the risk of an overdose; many physical problems crop up; the addict becomes vulnerable to emotional problems, suicide, and accidents.

Facilitators should be careful in applying the disease concept. Some authors and professionals who work with the children of alcoholics push this disease concept too far, telling the children they "should not" feel angry toward the alcoholic: "How can you be angry at someone who has a disease and is not at fault for that disease?" There are many problems with this line of thinking. First of all, not every alcohol or drug abuser is an alcoholic. Second, although people "should not be angry" at a person for having a disease, they can be very angry at that person for using alcohol when he knows what will happen once he starts drinking. The "should not be angry" message is an alcoholic-centered viewpoint. The LifeGuides Program is decidedly child-focused. If the children want to feel angry, whether or not the drug user has a disease, that is natural, appropriate, and quite understandable. If the disease concept helps participants feel less emotionally vulnerable to the alcoholic, then they should make use of it. If they feel that the alcoholic has been so outrageous in his or her behavior that forgiveness is not appropriate—at least at the present time—forgiveness should not become a major goal for the facilitator.

Discussion

The facilitators should help participants see the practical implications of the Mood-Swing Graph and the disease concept. The facilitators can say, "What does all this information mean to you?" and then read the following points:

- **"Well first of all, if you know or live with a person with drug problems, you are not alone.** Almost a quarter of all people in this country say that they have had problems at home because of alcoholism."

- **"You cannot cause the alcoholism of another person.** Clearly, a person's own feelings have a great deal to do with whether he or she becomes alcoholic. Furthermore, many researchers have studied this problem and concluded that those who become alcoholic often have some kind of physical traits that make them more likely than other people to become alcoholic."

- **"Alcoholism is a disease that no doctors or psychiatrists have ever been able to cure.** People can stop drinking, but if they start drinking again, they will fall back into alcoholism. Since no doctor or psychiatrist has ever been able to cure it, obviously, you cannot expect to try to cure it yourself."

- **"You cannot control another person's alcohol use.** The use is determined by the person's own feelings and, eventually, by the person's addiction. If a person is addicted to drugs, he or she will want them and get them regardless of what anyone else does."

- **"Although alcoholism is a disease, it is a treatable disease.** It cannot be cured, but if an alcoholic stops drinking, he or she can live a normal and very happy life. Many alcoholics have been through treatment, have stopped drinking, and have changed their lives around totally. There is hope for alcoholics and the people who live with them."

Facilitators can also ask these questions:

- "What do you think of what I've just said?"
- "Do you believe it? Is it hard for you to accept?"
- "Have you heard statements by other people that contradict what I just said."

Exercise:
Signals Worth Watching.

In the *Becoming Aware Participant Guidebook*, the "Signals Worth Watching" list corresponds to Dr. Richard Heilman's warning signs of chemical dependency. They are:

- **Preoccupation:** Does he look forward to getting his next drink or next hit, plan his day around when and how to get chemicals, talk constantly about alcohol and other drugs?
- **Gulping drinks or rushing the high:** Does he regularly smoke two or three joints in a row to get a quick high?
- **Increased tolerance:** Does it take more now to get high than it used to?
- **Hidden bottles or protecting the supply:** Does he keep bottles in secret places so he can take drinks during the day without anyone noticing? Is he so concerned about having enough chemicals for his own use that he hides them even from his chemical-using friends?
- **Medicinal drinking:** Does he use alcohol and other drugs to mask pain, deal with loneliness and depression, and cure hangovers?

- **Blackouts:** Has he ever had a blackout? How many?
- **Using more than intended:** Does he go to parties intending to have only one glass of beer or one joint but then end up getting smashed?
- **Using alone:** Do drinking and drug use take place less often at social gatherings and more often when he is alone?

Discussion

The following are some ways that information can be used in the LifeGuides class.

Facilitators can ask participants to look at the list of signals, explaining that these signals have been identified by experienced counselors as some of the traits to look for when trying to assess drinking or drug use. Facilitators can then ask:

- "Which of these signals have you observed? This can be in anybody, a friend or a relative."
- "Give some examples, if you can, of any of these signs."

Journaling

The facilitators can also ask participants to review these signals during the week. Participants can look for ways that some of these signs are shown by people they know.

It is seldom possible for participants to truly understand the scope of someone's drug use simply by using "Signals Worth Watching." Although all of these signals can be manifested in outward behavior, they are often internal signs, known only to the drug user. The signals participants do observe, however, can be very revealing of the situation the participant is facing.

Facilitators should especially look for indications of blackouts. Giving a strong message that blackouts are a serious sign, facilitators should be sure that participants understand the difference between passing out and having a blackout. (In a blackout, a person under the influence of alcohol continues to move about, talk with people, and even drive a vehicle; the person simply cannot remember anything from a blackout period. A person who has passed out is both immobile and unconscious.)

Shock Waves

How Alcoholism Affects the Family

Parental alcoholism and other forms of chemical dependency are very confusing to young people. They want to know why their parents are so unreliable, why they are so unfair sometimes, why they seem to believe so strongly in certain values and then violate their own value systems.

This section explains how the progression of chemical dependency has a parallel effect on the family and what happens to young people as this happens.

Facilitators should look for discrepant statements from participants when presenting this material. When participants hear information about the impact of alcoholism on families, they are likely to admit to the presence of problems but deny that those problems have affected them in any way. For instance, in one school a boy told a facilitator: "My father's drinking doesn't affect me at all. I haven't asked him a question in three years. I never ask anything of him and I never expect anything of him. He gets up in the morning, he eats, he goes to work, he comes home, he gets a six-pack, sits down on the couch, watches TV, and goes to bed. If I have something to ask him, I ask him as soon as he gets home, before he has a beer. His drinking just doesn't affect me."

A girl in a support group told the facilitator: "I learned early on that if my mother says we're going to take a family vacation, I'd better not plan on it. We just get all our stuff together and never go. I don't even give it a second thought now when she says we're going to do something, and it doesn't bother me at all."

This type of dissociation is also typical of children of divorce. A participant will say, "Since my father moved out, my parents' fighting has gotten worse, not better. My father doesn't even come to get me when he says he will. I'm so used to it, though, that I don't even notice it. I always have plenty of things to do. If he says he's coming over I say, 'Fine,' but I always plan to do something with my friends and just go ahead with it."

In each of these statements, the children have indicated that they have experienced some very clear effects from their parents' problems, while denying that they have any negative feelings about the issue.

Facilitators should note in the log any examples of this type of discrepant statement. When the information on denial is discussed, examples similar, but not identical, to the ones raised in class can be used.

Goals for Sessions on How Alcoholism Affects the Family

Goals for sessions on this subject area include:

- To help participants begin to see the many different ways they can be affected by chemical use in the family.

- To help them determine what aspects of their lives most need to be addressed.

- To provide a solid foundation that will help participants understand other issues in the LifeGuides curriculum, such as denial, feelings, and enabling.

Affirmations on Facing Alcohol and Drug Use in Those Close to Me

The following affirmations can be read in class before or after the sessions on this subject area. They may also be assigned for daily reading during the week. These affirmations can be found in the *Becoming Aware Participant Guidebook.*

- I am willing to look at any effects alcoholism or drug abuse has had on my life.

- I am willing to look at any effects alcoholism or drug abuse has had on my family.

- It is OK to talk about drug problems; it is very important to talk about them.

- My needs are important.
- I will talk directly to people I am angry with.
- It is OK to trust people.
- It is good to express feelings.
- I will learn to act as an individual, not merely as a member of a system.

Overview

- Films: "Lots of Kids Like Us" and "No-Fault Kids"
- Demonstration Techniques for The Effects of Alcohol Use on the Family
- Review of the Progression of Chemical Dependency
- How the Family is Affected
- Family Rules Change
- Exercise: Special Rules for Special Problems
- The Effects on Children
- Exercise: Shock Waves—How the Chemical Use of Another Affects Me
- Typical Reactions to Alcoholism in the Family
- Exercise: How Families React to Other Serious Problems

Films

There are many films available that describe the progression of alcoholism and its effects on families and children. These films can be especially helpful in classes for junior high school students. Appendix B includes recommendations for some specific films. "Lots of Kids Like Us," described on page 195, does an excellent job of showing the effects of parental alcoholism on children.

The film, "No-Fault Kids," describes the effects of divorce on children and is also described in Appendix B.

Demonstration Techniques for the Effects of Alcohol Use on the Family

Facilitators can use two different models to describe the effects of alcohol use on the family: the Parallel Mood-Swing Graph and the Family Mobile.

Parallel Mood-Swing Graph

This involves drawing the Mood-Swing Graph used in previous sessions and reviewing the way alcoholics' moods tend to swing and come back to normal when they use drugs. Then the facilitators say:

"In many families, everyone is strongly affected by the mood swings of the alcoholic. When the alcoholic is feeling good, the other people are feeling good. [The facilitator can draw the mood swings of a family using a different color ink or pencil from the graph already drawn.] When the alcoholic is in a good mood, the family's moods swing up here, but when the alcoholic is in a bad mood, their moods swing down here. [A line is drawn down to the bottom of the Mood-Swing Graph.] This happens to people who cannot separate themselves from the alcoholism or the alcoholic's problems. They cannot 'detach' as counselors say. They cannot take charge of their own lives and their own moods.

"Have any of you seen this pattern, where the moods of people around an alcoholic go up and down with the moods of the alcoholic?"

The Family Mobile

The family mobile introduced on page 96, in "Drug and Alcohol Use, What's Normal, What's Not," can be used again here. Facilitators can say:

"When a parent becomes alcoholic, they often don't take care of their responsibilities and may actually abandon the family. [The facilitator should unclip the father or the mother from the mobile.] When that happens, everybody else is let down. Sometimes, to get the family back into balance, an older brother and sister will try to move up here [facilitator unclips the oldest child and puts that child where the father used to be] in order to put the family back in balance. It is hard for the child to take on that role and it often doesn't work very well. Also, a child should not be in the position of taking on the position of a parent.

"Did anyone ever see a family in which the children had to take on the duties of the parent?"

Review of the Progression of Chemical Dependency

The facilitators can review briefly the material covered on the progression of chemical dependency. They can list the four stages of the process and point out how drinking increases in order to keep the feeling level high, that more and more of the chemical is needed for the user to even feel normal, and that behaviors increasingly violate the person's value system.

How the Family is Affected

The facilitators can refer back to "The Immediate Effects of Alcoholism and Other Family Problems on the

Children," on page 13 in "LifeGuides Overview," for additional information on this subject.

Here are some of the key points in the progression where people are affected by the alcohol or drug use of another family member.

Stage 2: Social/Recreational Use. When a parent or other adult in a family is in this stage, the effects of "chemical dependency" *per se* do not come into play. However, it is very possible that, simply in the manner in which the person anticipates and plans his use, he will be modeling a high degree of interest in or concern with drugs. If, after raking leaves for several hours, a father says, "Well, I think I've earned myself at least a couple of beers for that!," he is indicating that alcohol is very important to him. If whenever he is faced with a problem or a difficult decision he says, "I need a drink so I can think about this!," he is, again, showing that he is pre-occupied with alcohol.

Children are affected by this modeling because they see that the leaders of their families consider alcohol or other drugs very important. The children will be more likely to assume that alcohol will be central to their lives as well.

Stage 3: Harmful Involvement. Children become affected as adults expand the number of times each day and the number of occasions when they consider drinking appropriate. A child will start finding his parent more and more inaccessible because the parent is feeling high. As problem drinkers begin frequently violating their value systems, the other family members are affected in many ways:

• They may be present at the time a parent breaks a law or a rule of conduct, causing all family members to feel shame or guilt.

• Some of the values they are violating may have to do with parenting. Even though they want to be good parents, alcoholics tend to neglect their parenting responsibilities. The children become increasingly more isolated from them. As the parents decrease their involvement in previously enjoyable activities, the children start to lose out on more and more fun activities.

• Because of the conflicts in their value systems, alcoholics' denial becomes stronger in many ways:

  – They deny that certain events took place: e.g., that they were screaming at their spouses and children or that they were driving recklessly.

  – They deny that things are as bad as everyone else says. They try rationalizing, blaming, avoiding, at-tacking, compensating, looking only on the bright side, and all the other tactics of denial.

• If alcoholics must spend money to buy alcohol or other drugs, other family members do not have use of that money.

• If they spend time drinking and using drugs, others in the family do not get that time.

The fact that the alcoholic's denial system is so complete makes those who live with them feel crazy at times. In fact, here's what some interviewers found when they talked to the children of alcoholics:

"Nothing they saw or heard made sense. Children do not understand how there could be a bloody rampage in the house at night and the next morning no one acts like anything has happened; how the mother can allow the father to drink up the family budget when the children have holes in their shoes and no warm clothes; how the parents and society insist that children love and respect their parents when they are never lovable and frequently disgusting. The environment is so inconsistent, irrational and unresponsive that some children begin to conclude they are the crazy ones. It is not just the inconsistency and abusive behavior of the alcoholic that creates this feeling; it is also the apparent acceptance of such behavior by the non-alcoholic parent." (Booz-Allen and Hamilton, 1974)

Certainly, it is not like that in every home disrupted by alcoholism or other problems, but the feeling of being crazy because of inconsistent messages is fairly common.

Stage 4: Chemical Dependency. When a person shows loss of control over chemical use, the family goes into complete turmoil whenever the person drinks. It becomes a disaster for everyone in the family.

As an alcoholic's self-worth deteriorates, he drags the rest of the family down with him. Others in the family feel as bad about their own lives as the alcoholic does about his life.

Discussion

After presenting the above information, facilitators can ask participants to consider some effects they have witnessed. The facilitators can say:

"We have already seen the many different ways that alcoholics behave when they go through the stages of use, abuse, and chemical dependency. We have talked briefly about how those who know, work with, love, or live with an alcoholic or drug addict behave when the addict goes through the stages. Think of someone you know — it could be yourself, but it doesn't have to be — who has a great deal of contact with an alcoholic or drug addict.

- "What things did you see that person going through?"
- "Did you ever know someone who thought they were crazy or didn't understand what was going on in their lives?"

Family Rules Change

In families that are having trouble with alcoholism and other significant problems, new rules come into play. These include:

Don't Talk About Problems in the Family

This is the rule that tells all family members they do not talk about drinking or drug use or other family problems.

"Don't talk directly to anyone you are angry at" is a major part of this rule. When parents follow this rule, it causes them to talk to their children about their anger toward the other parent.

Do Not Trust People

Sometimes parents in troubled families will actually say no one outside of the family can be trusted. Children also learn that it is not possible to trust some people within the family.

Feelings Should Not be Expressed

The family rule may be that they **never** talk about negative events. A person may physically or emotionally abuse a child at night and, the next morning, be all smiles and friendly. Although the feelings of the abused person may be quite intense, to talk about those feelings would go against the grain and destroy the family myth that "we are a big, happy family."

These first three rules — *don't talk, don't trust, don't feel* — are considered by many professional alcoholism counselors to be the most common and most powerful of the rules adopted by alcoholic families. Some other rules are:

Children's Needs are Not Important

Children should not be concerned about their needs, but should adjust to help the family.

Stay in Your Place, Play Your Role

When family members try to break out of rigid and restricting roles, they often meet with a lot of resistance. More information about family roles can be found in "Moving On," beginning on page 153.

Exercise:
Special Rules for Special Problems

Facilitators can tell participants:

In your *Becoming Aware Participant Guidebooks* is an exercise, 'Special Rules for Special Problems,' which lists these family rules. Indicate on the chart which rules are 'very true,' 'not at all true,' or somewhere in-between for your family. Take about five minutes to do that now."

Discussion

After about five minutes, participants can meet in small groups or as a class. Facilitators can ask them:

- "Have you seen any of these rules in anyone's family?"
- "Have you seen them in your own family?"
- "Can you give an example of how some of these rules have been expressed to you?"
- "Have these rules changed over the last several years? Or has it been that way for as long as you remember?"

The Effects on Children

The following list includes effects found by researchers of parental alcoholism on the children living in the home (Cork, 1969). Facilitators can read the list and ask participants to think of which ones apply to them. Facilitators can ask participants for examples. Most of these effects can be caused by any disruptive family problem, not just parental alcoholism.

- The children's school work was affected.
- Their relationships with other family members were affected.
- Their relationships outside the family were affected.
- Their physical health suffered.
- They worried constantly about not being liked by peers.
- They worried constantly about being different.
- They were generally anxious and afraid of the future.
- They felt burdened by too much responsibility; had to grow up too fast.
- They constantly felt ashamed and hurt, were frequently upset, and cried easily.
- They were never self-confident.
- They felt unwanted by one or both parents.
- They were constantly angry and hostile toward parents and others.
- Some were overly self-reliant and felt unable to trust or depend on anyone.

- They felt uncomfortable with or fearful of the opposite sex.
- They were constantly defiant, at odds with authority.
- They felt hopeless and depressed, lacked ambition, and passively accepted their situations.
- They thought constantly of escaping from family or from responsibilities.

Exercise:
Shock Waves — How the Chemical Use of Another Affects Me

This exercise is found in the *Becoming Aware Participant Guidebook*. Because participants should not write explicit information about their families in their guidebooks (to protect confidentiality), the written directions for this exercise are intentionally missing. Facilitators can say:

In your guidebook is an exercise called 'Shock Waves — How the Chemical Use of Others Affects Me.' To complete the exercise, think of a person whose alcohol or drug use has had some affect on you. Do not write that person's name in the guidebook. Circle the numbers of the statements that apply to you."

If facilitators prefer to take additional measures to ensure confidentiality, they can ask participants to list the number of each statement that applies to them on a separate sheet of paper. They can then ask participants to write the total number of responses on a separate sheet of paper and hand it to them. After putting the total number given by each participant on a chalkboard or flipchart, facilitators can comment on the variation among the numbers. If it is obvious that at least half the class has had some negative effects due to someone's drinking, the class can break into small groups and be given the following directions:

- "Go down the list of effects. Share examples of when, if ever, you have experienced an effect or feeling described on your sheets."
- "How do you feel about what you see?"
- "Were you surprised by any of your answers? Were these things that you had ever thought of before?"

The facilitators can look for how open or guarded participants are at this stage in the process. Usually, sharing this information will create its own momentum of honesty. When one participant hears another's story, he or she will open up and offer examples as well.

Typical Reactions to Alcoholism in the Family

Many people have studied the stages families go through when faced with alcoholism in one of their members. Here are some of the general conclusions that many different researchers came to:

- **Denial of the problem.** Incidents of excessive drinking occur but the alcoholic explains them away. The spouse tries to avoid the topic and tends to believe that drinking is not a problem. Anyone trying to exert control meets with resentment and rebellion from the alcoholic.

- **Attempts to eliminate the problem.** As drinking episodes increase and last longer, the spouse tries to hide the problem from friends and employers. The husband and wife examine the reasons for drinking. They try to handle the problem themselves. The alcoholic spouse feels no one understands. The non-alcoholic spouse feels out of control and a failure. The alternate times of drinking and non-drinking impose conflicting requirements on the children. The non-alcoholic spouse is in conflict about whether to protect the children from the reality of drinking or to depend on them for everything and confide in them. The alcoholic may insist on attending functions with the children, embarrassing them with drinking episodes.

- **Disorganization.** This is a time of chaos in which the nonalcoholic spouse and children develop strategies for avoiding or controlling the alcoholic behavior. The nonalcoholic spouse is frustrated and unhappy with his or her own responses to the drinking. The children can get no help or understanding from either parent about changing their family situation.

- **Attempts to reorganize despite problems.** At the onset of a crisis, such as lack of money to pay bills or violence directed at spouse or children, the family begins to separate. Either the parents physically and legally separate or the non-alcoholic spouse reorganizes the life of every family member, with the exception of the alcoholic. The reorganization may involve seeking professional help for the family, getting a job, and discovering Al-Anon.

- **Efforts to escape the problems.** Either desertion by the alcoholic spouse or a decision to separate by the non-alcoholic spouse occurs. Children may be divided between parents or sent to live with relatives or older siblings.

- **Reorganization of part of the family.** Separated from the alcoholic, the family tries to establish a new life. However, the alcoholic spouse may still affect the family by calling, attempting violence against family members, or working on their sympathy to gain a reconciliation.

- **Recovery and reorganization of the whole family.** If the alcoholic spouse achieves sobriety, whether or not there has been a separation, the family may attempt to reorganize. This involves dealing with problems long hidden by the alcoholism.

List adapted from: A *Growing Concern: How to Provide Services for Children from Alcoholic Families,* U. S. Department of Health and Human Services, 1985.

Discussion

Facilitators can list the following typical reactions on a chalkboard or flipchart and ask participants if they have observed any of them and, if so, to give an example:

- Denial of the problem.
- Attempts to eliminate the problem.
- Disorganization.
- Attempts to reorganize despite problems.
- Efforts to escape the problems.
- Reorganization of the family.
- Recovery and reorganization of the whole family.

The facilitators can also ask: "How do you, personally, react? Give examples of your own behavior or attitude to any of these reactions."

Exercise:
How Families React to Other Serious Problems

Alcoholism is not the only problem that disrupts a family. Divorce, the illness or death of a family member, and anything else that keeps a parent from acting like a parent will put pressures on a family system. Facilitators can ask participants to review the list of typical reactions and consider how they would apply if there were no alcoholism in the family but the parents were getting divorced. Facilitators can then ask for examples of this.

Something to Think About

Participants' Risks for Future Problems

Many patients in treatment centers for drug problems are children of alcoholics. One thing these people often say with great surprise is, "When I saw my parents drunk when I was a kid, I swore I would never end up like that. Well, here I am, drinking just as much and getting into just as much trouble as they did."

There is clear evidence that, although they do not necessarily become addicts, children with parents who have drug and alcohol problems are at more risk than other people their age for having serious problems with chemicals. This section helps participants become aware of this risk.

Adults who work with the children of alcoholics must avoid giving them a label that also becomes a self-fulfilling prophecy. It is a goal of the LifeGuides Program to make these youths aware that they are at high risk of becoming chemically dependent or of marrying a chemically dependent person. Facilitators must be careful, however, not to use the label "child of an alcoholic" as though that particular aspect of the person's life totally defines his or her present identity and future actions.

To introduce this section, facilitators can summarize the information provided under "The Children of Alcoholics Face a High Risk of Having Drug Problems" on page 116 and "The Long-term Effects of Parental Alcoholism" on page 118.

The Insight Class. Community Intervention's Insight Class Program™ provides educators and other concerned professionals with a method for helping young people evaluate their use of chemicals. If a school or agency provides an Insight Class Program™, it might be helpful to have LifeGuides participants attend one of the three-week, nine-session cycles. Participants who are using alcohol and other drugs on a regular basis should be strongly encouraged to attend an Insight Class.

Goals for Sessions on Participants' Risks for Future Problems

Goals for sessions in this subject area include:

- To make participants aware of the special risks they have for chemical dependency or drug abuse.
- To emphasize the need for them to say stay drug-free while they are in the LifeGuides Program.
- To challenge their assumptions that they could never be like their parents.
- To provide our participants with an opportunity to assess their own risks for drug and alcohol use.

Affirmations on Facing My Own Risks for Drug Problems

The following affirmations can be read in class before and after the sessions on this subject area. They may also be assigned for daily reading during the week. These affirmations can be found in the *Becoming Aware Participant Guidebook.*

- I will honestly and openly examine my risks for chemical dependency.
- I will honestly and openly examine my risks for other long-term problems.
- I realize that, although I may be at risk for certain problems, this does not mean I cannot avoid those problems.
- I will take responsibility for myself and for my life.
- I will not be influenced by the behavior of my friends who may face lesser risks than I.
- I will not imitate the negative behaviors of those around me.
- I can get along quite well without drugs.

The Children of Alcoholics Face a High Risk of Having Drug Problems

Children of alcoholics run a higher-than-average risk of becoming alcoholics or at least of having severe problems related to chemicals. Vaillant and Milofsky (1982) conducted a 33-year follow-up study of about 400 men who had served as the non-delinquent controls in a longitudinal study of delinquency. In their effort to discover which of several possible predictors of adult alcoholism had been present in these people's youth, the authors found two important factors, heredity and ethnicity. Regarding heredity, the researchers found that men with several alcoholic relatives were three times as likely to become dependent on alcohol as those with no alcoholic relatives.

When they looked at the effects of ethnicity, they discovered that the Irish were seven times more likely to be alcohol dependent than descendants of Mediterranean ethnic groups (Italian, Jewish, Greek, Portuguese, and Syrian), and those of Northern European descent were six times as likely to be alcohol dependent as the Mediterranean.

In *The New Drinkers* (1980), Reginald Smart cites a number of studies showing that the rates of alcoholism among the parents of those diagnosed alcoholic range from 50% to 60%.

In a study of seventh and eighth graders in Minnesota (Namakkal and Mangen, 1979), students with family members who had been through treatment programs for alcoholism or drug abuse reported significantly greater personal use of all illicit substances examined. Overall, 17.2% of students reported that a family member had undergone treatment for alcoholism. Of that group, 24.9% reported current marijuana use of at least twice weekly, compared with 14.7% of the other students. The incidence of daily use of hard liquor for students with parents who had completed treatment was 4.1%, compared with 1.6% for the rest of the students. Furthermore, 28.7% of the students with parents who had drinking problems reported using hard liquor at least once a week, compared with 18.1% of other students.

- I do not need drugs to help me meet other people.
- I can meet other people and make friends without using drugs.
- I can overcome my sadness without using alcohol or other drugs.
- I will recognize my personal risks for drug use and take responsibility for not using alcohol and other drugs.
- I can cope with my problems in school, at home and anywhere else without using alcohol or any other drugs. I realize that using alcohol and other drugs will actually make my problems worse for me in the long run.
- I will seek the help of others if I find drug and alcohol use is harming my life.

Overview

- Film: "My Father's Son"
- Many Opportunities to Point Out Participants' Risks for Drug Problems
- Exercise: Six Signs of Risk for Serious Drug Problems
- Risks for Problems in Relationships

Film

"My Father's Son," described on page 195 in Appendix B addresses the risks that children of alcoholics face for becoming chemically dependent.

Many Opportunities to Point Out Participants' Risks for Drug Problems

Throughout the LifeGuides Program, in presenting the material and processing exercises facilitators will have numerous opportunities to point out participants' risks for drug abuse or chemical dependency. In talking about summer vacation, for instance, participants may indicate that their drinking and drug use increases during that time. When discussing feelings, they may indicate that they sometimes use alcohol and other drugs to feel better when they are angry or sad. Discussions on relationships or making friends often involve references to drug use.

The most important thing for the facilitators to keep in mind is **not to ignore references to drug use.** For instance, facilitators should pursue something as seemingly innocuous as a participant saying, "He got mad at me because I spilt beer on him." They might ask the participant what he was drinking and how much, how

typical was that of him, why he needs to drink to have fun, and so forth. The inquiry should not sound like a third-degree grilling, but the participant should know that drug use is not considered normal.

Exercise:
Six Signs of Risk for Serious Drug Problems

To introduce this exercise, facilitators can say:

"Today we are going to sum up what we have learned about ourselves and our risks for drug problems. Look at the 'Six Signs of Risk for Serious Drug Problems,' in your *Becoming Aware Participant Guidebook.* I'm going to walk you through these now. Make sure you put a 'yes' or a 'no' next to each one, depending on whether you think that that risk indicator applies to you."

Facilitators can then read each item to the participants, elaborating when it seems necessary.

- "Getting low grades in school" (Ds & Fs).
- "Independent use of alcohol outside the family before age thirteen. Don't mark this one just because a relative has given you a sip of beer or a family member gave you a glass of wine to drink on a religious or festive holiday."
- "A lack of religious affiliation. If you don't attend church and don't have any clear religious feelings, check this one."
- "Anxiety, depression, and other emotional problems."
- "Low self-esteem."
- "Family problems, feeling your parents don't spend enough time with you or don't show enough care or concern about you."

Discussion

Facilitators can process this in a variety of ways. If they feel the class is open, honest and trusting enough, the participants can be asked to discuss their specific responses. The facilitators might say:

- "Let's go round and see how many risk factors we each checked off."
- "Which risk factors did each of you check off?"
- "Do you all agree with __'s risk factors?" "Do you think he's got them all?" (This, of course, is more confrontive than some classes can tolerate. It is up to the facilitators to decide if this type of class discussion of risk factors is appropriate).

The Long-Term Effects of Parental Alcoholism

Many researchers and authors have described the long-term effects of parental alcoholism on the children (cf., Cork, 1969; Booz-Allen and Hamilton, 1974; Woititz, 1983). The findings below verify what the heart and common sense have long predicted: Children from alcoholic homes are bound for troubled lives. All of these effects can be the result of a number of different family problems. Among the most common long-term problems are:

■ **Lack of self-confidence, low self-esteem.**

■ **Problems in relationships both with the opposite sex and with the same sex.** The children of alcoholics have difficulty understanding what a healthy or intimate relationship should be like. They have trouble choosing boyfriends, girlfriends, and spouses. Because of low self-esteem and lack of healthy models in their lives, they often tend to choose people who do not treat them well.

■ **Extremes in the way they approach work.** Few, it seems, take a measured, moderate approach to their jobs and careers. They are frequently overachievers who work very hard for approval; they become workcoholics. On the other hand, many of them lack direction and are very irresponsible.

■ **Depression and suicidal tendencies.** The Booz-Allen study, for instance, found that 18% of the children of alcoholics they interviewed suffered from depression and 12% manifested suicidal tendencies.

■ **Difficulty finding enjoyable things to do.** The concept of fun often eludes them.

■ **Extremely self-critical.** Whether they are very responsible or very irresponsible, they tend to judge themselves harshly.

■ **Rigidity.** They get locked into rigid patterns of behavior they have learned in their families and do not know how to break out of those patterns.

■ **Emotional blocking.** Their emotions become deadened. They don't understand feelings and really can not feel.

Facilitators can then conclude the exercise by saying:

"These six areas were studied by researchers who found that kids responding 'Yes' to four of the risk factors are 4½ times more likely to be involved in heavy drug use, those with three risk factors were 2½ times more likely to be involved, those with two risk factors were twice as likely, and those with one risk factor were 1½ times more likely to experience serious drug problems.

"Remember, these risk factors are in addition to any risk factors you might face if your parents are alcoholic."

Risks for Problems in Relationships

Obviously, people whose families have been troubled by the alcoholism of a parent run a clear risk of having drug problems themselves. Alcoholism isn't the only behavior problem children can learn from parents, however. Many attitudes and behaviors are passed on. People who have worked with families for years — school counselors, therapists, doctors, clergy, and others — have often noted that children often live their lives very much like their parents live theirs, even when they are most determined not to.

For example, people who were physically abused by their parents are determined that they will never abuse their own children. But if they start feeling pressure when one of their children starts misbehaving, they tend to fall back into the patterns they learned as children. A great many men who beat their wives or children were also beaten when they were young.

In choosing marriage partners, people often follow a pattern similar to their family pattern. People who have grown up with alcoholic parents have witnessed firsthand the destruction that alcoholism causes. Nonetheless, people who work with families report that children of alcoholics tend to marry alcoholics.

People who have grown up in homes in which there was a lot of fighting are often determined never to fight like that with their spouses. Unfortunately, however, their parents didn't teach them healthy ways of resolving conflict. Instead of yelling, as his parent did, a husband may simply refuse to talk to his wife for a week. This can be extremely hard on a relationship.

Discussion

Facilitators can ask the class the following questions:

• "What do you think of the idea that we tend to do some of the things we were determined not to do?"

• "Have you ever seen this pattern in any of your friends or acquaintances?"

• "Do you know anyone who fights with his parents all the time, but, in fact, is similar to them in many ways?"

• "Think of the ways you are similar to your parents. What are the positive traits you have learned from your parents? This can be anything — something small, such as how to fix or clean something, or a bigger issue, such as how to help friends when they need it.

• "Are there other traits you have learned from your parents that you are happy with? What are some you are not happy with?"

Phase II: Taking Care

Denial

Dance of Deception

As alcoholics or drug addicts become more harmfully involved with chemicals, their denial systems become thoroughly natural to them. Addicts actually do believe many of their own excuses and rationalizations. They convince themselves and their families that their view of the world is, in fact, reality.

Denial of family problems powerfully affects children of alcoholics:

- They get confused and start feeling crazy when the events they witness and the feelings they experience are discounted.
- They feel a tremendous degree of stress from trying to avoid talking about family secrets, both with family members and with those from outside of the family.

Many family issues, such as marital problems, sexual abuse, or the emotional problems of the parents, are also surrounded by layers and layers of denial. In this section, the techniques of denial used by families affected by alcoholism illustrate the ways that families disrupted by a variety of problems react to the pressures they face.

In the discussion about the Mood-Swing Graph, on page 100 in "Drug and Alcohol Use, What's Normal, What's Not," participants were provided with an overview of the progression of chemical dependency and shown how defenses increase as drug use increases. The information and exercises in this next section give participants an expanded vocabulary and some concepts to help them gain a deeper understanding of the Mood-Swing Graph and the effects of chemical dependency or other problems on their families.

Goals for Sessions on Denial

Goals for sessions in this subject area include:

- To help participants understand the typical processes of denial manifested by alcoholics and others with emotional, marital, or behavioral problems.
- To help participants understand that such people are often genuinely unaware of the denial techniques they use.
- To help participants identify techniques they have seen used in their own homes or by others they know.
- To help them understand how they currently use denial in regard to family problems and other problems in their lives.
- To begin to explore how this denial leads them to block even their most basic feelings.
- To help participants look at the way they use defenses and to understand how defenses keep them isolated and stuck.

Affirmations on Honesty with Self and Others

These affirmations can be used as warm-ups for each session in this subject area or participants can recite the affirmations daily during the week. These affirmations can be found in the *Taking Care Participant Guidebook*.

- I trust myself.
- I trust my eyes, my ears, and my feelings.
- I will not let anybody hide the truth from me.
- I will accept the truth in my life.
- I welcome the truth as the most important tool for making my life better.

- I am not afraid of the truth about myself, my family, or my life. I want to find out more about myself.
- I want to look beyond the walls of my defenses, which keep me from growing.

Overview

- Films
- Move Slowly in Confronting Denial
- Exercise: What's "Denial" Mean to You?
- Reading: "Don't be Fooled by Me"
- Masks Over Masks
- Exercise: Taking Off the Masks
- Exercise: Shedding Our Defenses
- Exercise: A Few Fast Moves
- Exercise: A Few Fast Family Moves

Films

Younger participants and those who are new to the LifeGuides Program will find the concept of denial difficult to grasp at first. By using films to point out examples of denial, facilitators can help them understand the meaning of the word and the many ways in which denial is manifested. For instance, depending on what transpires on the screen, the facilitator might say, "Did you see how that girl told her friend that everything was fine at home. She really believed it, I think. That's what we call 'denial.' "

The films "Open Secrets" and "My Father's Son" both have examples of denial. These films are described in Appendix B, pages 195 and 196.

Move Slowly In Confronting Denial

Rationalizing, minimizing, and lying all become second nature to children from alcoholic and other disrupted family environments. These behaviors affect how they interact with others — in a LifeGuides class as well as outside of class.

Adults should not attempt to crash through, in an abrupt and confrontive fashion, the system of denial that children use to avoid looking at their family problems. Children from disrupted family environments tend to be aware of problems, but do not recognize, or will not admit that they recognize, any connection between those problems and the way they feel. This can be viewed as dissociation, a lack of connection between awareness and emotions. The facilitators can let participants live in this apparently contradictory state, at least for a time.

Participants who do not deny that events took place but, rather, deny any negative feelings related to those events can be gently challenged when the facilitators think it is appropriate and the participant is ready to accept such challenging. For instance, a participant may describe a violent fight his parents had and then say, "But that doesn't bother me, that's their problem." A facilitator could ask another participant, "John says that doesn't bother him. What do you think?"

After several such interventions, the facilitator can use the term "denial" to label those behaviors and provide some conceptual structure to the participants.

There are several different routes the facilitators may choose for this subject area. The information given in this section in "Masks Over Masks" and the exercise "Taking Off the Masks" focus on the deeper down, more complex defenses people use to keep themselves and others from seeing who they really are and what they really feel. The other exercises focus more on the techniques alcoholics and drug users employ to keep others — and sometimes themselves — from understanding how serious their chemical use is.

Exercise:
What's "Denial" Mean to You?

This simple introductory exercise will work well with older and more verbal participants. Younger, less verbal participants may find it hard to express themselves on this issue. Facilitators can simply ask:

- "What does the word 'denial' mean to you?"
- "Will someone give me an example of denial that you've observed in someone else?"
- "Tell me one way that you might have been fooling yourself in the last week."

This exercise can be a homework assignment. Facilitators can ask participants to keep track of any way they use denial during the week and to look at all the different techniques they use.

When participants give an example, the facilitators should try to label the kind of denial used. Most types of denial will fall under one of the categories described in "A Few Fast Moves," on page 125.

Reading:
"Don't be Fooled by Me"

Facilitators can ask one of the participants to read the poem (author unknown), "Please Hear What I'm Not Saying," found in the *Taking Care Participant Guidebook.*

Discussion

The facilitators can try to elicit participant reactions to the poem. Some statements they can make include:

- "The person in the poem begs other people not to be fooled by him. Why do you think someone would want people to see through their defenses?"

- "The person says that 'pretending is an art that's second nature with me.' What does that mean to you?"

- "The poem says, 'I panic at the thought of my weakness and fear being exposed.' Has anyone ever felt that way?" (The facilitator can introduce participants to the idea of shame here. Shame will be discussed in more detail in sessions related to feelings.)

- "The speaker in the poem begs people to 'Beat down the walls with firm hand.' What happens if someone doesn't beat down walls, if the walls stay up?" (Facilitators can make the point here that, unless people let go of their defenses, they can never face those issues that keep them feeling unhappy.)

Masks Over Masks

Presenting the following information is one way facilitators can introduce participants to the concept of denial. Before starting this talk, a facilitator can write the following words on a blackboard or flipchart:

Masks

Anger

Shame

Fear

Loneliness

A facilitator can then say:

"Lots of people talk to counselors. Some do it because they feel bad, some do it because their behavior makes other people feel bad. And some do it just because they want to make their lives better in some way. One reason people talk to counselors, psychologists, pastors, and others is to seek help in making changes. When people start to make changes, counselors often discover masks over masks over masks.

"The first mask is made up of many different behaviors that people use to control their lives. Even though they may want to change, they are afraid of what will happen when they do change. They try to control, manipulate, and keep things the way they are. People become workaholics, perfectionists, con artists, alcoholics, druggies, overeaters, undereaters, exhibitionists, compulsive shoplifters, and many other things. Their behaviors distract them and others from the pain they are feeling underneath.

"When counselors try to get people to change, they have to confront them or frustrate them or, in some other way, stop the manipulations people use to control their lives. Unless some control is given up, new discoveries and new ways of behavior cannot be tried.

"The trouble is, underneath most of these masks of manipulation is anger. Anger can come across as:

Being sarcastic

Shouting

Threatening

Attacking

Glaring

Being disruptive

Complaining

Being insulting

Making a joke out of important things

Laughing at people

Being silly

Not listening

Lying

Acting superior

"These are ways that people try to disrupt the process of change. Even depressed people who seem as if they do not have the energy to lift a finger will become very angry when they are pressured to make the changes they have to make to get rid of their depression. And when people get beyond their anger, they are not at the end of their search. Under the anger they find shame.

"Shame relates to the problem that needs changing. People who feel shame feel bad and worthless. But when counselors and others encourage people to go a little deeper, what they see underneath the shame is fear. The fear is the fear of rejection and abandonment, fear of the unknown, fear of new things, and most of all, fear of loneliness and isolation.

"When counselors run into manipulation, anger, shame, and fear, it is easy for them to forget about loneliness. When one sees manipulative behaviors or anger in friends or acquaintances, it is easy to forget that deep down they may be very lonely.

"When someone acts out in anger, people tend to get angry right back at them. That causes them to feel shame, to become fearful, and to feel isolated. The irony here is that fear of loneliness leads to loneliness. It becomes a vicious cycle. Out of fear, people go back to manipulation, being controlling, and refusing to listen to others, to change their behaviors, or to open up to others.

Exercise:
Taking Off the Masks

In the *Taking Care Participant Guidebook,* there is an exercise called "Taking Off the Masks." Facilitators can tell participants to look at the feelings given under "Underlying Feelings" and then ask them to "think of a time when you have felt one, two, or more of those feelings. Circle those feelings. Look at the words under the next heading, 'Attempts to Hide from These Feelings.' Circle the defenses you use — the ways you act — to keep yourself or others from knowing how you feel. Draw lines connecting the circles under the first heading with the circles under this heading. After that, go to the last heading, 'How I Looked to Others,' and circle the words that apply."

Facilitators should allow ten minutes for people to complete the exercise. Facilitators should observe participants closely as they complete the exercise, watching their facial expressions and what they are doing. They can note people who cross out things after they circle them.

Facilitators may choose to process the exercise from the bottom of the page, "How I Looked to Others," to the top or from the top down. Processing from bottom to top, outside to inside, facilitators would ask:

- "What words or phrases best describe how you looked to the outside world?"
- "What techniques or attempts to hide lead to that particular image or style?"
- "What underlying feelings did you circle?"

Participants who are willing to share the details of an event, if it is not too personal or likely to be overwhelming — e.g., an assault or sexual abuse — would be at some advantage, since talking about a particular event often helps clarify feelings. Facilitators can control the level of disclosure by saying, "Maybe someone would like to tell us about a particular event, if it isn't too personal, to see how this process works in real situations."

This exercise presents an opportunity for facilitators and others in the class to share their observations. After a person has described the defenses he or she uses, the rest of the class can add some they know the person has used outside or inside the class. Facilitators can point out the defensive techniques they have observed in or out the class.

Exercise:
Shedding Our Defenses

This is a variation of "Taking Off the Masks." To do this exercise, the facilitators need a supply of self-stick note pads (e.g., Post-It Brand Notes). Participants are to write down all the defenses they used in the "Taking Off the Masks" exercise, putting each defense on a separate self-sticking sheet. These are the defenses they circled under "Attempts to Hide From These Feelings," in their guidebook. The participants then stick the notes on themselves. This is symbolic of the idea that people's defenses stand between them and the rest of the world.

The facilitators then ask each participant in turn to take off his or her defenses, one at a time. When they do this, they should speak some positive affirmation. For example, a participant can say, "I'm not going to attack people when I feel scared," and then remove the "attacking" defense and throw it away. Another might say, "I'm not going to be a clown to hide my feelings," and then pull the "being a clown" defense off, and throw it away. One of the facilitators can participate in the exercise to give participants an idea of the kinds of affirmations to use.

If it seems too forced for participants to state their intention not to use certain defenses anymore, they can simply say, "I don't need this defense anymore" as they remove the piece of paper.

Facilitators can also suggest that participants give an example of the defense they are shedding: "Sometimes I'm sarcastic when I get angry at people. I don't need to be sarcastic. I'm going to make an effort not to do that."

Exercise:
A Few Fast Moves

This and the next exercise focus less on deep-down, hidden defenses and more on the specific defenses people use both to deny the effects of their own or another's behavior on their lives and to prevent others from recognizing these effects. This is a more easily understood concept of defenses. Even though these defenses are close to the surface, many of those who live with alcoholics or others with problem behavior use them unconsciously.

A facilitator can tell the participants that defenses are the ways people think or the things people do to avoid thinking unpleasant thoughts, seeing unpleasant things in themselves, and making changes that are difficult or frightening.

A Few Fast Moves

Rationalizing (making reasons or excuses)

- "I have too much pressure on me, I need to unwind with a drink."
- "This house is always a mess and the kids are always so rowdy. I need a drink just to tolerate it."

Blaming (other people or other things for problems or for the chemical use)

- "If my boss wasn't such a jerk, I wouldn't need a drink at lunch time."
- "It's my boss's fault. He is always on my case. There's just too much pressure."
- "It's my wife's fault. The house is a mess, she is a lousy cook, she is always on my case."
- "It's my friends' faults. I just like to keep them company, and they are always pushing drinks at me."

Avoidance (staying away from reminders and problems)

- "I figure, if I don't drink at home and just stay at the bar, my family can't hassle me about it."
- "Look, I'm not in the mood to talk about my drinking. Just leave me alone!"
- "So Fred is coming over tonight. He's so much into that Alcoholics Anonymous stuff I can't stand it. I'm leaving."

Anger and attacking (in order to shift the blame or to cover hidden feelings of guilt; putting the other person on the defensive)

- "Look, if you don't get off my case, I'm going to sit here and drink until I can't even see."
- "Don't talk to me about being drunk! You're the one who's not taking care of business around here. Get in that room and do your homework before I have to make you!"

Compensation (trying to make up for the harm done)

- "My wife isn't mad at me anymore. I know I hit her when I was drunk last night but I brought her flowers and I've been working real hard around the house since then."
- "Look, I told you I was sorry for embarrassing you at that party last night. What else do you expect of me? I said I was sorry."
- "Look, I know I forgot to go to the school play. Tell you what. I'll take you to a movie tonight."
- "My boss thinks I'm a drunk. I'm going to prove him wrong. I'm going to get every bit of work done that I've been behind on and give it to him by Friday."

Looking only on the bright side (to avoid seeing real problems)

- "Quit talking about my drinking. I'm bringing home a paycheck and I'm still selling my quota."

- "I figure that since I still can go out and run three miles I must be in pretty good shape. That alcohol isn't doing too much to my body."
- "You just don't have a sense of humor. Everybody at the party thought I was very funny."

Delaying tactics (putting off quitting)

- "I think it's this job of mine. I will stop drinking if I could get a job where other people don't drink."
- "I'll quit as soon as summer vacation is over. It's just too hard to stop drinking when I'm up here at the lake."

Helplessness (thinking that one cannot quit using and that one is not responsible for what happens in life)

- "There's no way I could quit. The guys I work with are always drinking."
- "Housework is so boring. There is no way I could get through the day without something to drink."
- "I like baseball and I can't go to a game without someone buying me a beer."

Others are worse (focusing on the problems of others)

- "Quit talking about my drinking. Tom's wife is so bad she has had to go to treatment!"
- "This is my first DWI. I know guys who have had three or four."

Continued on next page

Continued from previous page

- "All I ever drink is beer; your lazy brother has got a bottle of whiskey on the counter all the time."

Making rules (thinking that if special rules about using are followed, all is OK)

- "I'm having trouble getting to work with a hangover. From now on I'll only drink on the weekends."
- "I'm not going to be a drunk driver. As long as I get my wife to drive, I'm OK."
- "No more drinking during the lunch hour. I made so many mistakes yesterday afternoon I could get in trouble."

Used to have a problem (putting a problem in the past helps to avoid facing the present)

- "I really enjoyed that Alcoholics Anonymous meeting you brought me to. But I haven't had any trouble with my drinking in over a month. I don't think it will be a problem from now on."

- "I haven't had anything but a beer for the last six months. No more hard liquor for me."
- "I used to yell at my kids all the time. But now I'm OK. I just fall asleep."

Minimizing (thinking the amount of chemical used and the harm done is very little)

- "You are exaggerating. I really don't drink that often."
- "I know you think I insulted your friends at the party, but you're making a mountain out of a molehill. They had a good time."
- "Look, it's not like I hit another car, is it? At least I was able to pull off to the side of the road."
- "Well, I have had a little trouble at work but it's really no big thing. They love me there."

Don't care (recognizing consequences, but denying concern about the consequences)

- "Really, I don't think I'm cut out to be a family man. She's probably smart to leave me."

- "That place is for idiots. I can get a much better job somewhere else."

It won't happen to me (admitting use, but not believing that the same consequences will follow)

- "That judge is a good guy. He will know that I was just having a good time."
- "Some of the women at work had to talk to a drug counselor. Not me. I can take care of this problem on my own."

Projection (thinking that others behave the same way)

- "I bet my boss drinks ten times as much as I do."
- "Don't tell me your teachers notice my drinking. I'll bet they're drunk out of their minds every night."

Some feelings related to chemical use include shame, guilt, a sense of loss, helplessness, embarrassment, and panic. To protect themselves from these feelings, users and those they live with raise a wall of defenses in their minds and then manifest those defenses in their actions. Defenses affect what information a person receives, what events the person remembers, and how he or she interprets the events. Defenses prevent the chemical user and others from making responsible and sensible decisions.

To start the exercise, a facilitator can ask participants to turn to "A Few Fast Moves," in their *Taking Care Participant Guidebooks.* Responses to these items can be processed in a number of ways. Facilitators can ask participants to check the defenses in each section that they have observed in others, or facilitators can ask how many items each participant checked overall or in each section.

If facilitators are taking a more information-oriented approach, they can move through each section and talk about people they have known who manifested such defenses and how their statements compare to their actual behaviors.

Note that in the participant guidebook there are no headings for the different groups of defenses. If there is time, facilitators can ask participants to label or give a general description for each group of defenses. This can help them develop a more flexible way of looking at this issue. Names for the various groups of defenses in "A Few Fast Moves" are provided in the facilitator's list of defenses on page 125.

Exercise:
A Few Fast Family Moves

Although all of these defenses may be used by the alcoholic or drug user, they are also used by family members and others who are around the user. Facilitators can ask participants to label or give a general description for each group of defenses in the "A Few Fast Family Moves" exercise in the *Taking Care Participant Guidebook.* The following list includes labels and defenses.

Projection
"Don't call my dad a drunk. He doesn't drink any more than your dad."

Rationalizing
"If your mother had to raise three kids on a waitress's salary like my mother does, she might drink a little too."

"I don't care what the papers said. My dad was just pulling away from the curb and the cop wanted to pull him over."

Avoidance
"Say, Sue. Maybe we shouldn't go to my house today. We're redecorating."

Anger and Attacking
"If you ever say one more word about my parents—just one—I'm going to belt you."

Compensation
"I'm really sorry my father said those things to you. He didn't mean them. He's a nice guy. Let me take you to a movie. I'll pay."

Looking Only on the Bright Side
"What do you mean, you think mom drinks too much? She's the hardest worker and best mother a kid could have!"

"I get to do anything I want to. I get to go out anytime I want, and I don't have to answer to my parents like you do."

Helplessness
"Your father has had a very hard life. His father left home when your dad was only three. It's just hard for him to deal with things sometimes."

Others are Worse
"You kids should be grateful for what you have. There are kids I know who don't even have decent clothes to wear."

Making Rules
"If dad promises not to drink when I have friends over, everything will be OK."

Used to Have a Problem
"A couple of months ago things were really bad around our house. Things are going a lot better now." (Maybe because mother has gotten a job and is doing her drinking away from home, or dad is out of town a lot.)

Minimizing
"I know he calls me names when he's drinking, but it really doesn't bother me. I think that happens in most families."

Discussion
In talking about the ways people defend alcoholic family members, facilitators can point out that there is usually more shame related to a parent's use of drugs than to a child's own use. No matter what children know to be the truth in their families, no one likes to hear their parents criticized.

Enabling

The Helping That Hurts

"Enabling" refers to all the words and actions people employ to help alcoholics and other people with problem behaviors avoid the consequences of their own actions. While enabling is usually considered an unnecessary activity that serves only to keep addicts and others stuck in dysfunctional behavior patterns, Life-Guides facilitators should be wary of giving participants the message that enabling is always wrong. It is one thing for a relatively secure, middle-class woman with her own career to tell her husband she will not make excuses to his boss for him anymore, and that if he wants to lose his job because of his drinking, that is his problem. It is quite another thing for a woman whose family is living in or at the edge of poverty to be so detached about her husband's job.

While long-term, consistent enabling will be fruitless, enabling an alcoholic to keep his life together over the short run may often be appropriate and necessary. Furthermore, for children and women living with abusive men, enabling behaviors may have to be used until the family members feel they are safe from abuse.

As with denial, then, facilitators want to let participants know that enabling is both natural and almost inevitable. Furthermore, if what a family needs is a temporary reduction in stress and tension, enabling may be necessary. To stop enabling is to begin a process of intervention; intervention usually means an increase in stress and tension.

Goals for Sessions on Enabling

Goals for sessions in this subject area include:

- To introduce participants to the concept of enabling: What it is, how it works, and how it affects a family.
- To help participants see how members of their families, including themselves, enable.
- To help participants choose, if possible, at least one enabling behavior they will try to stop this week.
- To reassure participants that, no matter what they may hear, enabling is not always bad and, in some cases, it is necessary in order to cope with daily life.

Affirmations on Letting Others Take Care of Themselves

These affirmations can be used as warm-ups for each session in this subject area, or participants can read the affirmations daily during the week. These affirmations are found in *Taking Care Participant Guidebook*.

- The best thing I can do for another person is to be honest with that person and give that person an opportunity to take care of himself.
- I help a person more by allowing that person take responsibility than by taking care of her responsibilities for her.
- I am an important person.
- My needs are as important as other people's needs.
- I am young and need to spend these years helping myself grow and develop.
- I am young and want to play and enjoy my life.
- I am not going to let my younger years slip by without enjoyment.
- I can attain the serenity to accept the things I cannot change, the courage to change the things I can, and the wisdom to know the difference. (This "Serenity Affirmation" is an adaptation of the "Serenity Prayer." Rephrasing it as an affirmation helps avoid conflicts with laws on prayer in the schools.)

Overview

- Film: "Open Secrets"
- Exercise: Enabling is Hard Work
- Introductory Comments to Participants
- Exercise: Enabling — The Helping that Hurts
- Exercise: Case Examples of Enabling

Film

"Open Secrets," described in Appendix B, on page 196, offers some examples of enabling. Facilitators can point out examples of enabling in the film to help participants grasp the meaning of the word and the many ways in which enabling is manifested.

Exercise:
Enabling is Hard Work

The facilitators or participants can pick the largest person in the class and tell him that he is to lie on the floor and stay completely, absolutely limp. The job of the class is to help him stand on his feet, make him look straight ahead and, using their own hands, keep a big smile on his face. All members of the class are to participate in this task. Once they get the person standing on his feet, they are to hold him in that position for one minute, smile and all. Then the facilitator will tell two of the people holding him that they must do some other task, such as put all of the chairs into one straight line. If it is difficult for the remaining people to hold the limp person up, those working on the additional task must complete it as quickly as possible and get back to helping the group.

This exercise should not take more than two or three minutes.

Note: In some schools, there may be norms or regulations against learning activities that involve touch. Facilitators must determine whether the social climate in the school and community is such that most adults would find this type of exercise acceptable. If not, facilitators must either drop or alter the exercise appropriately.

As an alternative to physically holding the person up, participants could spend five minutes trying as hard as they can to make the person happy. The class members could tell the person jokes, get the person a glass of water, fan him to keep him cool, and do anything else the person wants that is possible and acceptable.

Discussion
The facilitator can then ask:

- "How hard was it to do that?"
- "How did you feel when you had to go and do other tasks and then rush back to help hold the person up?"
- "How much time do you think we spent doing this?"
- "How would you like to do it for a whole day?"
- "How would you like to do it for a whole week?"
- "For a whole year?"
- "For twenty years?"

"Enabling a person in his daily life is very much like constantly trying to pick him up, hold him straight, and keep a smile on his face. This gives you some idea of the energy that enabling takes away from people."

Introductory Comments to Participants

Facilitators can present the following background information to participants:

"Enabling refers to all the words and actions people employ to help alcoholics and other people with problem behaviors avoid the consequences of their actions. While enabling is usually considered an unnecessary activity that serves only to keep people stuck in negative behavioral patterns, we're not going to tell you, as you might hear from other people, that enabling is always wrong. As with denial, enabling is almost inevitable. Furthermore, if what a family needs is a temporary reduction in stress and tension, enabling may be necessary.

"People can enable in a wide variety of situations. Teachers can enable students if they feel sorry for them. They might excuse a student from handing in homework because they know the student has trouble at home. Spouses and children of alcoholics enable, or at least have many opportunities to observe enabling in practice. Here are just a few:

- "Protecting the alcoholic from himself by looking for his hidden bottles and emptying them out.

- "Telling lies to employers, relatives, or even other family members to prevent them from knowing that the alcoholic has been drinking or what he has done while he was drinking.

- "Consistently cleaning up the messes the alcoholic has made around the house—making sure that the empty beer cans are out of sight, the vomit on the floor is washed away immediately, his clothes are picked up, etc.

- "Smoothing over problems with people whom the alcoholic has hurt or offended.

- "Always helping him when he is drunk—getting him undressed, getting him to bed, bringing him coffee in the morning.

- "Taking over all the family responsibilities the alcoholic has let slide—making sure the younger children are fed and helped off to school in the morning; doing their chores, etc.

- "Using any of the denial techniques that have already been described. Denial is an enabling behavior.

- "Doing the chores that the alcoholic should do.

- "Paying liquor bills for him.

- "Encouraging him to drink at home so he won't get into trouble.

- "Cleaning up the bed when he vomits on it and then complaining about it.

- "Paying for his liquor and then pouring it down the sink.

- "Telling him not to feel sorry for himself, then consoling him when he's feeling sorry for himself.

- "Trying to tie up his free times so he won't have time to drink.

"Sometimes kids enable both their parents — whether or not alcohol is involved — to keep the parents from fighting. Kids can be especially sensitive to this if their parents have already separated and are trying a reconciliation. In these cases, children enable by:

- "Always being 'perfect children' so that the parents cannot argue about them.

- "Cleaning the house so that neither parent can complain to the other about a messy house."

Exercise:
Enabling—The Helping That Hurts

In the *Taking Care Participant Guidebook* is the "Enabling: The Helping That Hurts" exercise. Participants are to review the checklist of enabling behaviors and check off every enabling behavior they have observed (the "O" column) or actually participated in (the "M" for "me" column).

Discussion

In small groups or as a class, participants can discuss when they have observed such behaviors or done these behaviors themselves. The facilitators can then ask:

- "How many items did you check in the 'O' column?"

- "How many in the 'M' column?"

- "Which item in the 'M' column caused the most serious problem for you?"

- "Which item in the 'O' column bothers you the most?"

- "What do people — yourself or someone else — get out of each of these enabling behaviors?"

- "What do people lose when they enable? What are the consequences of enabling?"

- "One of the most important ways that people enable is to support the another person's defense system. Think of all the ways you have observed someone defending another person whose behavior was causing problems."

Exercise:
Case Examples of Enabling

A facilitator can read or ask a participant to read each of the following examples. After each example are discussion questions the facilitators can ask of the participants.

Betty is a grade A student and a cheerleader. Her mother, who is a single mom, works as a nurse at night. When she comes home at 8 a.m., she likes to have several drinks to "unwind" and shed the tension caused by her job. When Betty gets home from school, she usually makes coffee for her mom and the evening meal for the kids. She has accepted this because of how hard her mother works and the unusual hours she works. It creates a great deal of stress for Betty, however, whenever she wants to go to a special event or to a ballgame. She must run home, help her mother out, then get back to the event. This Friday, the basketball team and cheerleading squad must leave at 3:00 p.m. to go to a game in another town. Betty calls her mom to tell her she is not going to come home but nobody answers the phone. She decides to go to the ballgame anyway.

- "What do think of Betty's decision? What do you think will go through Betty's mind?"

- "What do you think her mother will do?"

- "Do you think it would have been any better for Betty to talk this over with her mother the night before?"

- "Are there other ways she could have gotten what she wanted?"

- "Do you think she is irresponsible for not making supper for her younger brother and sister?"

Tom is an only child living with his divorced mother. She takes care of her job and her home duties, but she is very emotionally dependent on Tom. Although she does not drink every day, whenever she does drink she gets very drunk. At those times, she demands that Tom stay with her to keep her company because she feels so lonely.

She says that after all she has done for him and all the hours she's worked to buy him clothes and pay for the special classes he wants to take, he owes this to her. Even though his mother is single, she has done very well in her career and has been able to give Tom whatever he wants. This night, Tom wants to go out with his girlfriend and his mother wants him to stay home. She does not like this girlfriend or any of his previous girlfriends. After his mother tries to guilt him, she threatens him. She says that if he does not stay with her, she is not going to give him anymore money for clothes, lessons, or recreation.

- "What do you think Tom should do?"
- "How do you think he should do it?"
- "What do you think his mother will do that night? Later?"

Jim is a senior in high school and the oldest of three children. His father and mother have just separated and he lives with his mother and the other two children. Tonight, Jim is babysitting the other two kids when his father calls. His father wants Jim to talk to his mother for him, explain that he is sorry for getting mad and hitting her last week. He wants Jim to talk his mother into taking him back.

- "What do you think Jim should do?"
- "How do you think he should do it?"

Eleven-year-old Ann lives at home with her father and mother. Her mother usually works the late-night shift on the weekends, and Ann does all the laundry and cleans the house. Her father is very strict. A couple of weeks ago Ann would not do her chores because she wanted to play. Her father grabbed her by the hair and slapped her hard across the face. Today, the local recreation center has a trip planned to an amusement park. Ann wants very much to go. Her father says that she has to wake her mother up to do the chores, or Ann has to do them herself.

- "What do you think Ann should do now?"
- "What do you think Ann should do in the long run?"

Feelings

Where They Come From, Where They Take Us

Whether they are drug users, children of alcoholics, or pretty "normal," young people seldom have a chance to explore their feelings with others. For children from alcoholic and other disrupted family environments, the discussion of feelings can be particularly meaningful because:

- Dysfunctional family environments tend to produce long-term feeling states of anger and depression.
- The feelings of an alcoholic or otherwise unstable parent will swing wildly and cause tremendous confusion.
- The children may be living in family situations where it is not considered appropriate to discuss feelings.

Goals for Sessions on Feelings

Goals for sessions in this subject area include:

- To deepen participants' understanding of the Mood-Swing Graph and the roles that feelings play in the progression of chemical dependency.
- To introduce the language of feelings so that participants can use it in the class as well as in their daily lives.
- To teach participants to recognize and label their feelings.
- To help them assess how sad or happy they are.
- To teach them that anger almost always covers up other feelings.
- To help them realize that their feelings are tightly connected to the feelings expressed by their parents.

For all discussions about feelings, facilitators should remind participants of the "Feeling List" in the *Taking Care Participant Guidebook*.

Affirmations About Feelings

These affirmations can be used as warm-ups for each session in this subject area or participants can read the affirmations daily during the week. These affirmations are found in the *Taking Care Participant Guidebook*.

- I can feel happy right now.
- Sad feelings pass.
- My life is improving.
- I will feel better and better as the class goes on.
- I do not have to feel bad because someone else feels bad.
- All of my feelings are OK for me. I should not be ashamed of any of my feelings.
- It is good to talk to other people about feelings.
- I look forward to sharing my feelings with other people and having them share their feelings with me.
- I will grow closer to other people by sharing my feelings.
- Other people will like me more when they know how I feel.
- A strong person and a good person can feel sad.
- I like myself when I cry.
- Crying is good for me.
- I am going to do healthy things to make myself feel happy.

Overview

- Film: "Friends for Life"
- The Use of Expressive Techniques Will Help Reveal Emotions
- Exercise: The Feeling Cube

- Exercise: Feeling-level Reactions to Family Stories
- Exercise: Fill in Your Feelings
- Exercise: Happy, So-So or Sad
- Shame: The Feeling That Takes You Nowhere
- Exercise: Memories of Shame
- Exercise: The Worst of Times
- Mind Messers and Day Makers: How We Think Can Affect the Way We Feel

Film

"Friends for Life," described on page 197 in Appendix B, emphasizes the necessity for young people to help friends who are depressed or suicidal.

The Use of Expressive Techniques Will Help Reveal Emotions

Drawing, making collages, and a variety of other art projects can be extremely helpful for participants who are learning about feelings. A simple suggestion such as, "Everyone draw how they are feeling right now," can help participants get in touch with their feelings and help them release those feelings.

These expressive techniques can be used with any group of participants, from junior through senior high school. In general, the younger children can be given more elaborate tasks and more tools to work with. If they draw a "family diagram" (see page 95), they can use bright colors to define relationships or even different colors of glitter. Facilitators can provide some for the use of color: red means anger, blue means sadness, black means very sad, green means peaceful, and pink, orange, or yellow mean happy.

The senior high school students will be less likely to get involved in that type of art project, but they will readily draw pictures, caricatures, or abstract creations.

Exercise: The Feeling Cube

On a chalkboard or a sheet of paper, facilitators list and number six basic feeling areas: 1. glad; 2. afraid; 3. confident; 4. sad; 5. mad; 6. ashamed. Each participant then rolls a die and gives an example of the feeling corresponding to the number cast. For example, the participants who get the number "1" will talk about a time in their lives when they felt glad; those who get a "4" will talk about a time when they felt sad. Participants can refer to the "Feeling List" to get some ideas

about other words related to the six basic words on the board.

Exercise: Feeling-level Reactions to Family Stories

Facilitators can introduce this exercise by telling participants:

"Feelings have much to do with how we live our lives. People who are very sad will seek ways to feel better about themselves or better about their lives. They may do this in a healthy way, such as you are doing in this class, or in less healthy ways, such as using drugs, depending on a relationship with another person to make them feel better, or constantly shopping.

"In families where the parents are having problems, feelings can be a very touchy issue. Let me read you some typical things that happen in many homes. As you listen to these stories, write down the feelings you hear mentioned, the feelings you presume a person would have in that situation, and your own feelings when listening to the story. [The facilitators can write these categories on a chalkboard or flipchart.]

"At night Tom lay up in his bedroom trying to sleep. He finds it difficult, however, because his parents are shouting and screaming at each other. He hears his father call his mother a stupid, worthless *#!!, then he hears his mother slap his father. She starts sobbing and his father stomps out of the house. The next morning, when Tom comes downstairs, his mother is smiling at him and asks him if he slept well. When his father comes down, she smiles and asks him what he would like for breakfast.

"Eight-year-old Jennie's family is having financial problems. Her father works as a machinist and can make a lot of money, since there is plenty of work in the community. However, for the last several months he has not been going to work regularly and has just been fired from his job. Although he occasionally goes out to look for work, he mostly sits around the house, drinks, and complains about his life. Whenever Jennie's mother talks to Jennie's grandparents or other relatives, she smiles broadly and talks about how great things are going at home. She talks about her husband wanting to make some changes in his life by exploring exciting new ideas. She never acts as though she feels sad."

Discussion

After reading each story, facilitators should give participants time to write down their responses. Then they can ask participants if any of them would like to read some of the things they wrote. If necessary, facilitators can call on certain participants. The facilitators can also assist the participant through the process of "tracking a feeling."

Tracking a Feeling

When participants appear to react to a particular story but also have difficulty saying what their feelings are, facilitators can try these questions to help clarify the nature and intensity of the feeling:

• "Where in your body do you feel the most?"

• "Is it hot or cold, sharp or dull?"

• "When did you start to feel it? What words or phrases were being said?"

• "Which word comes closest to your feeling: glad, sad, afraid, confident, ashamed?"

The facilitators can teach this approach to participants so they can use it in and outside of the LifeGuides class.

Exercise:
Fill in Your Feelings

Participants can refer to the "Fill in Your Feelings" sentence completion exercise in their participant guidebook. They can take several minutes to complete the sentences in that form.

Discussion

After participants have completed the form, the class can discuss responses one item at a time. The facilitators should be sure not to demand more self-revelation than participants are comfortable giving. Instead of asking each person to say how they responded to the items, the facilitator might ask:

• "Does anyone want to say what they wrote down for the first sentence?"

• "Did anyone else put something like that down?"

This exercise will reveal not only much about participants' feelings but information about their relationships as well. (If participants are honest.) For instance, a participant might say, "The one thing that made me happiest last week was when my boyfriend told me he loved me"; or, "I feel good whenever I'm with my boyfriend." Such responses indicate that the participant might be very dependent, if not co-dependent, on her boyfriend.

Exercise:
Happy, So-So, or Sad

"Happy, So-So or Sad" in the *Taking Care Participant Guidebook* can be given during the LifeGuides Interview or during sessions on feelings. This exercise focuses on how participants are feeling about their lives. Participants who indicate that they feel "terrible" or "unhappy" about major areas of their lives merit close watching. Facilitators who are concerned about serious depression in a participant should see the person individually or have the person be seen by an experienced counselor. For more information about screening for depression and suicidal tendencies in adolescents, see Community Intervention's publication *Adolescent Suicide: Identification and Intervention.*

Discussion

If the facilitators think it would be helpful, the following general process questions concerning the "Happy, So-So, or Sad" exercise can be asked during sessions on feelings:

• "How did you feel when you were reading those questions?"

• "How do you feel now when you look them over?"

• "Some of those things are negative. Do you find yourself saying those things to yourself again and again?"

• "Do you think that the feelings you had when you answered the questions or are having now have anything to do with someone else's behavior?"

Shame: The Feeling that Takes You Nowhere

The concept of shame is central to the feeling lives of children from alcoholic and other disrupted family environments. One author (Kaufman, 1980) defines shame as "the piercing awareness of ourselves as fundamentally deficient in some vitally important way as a human being. To live with shame is to experience the very essence or heart of the self wanting."

When people are feeling good about themselves and they make a mistake, they are likely to say to themselves: "Yep, I messed up. I think I see why I did that, but I know I can do it better next time." When a person is not feeling too good about himself, he is likely to take it more to heart and criticize himself as a person: "How stupid could I be? I'm just no good. I'm hopeless. I'm going to quit."

Although it is hard to describe the essence of shame, that second response comes close to it. Shame can be overwhelming and intense, or it can be extremely uncomfortable though not quite so all-consuming. People are more likely to feel shame as a result of a particular event if:

• The event takes place in public.

• It involves a person they love, trust, or depend on.

• It involves rejection of themselves.

Broken promises can be very shaming. For example:

Allen was told by his father that he would come and watch him play basketball on Friday. His father has never seen him play and Allen told his friends he was very excited. But Allen's father didn't show up. After the game, he found out that his father stayed late at work and never bothered to call home. The next day, when his friends asked him why his father didn't come to the game, Allen became angry and told them to shut their mouths.

There are some special elements in this simple story that lead to shame. First of all, a parent was involved. Allen had a great need to be admired by his father. He also was vulnerable because he allowed himself to become excited and happy about the possibility of his father watching him play. Furthermore, he let other people know that he was excited and looking forward to having his father attend the game. Therefore, when his father did not show up, he was publicly embarrassed.

Allen's reaction to his feelings of shame was anger. This is very typical. People who are feeling shame almost never admit to it. Instead, they use some other defense, quite often anger.

People have many different and long-lasting reactions to shame. People who are shame-based tend to do things that make them feel good in the short run, but make them feel ashamed in the long run: they overeat, become bulimic, abuse drugs, or shoplift, for instance. These behaviors can feel good when people do them, but they are basically self-destructive. In some ways, this kind of reaction is like a self-fulfilling prophesy. If a person thinks he is unworthy, he is more likely do things that make him feel unworthy.

Shame is Different From Guilt

Guilt is a feeling people have when they think they have *done* something wrong. For instance, a person forgets to meet a friend he had agreed to meet, or he hurts somebody's feelings just because he was in a bad mood. The person may feel guilty for what he has done, but if he has a pretty good self-concept, he does not feel like a totally bad or unworthy person because of that one action.

Shame, on the other hand, arises out of things that are done *to* people. People who are victimized by physical or emotional abuse when they are young tend to feel a great deal of shame. They feel they are unworthy people, and this then generalizes to everything they do. Every mistake they make makes them feel not guilt, but complete shame. Shame is the victim's feeling. It comes because bad things happened to the person even though he didn't do anything wrong. Eventually, when enough bad things happen to someone, the person starts to feel as if he deserves it.

Often, people feel more ashamed about what other people do than about what they do themselves. For instance, a boy might get into trouble for breaking a neighbor's window and feel guilty about it. On the other hand, the boy might get yelled at by his neighbor for something his brothers, sisters, or parents did and feel very ashamed. If someone tells a child, "Your father's just a no-good, lazy bum," the child's likely to feel more shame than if the child was accused of something.

Exercise:
Memories of Shame

Facilitators can ask participants to think of a time when they have felt shame, and then ask:

• "Who was involved?"

• "What was your main reaction to the shame?"

• "How often did events like this happen to you?"

"The more that shaming events are repeated in our lives, the more they become deeply ingrained. When they are deeply ingrained, we tend to feel shame not only with those people with whom we originally felt shame, but with many other people as well. The shame becomes generalized. It becomes part of how we look at ourselves. We not only see ourselves as worthless, we feel we are often seen that way by others as well."

Exercise:
The Worst of Times

In the exercise "The Worst of Times", participants are very likely to recall some immediate, family-related incident. Participants are not expected to share the details of any incident they envision during the exercise, but only to describe and discuss the related feelings.

Facilitators can ask the participants to sit quietly and close their eyes, and then tell them:

• "Keep your eyes closed and concentrate on your breathing. Take a deep breath, hold it for a second, then let it out. Try to put all other thoughts out of your mind and just focus on what it feels like to take the air into your lungs and let go of it."

Facilitators should pause for a few seconds, allowing participants to inhale and exhale several times. Then continue:

- "I want you to turn your attention to a period in your life when you were going through a very rough emotional time, a time when you felt emotionally terrible. We are not going to ask you to tell us any of the details of this time, so don't worry about that. Just think of a hard time you had."

Facilitators should pause for a few seconds, then say more quietly:

- "What was going on with you at that time?"
- "Who were the important people involved?"
- "What did they look like, what were they saying or not saying? Think about this for a few minutes."

Pause again.

- "What feelings did you have at that time?"
- "What sorts of feelings do you have now when you think about it?
- "Do you feel anything in your body, in your stomach, in your head, in your muscles, in your neck, or in your jaw? Focus on what that feels like.
- "Did you spend most of your time by yourself or with other people?
- "What sorts of things did you stop doing?
- "What sorts of things did you start doing? Did you think about running away, quitting school, or any other way to escape? Did you talk to people about the problem?
- "Did you want to keep this problem a secret from others or did you ask for help?
- "What sort of person would you have liked to talk to about it?
- "Did you use more alcohol or other drugs at that time?"

Pause.

- "In a minute I am going to ask you to open your eyes again. At that time, we're not going to talk about what actually happened to you to make you feel bad. We're just going to talk about the feelings you have right now and the feelings you had at that time."

When the participants have opened their eyes, facilitators can ask each person to respond to the questions asked during the exercise. Facilitators can use a number of follow-up questions and might also ask participants to look at the "Feeling List" and tell the class which of those feelings they had.

It is very important to emphasize the need for sharing feelings with others. Facilitators might say:

- "For those of you who talked to someone about the problem at that time, how did talking help?"
- "What sort of people did you want to talk to?"
- "What were the characteristics that you looked for?" (Facilitators can look for answers that include trusting or understanding someone who had gone through the same problem.)
- "Do you think some people in this class have some of these characteristics?" (Participants do not have to answer this out loud.)

Mind Messers and Day Makers: How We Think Can Affect the Way We Feel

Facilitators can say:

"In many ways, how we think about things can affect how we feel. In your *Taking Care Participant Guidebook* is a list of "Three Major Mind Messers," thoughts which, if you believe them, are bound to make you feel sad, mad or bad." The list includes:

- Everyone must love me or at least like me. If they don't, I will feel awful.
- I cannot make mistakes. Mistakes are terrible.
- People and events must turn out the way I want them to. If they aren't or they don't, it is awful.

"Now, most of us do not say these thoughts as directly as these mind messers, but in many ways, we believe them. For instance, a girl might go to a party with a new and colorful dress. Eight people walk up to her and say they love it, that it is very daring, but tasteful as well. When one person comes up and says, 'You look ridiculous in that dress,' the girl feels terrible and leaves the party."

Discussion

The faciltators can ask:

- "Has anyone ever been in that position?"
- "Can you give examples of other ways we feel we must be loved, liked, or accepted by everybody?"

"On the same page of the participant guidebook are some ideas to help you rethink the negative ways of talking to yourselves:

- "Being loved and accepted by everyone is nice, but I can live without it. I am still a human being and worthy of respect even if there are some people who don't love and accept me.

- "It's OK to make mistakes. It is fun to do things without making mistakes and very satisfying, but you can't be perfect all the time. No one can.
- "People are going to do what they want to and events are going to turn out a certain way, whether I want them to or not. I can affect some events and some people, but I will never be in complete control."

Anger and Conflicting Feelings

It can be very confusing to live in a home disrupted by alcoholism and other family problems. The children wonder, "How could someone who loves me get so angry at me for no apparent reason."

In families affected by alcoholism, the disease itself can explain these wild mood swings. When people lose control of their drinking, the alcohol controls their moods. The more they drink, they more they hate themselves for doing it. They may have already promised themselves they wouldn't get drunk again and so get angry as soon as they start drinking. Unfortunately, those around the drinkers are the ones who usually get blamed for the problems.

The moods of the people around them mirror those of alcoholics. They find themselves furious one minute, then confused and guilty the next day when the person they were angry at is behaving appropriately again.

Parent conflicts can cause confusion for the children. Parents who are angry or upset due to problems with their spouses can easily turn their anger on their children, who often do not know why they are the targets of anger. The children will be angry, frightened, and confused by the sudden changes in moods by adults in their homes and will have many conflicting feelings toward those adults.

The boys in LifeGuides classes tend to have a great deal of anger in regard to their fathers. Sometimes they take it out by becoming bullies or by being aggressive with their girlfriends and the staff at school.

Goals for Sessions on Anger

Goals for sessions in this subject area include.

- To help participants understand that conflicting feelings are normal and acceptable.
- To help them identify their conflicting feelings.

- To help them take actions to improve their general feeling states.

Affirmations on Accepting All My Feelings

These affirmations can be used as warm-ups for each session in this subject area or participants can read the affirmations daily during the week. These affirmations are found in the *Taking Care Participant Guidebook*.

- I am a good person.
- I am a good person and sometimes I get angry.
- I am a good person and sometimes I get angry at people I love.
- I am a good person and sometimes I get very angry at people who love me.
- It is natural to feel angry.
- I can express my anger without hurting other people.
- I will express my feelings this week without hurting other people.

Overview

- Helping Participants Recognize, Accept, and Deal with Their Anger
- Exercise: Observing Anger
- Exercise: Accepting Contradictory Feelings
- Exercise: Anger with a Smile
- Anger: How Are We Like Our Parents?

Helping Participants Recognize, Accept, and Deal with Their Anger

Whenever participants express feelings of anger, facilitators should acknowledge them and declare that anger is an acceptable emotion. This will be a new experience for many participants who have been told either that they aren't angry even when they say they are or that their anger is unjustified.

If the anger is expressed in class in any destructive way, such as throwing things, making threats, or using abusive language, the participant must be told that such behavior is unacceptable. The behavior, however, must be separated from the feeling: the *feeling* is acceptable, the *behavior* is not. To process the anger further, facilitators can ask:

- "What would you like to do about your anger?" (Usually this will elicit a number of different suggested alternatives, including violent actions. The participant might say something like, "I'd like to kill my dad!" The facilitator could reply, "No you can't kill him. But what are some other options?" In that way, facilitators will elicit a variety of options for dealing with the situation or for dealing with the angry feelings.)

- "How can you get this out of your body? How can you do something to let off steam so you don't go and get into trouble at home or in school or with your girlfriend or boyfriend?" (If there are two facilitators, one of them could take the angry person outside to work anger off in some physical way.)

- "Sometimes anger can be used for constructive ends: Go out and mow the lawn, clean your room, paint something, or fix something."

- "If you're angry, that usually means you're hurt. How has that person hurt you?"

- "What are you getting out of being angry."(The facilitator can note here that some young men want to hang on to their rage because it makes them feel powerful and intimidating. They often do not want to let go of that power.)

If necessary, facilitators can suggest that a participant go out and run or try some other exercise until he feels some of the angry energy dissipate. In counseling sessions, it is normal to ask group members to yell, scream, or beat pillows when they feel extremely angry. However, in a school setting, such behavior may be disruptive to other students unless the room is sufficiently isolated from other classrooms.

Many counselors use the "empty chair" technique with rageful people. They have the young person sit opposite an empty chair and ask, "What would you say to your father if he couldn't say anything back and if, when you snapped your fingers, he couldn't remember anything?" This technique could be used safely in a school situation. Before doing this, however, the counselor should be confident that the person participating in the exercise is a relatively healthy person with no serious underlying pathology. Otherwise, the person may get in touch with rage that she does not feel in control of. Facilitators should feel comfortable with the process, having used it or experienced it during training in support group facilitation. Also, it should be used only with classes that have developed trust and concern for each other.

Exercise:
Observing Anger

The facilitators can ask:

- "When was the last time you saw somebody angry? Without naming the person, briefly describe what happened."

- "What are some different ways that a child's drinking makes his or her parents angry? What different ways does drinking arouse anger in the home?"

Facilitators can ask the participants to think about how they use anger.

- "What makes you angry?"

- "Do you ever get so angry that you don't know what to do with that anger?"

- "How does that anger come out?"

- "How do you usually look at the situation that came up?"

- "How else can you react?"

- "How is your anger self-destructive?" (Facilitators can probe for such behavior as being in trouble with authorities, physical problems, lack of sleep, and so forth.)

- "How do you get that anger out without hurting yourself or someone else?"

Exercise:
Accepting Contradictory Feelings

No matter how much anger there is in children's relationships with their parents, almost all children will have conflicting feelings toward their parents. Let's look at Ann's situation.

Ann loves her father very much. He is a fun person to be with and extremely intelligent. He enjoys his daughter and likes to challenge her intellectually. Sometimes they will sit down and play Scrabble together. This makes Ann feel very good. After three or four drinks, however, her father's personality changes. He starts calling her "stupid" and "dumb" because of the words she makes up. If he continues to drink, he will usually finish the game by telling her how worthless she is.

Now, even though Ann loves her father, by the time she is done playing Scrabble, she may be extremely angry at him and even hate him.

When there is serious trouble at home, the children will have a wide range of feelings toward their parents. In the *Taking Care Participant Guidebook* is a list called "Real Life, Real Feelings." The list was made by a group of children troubled by parental alcoholism and other family problems. They were asked to list the words that came to mind when they thought about their relationships with their parents. Participants should look at the list now.

Discussion

The facilitators can ask:

- "Before you check off any feelings or attitudes, what do you notice when you look over this list?" (Facilitators should note, if participants do not comment, that there is a wide range of feelings and that some of the feelings seem contradictory.)

- "Think of one person in your life about whom you have had very intense feelings. This should be a person who is important to you. Now check all the feelings you have had toward that person."

- "Which of these feelings or attitudes do you consider positive? Negative?"

- "Did anyone check only items they consider positive? Negative?"

Exercise:
Anger with a Smile

Many people do not express anger directly. Rather, they will be indirect about it:

Mary's mother is always after her to be better: "If you'd only comb your hair you would look nicer. If you would only study harder you would learn more. Nice girls don't chew gum." Whenever her mother tells her these things, Mary feels like shouting at her. Instead of that, Mary simply does the opposite of what her mother wants her to do. When her mother asks her to clean her room, she will say, "Yes, Mom, right away." However, she never does it and she never changes.

Discussion

The facilitators can ask:

- "Has anyone ever seen this method of expressing anger? In whom?"

- "Have you ever used this?"

This is called passive-aggressive behavior. It is passive in its outward appearance but aggressive in intent. It is a very common way of expressing anger. It is also a way people transfer anger, to try to get another person to feel their anger.

Anger: How are We Like Our Parents?

Facilitators can explain to participants that most people express anger in ways they have seen it expressed at home, and then ask:

- "How do your parents express anger?"

- "How similar are you?"

- "How would you like to be different from your parents in this regard?"

- "How would you like to be like them?"

Self-esteem

Liking Ourselves

Improving the self-esteem of participants is a major goal for the entire LifeGuides Program curriculum. The information and exercises in this section offer participants an opportunity to examine closely how they feel about themselves and where those feelings come from.

Goals for Sessions on Self-esteem

Goals for sessions in this subject area include:
- To help participants get in touch with how they feel about themselves so they can gauge improvement.
- To help participants see how what they get or don't get from their families affects their self-esteem.
- To help them see how perfectionism can contribute to low self-esteem.

Affirmations on Self-esteem

These affirmations can be used as warm-ups for each session in this subject area or participants can read the affirmations daily during the week.
- I will be in control of my emotions. My emotions will not be in control of me.
- I can handle disappointments.
- I can admit to, accept, and correct my mistakes.
- I can find humor in my mistakes.
- I am a capable, competent person. I do not have be perfect in order to be competent.
- I do not have to be all-powerful to be self-sufficient.
- I accept my shortcomings as part of who I am. I am willing to try to change the things I believe most need changing.
- I am a lovable person.
- I am not lonely when I am alone.
- I do not blame other people for my problems.

- I am a strong person.
- I can cope with the troubles in my life.
- I am learning and changing.
- I am a wonderful person.
- I am learning more and more each day.
- I am learning to be assertive.
- I do not give in to other people when I don't want to.
- I can be happy even when I am alone.
- I am not afraid of today.
- I am not afraid of tomorrow.
- I take responsibility for my life.

Overview

- Exercise: Extra Work on Affirmations
- Tasks and Challenges Improve Participants' Self-esteem
- Exercises: Short and Simple Positive Feedback Games
- Exercise: How I See Myself
- Exercise: The Guilt Disposal
- Perfectionism Contributes to Feelings of Guilt and Low Self-esteem
- Exercise: Family Building Blocks — Foundations of Self-esteem

Exercise:
Extra Work on Affirmations

The affirmations take on particular significance when the focus is on self-esteem. The affirmations listed above are also listed in the *Taking Care Participant Guidebook* along with several other general affirmations. The list can be used in a variety of ways. Participants can be asked to pick at least one from the list at the beginning of a class and say it out loud. After each member of the class has spoken an affirmation, there can be another go 'round in which each participant has to speak two affirmations.

Another way facilitators can use the "General Affirmations" exercise is to go around the class and have each person pick three or four affirmations and say them to the person next to him or her. Again, the number of affirmations can increase with each class session.

The facilitators can also ask participants to give an example of how they can actually live out an affirmation in their daily lives in the coming week.

Children from alcoholic and other disrupted family environments find it very difficult to say positive things about themselves. Facilitators can ask participants to speak *specific* affirmations chosen by the facilitators. The participant may find it very difficult, but the facilitator could ask that person to repeat it several times. The other members of the class can also repeat the affirmation to the person.

Participants can read the affirmations every day. They also can be asked to write down how they behaved or felt in regard to each affirmation during the week.

Tasks and Challenges Improve Participants' Self-esteem

Giving participants tasks to complete or challenges to face can be very positive for their self-esteem. When participants do something positive for themselves or for the rest of the class, they feel better about themselves. This gives other people an opportunity to praise them. Facilitators will want to think of tasks appropriate for the age and abilities of the participants. Certain participants can be chosen to:

* Line up the chairs in the classroom in a manner appropriate for that session (usually a circle).

* Rearrange the room when the class is done. (This is probably less reinforcing than preparing for the class since other participants will not see the results.)

* Choose an opening exercise for the next class (perhaps the topic can be assigned).

* Prepare a skit for the class on a particular subject.

* Bring a treat to the next class.

* Set up the film projector and show the film.

* Come up with some ideas for a class field trip.

All participant accomplishments give the facilitator and the rest of the class a chance to say, "Great job! You really helped me a lot. Thanks."

Exercises:
Short and Simple Positive Feedback Games

Beginning or ending LifeGuides sessions with a positive feedback game will not only make participants feel better about themselves, but improve the group process as well. Here are some approaches:

* **Go-round focused on one person.** "Let's go around the class and give George an idea of what we like best about having him as a class member."

* **Writing positive statements.** Participants can have sheets of paper taped to their backs, to a chalkboard, or on their desks. People then go to each sheet of paper and write some positive quality they see in that person. The material on the sheets can be used in a variety of ways:

  – Participants can read their lists to themselves.

  – Participants can read the lists out loud to the others.

  – In pairs, each participant can read the other's list directly to that person.

  – In triads, the first participant can read the listing describing the second participant to the third person, while the second person simply listens.

  – To gain assertiveness, participants can read out loud, with as much conviction as possible, the traits on the lists they believe are most true of them. Each participant will have to choose at least four.

* **The ball-of-yarn exercise.** This exercise is most often used for group closure rather than an opener, but it works as both. Facilitators can give a ball of yarn to a participant and tell him or her to hold the end of the yarn and then pass or toss the ball of yarn to another person in the group. As the person passes the ball, he or she says something positive to the person receiving the ball. Each person in succession will do the same thing. By the end of the exercise, there will be interconnecting lines among the class members.

Each of these methods of hearing positive feedback will affect people differently. The positive-trait lists can be recorded by participants in their guidebooks.

Exercise:
How I See Myself

The questions in "How I See Myself," in the *Taking Care Participant Guidebook,* relate to self-concept. They are not questions that should be processed in the class unless it has developed into a close, trusting group.

Facilitators can ask participants to answer these questions during the week. Participants can then turn their guidebooks in to facilitators as they get to class. Facilitators can either take a few minutes to review the responses and then begin class, or one facilitator can review the responses while the other facilitator guides the class through one of the "Short and Simple Positive Feedback Games."

Although individual responses will not usually be discussed in the class, these questions help screen participants for low self-concept. Anyone with extremely low self-concept — as indicated by these items and other sources of information — should be seen individually by a facilitator to let the participant know that someone cares and is willing to listen if the person feels depressed. Referral to a professional counselor in or outside the school or agency may also be necessary.

If the facilitators think it would be helpful, the following general process questions concerning this exercise can be asked:

- "How did you feel when you were reading those questions?"
- "How do you feel now when you look them over?"
- "Some of the statements are negative. Do you find yourself saying those things to yourself again and again?"
- "Do you think that the feelings you had when you answered the questions or those you are having now have anything to do with your use or someone else's use of chemicals?"

Exercise:
The Guilt Disposal

Facilitators can have participants write down, anonymously, things that make them feel guilty. A facilitator can then pass around a bag. Participants read their lists to themselves quietly, then tear them up into small pieces and throw them into the bag. The facilitator then disposes of the bag after the class.

Perfectionism Contributes to Feelings of Guilt and Low Self-esteem

Facilitators can explain the downfalls of perfectionism by saying, "Some people believe that the way to develop a healthy self-concept is to be perfect. They strive to be perfect in sports, in class, or with their families. However, the trouble with this perfectionism is that it is impossible. Therefore, people who attempt to be perfect

usually end up feeling guilty about their imperfections and bad about themselves.

"What we need is what someone has called 'The courage to be imperfect'; a willingness to accept our faults, imperfections, and shortcomings as part of our human nature. This does not mean that we will not try to improve ourselves. It does mean that we don't have to be perfect in order to like ourselves or to be worthy of love."

Exercise:
Family Building Blocks: Foundations of Self-esteem

Families build our children's self-esteem in many ways. They:

- **Provide love**: "If someone loves me I must be worth loving."
- **Provide guidance:** "If I learn to be competent, I will feel competent."
- **Provide boundaries and rules**: "If I have clear, consistent, honest rules, I know where I stand; I know if I'm acting correctly."
- **Provide support:** "When other things in my life are going poorly, the family supports me and I feel better about myself."
- **Provide a value system to believe in:** "Having a value system makes me feel more secure in my day-to-day life; every little thing doesn't bother me if my behavior is consistent with what I believe to be right."

"Family Building Blocks: Foundations of Self-esteem" is found in the *Taking Care Participant Guidebook*. After looking these statements over, participants should indicate how each statement applies to their family by marking (A) applies completely, (D) does not apply at all, or something in-between. Note: The "A" and "D" are used in the participant guidebooks to protect confidentiality. The meaning of the codes will not be immediately apparent to anyone outside the class who happens to see a participant's guidebook.

Discussion
This exercise can help participants begin the process of acceptance and detachment. The participants can see what they are getting from their families and what they are not getting. They can start to consider how they can get what they need elsewhere.

Participants should not be pressured into revealing specific information about their responses. If they prefer, they can just review the "Family Building Blocks" exercise without writing their responses in their guidebook.

Coping with Daily Challenges

Exercises in this section help participants take a close look at the specific stresses they are facing and at the responsibilities they are expected to fulfill. Participants will look at whether or not they are fulfilling those responsibilities and if not, what is preventing them from doing so.

When reviewing the daily challenges, facilitators can remind participants of the material that has gone before — the progression of chemical dependency, denial, enabling, feelings, and self-esteem — and point out how all of those issues affect the stresses they may be feeling in their daily lives.

Facilitators should watch for participants who attempt to deal with family problems by being "perfect." Perfect children often have a great deal to do to compensate for family problems, and that can be overwhelming. Sometimes they spend so much time taking care of other peoples' problems, they don't have enough time to take care of their own.

Goals for Sessions on Coping

Goals for sessions in this subject area include:
- To help participants review what their responsibilities are.
- To help them get an overview of how much they are taking on and how much they are letting slip by.
- To help participants identify the areas in their daily lives that cause them stress.
- To help them see the relationship between their enabling and other survival behaviors at home and their ability to fulfill responsibilities both in and outside of the home.
- To help them develop coping strategies for the areas they are most concerned with.
- To introduce participants to the LifeGuides tapes.

Affirmations on Coping with Daily Challenges

These affirmations can be used as warm-ups for each session in this subject area or participants can read the affirmations during the week. These affirmations are found in the *Taking Care Participant Guidebook*.
- I am going to live one day at a time.
- I will focus my energy on the present moment and leave other problems for later.
- I am responsible for my own life. I am not responsible for my entire family.
- I can attain the serenity to accept the things I cannot change, the courage to change the things I can, and the wisdom to know the difference. (This "Serenity Affirmation" is an adaptation of the "Serenity Prayer." Rephrasing it as an affirmation helps avoid conflicts with laws on prayer in the schools.)

Overview
- Exercise: Ten Up, Ten Down
- Exercise: My Life, Right Now
- Exercise: Life's Daily Challenges
- Exercise: Pack Up Your Sorrows
- Exercise: Make a "Designated Worry Time" for Yourself
- Exercise: Role-Play on How to Tell a Friend About Family Problems
- Exercise: Inventory of Stress-Reducers
- Exercise: The 60-Second Tension Check
- Exercise: Progressive Relaxation
- The LifeGuides Audiotapes

Exercise:
Ten Up, Ten Down

Facilitators can give the participants the following instructions.

"In your *Taking Care Participant Guidebook* there is an exercise called 'Ten Up, Ten Down.' Take about ten minutes now to fill that out."

Discussion

Facilitators can either ask each participant to respond out loud to the following questions or just ask participants to consider each question without responding:

- "What do you think of your list?"
- "Are you satisfied with what you see?"
- "Which list was longer?"
- "Can you change the things that you don't like about yourself or your life?"
- "How do you feel, on a scale from one to ten, when you look over the list?"
- "What did you mark down on the Overall Life Satisfaction scale?"
- "How hard was it for you to list the ten things you like about yourself or your life? Sometimes young people find it very difficult to write those things down."

Exercise:
My Life, Right Now

Participants can be asked to go through each of the questions in "My Life, Right Now," in the *Taking Care Participant Guidebooks.*

The questions about school can help build trust between students and facilitators, since the questions give participants a chance to gripe about the adults in their lives without being criticized. Facilitators should note any defenses each participant uses during this exercise.

Exercise:
Life's Daily Challenges

Facilitators can give participants the following instructions: "Lets look at a list of the basic daily challenges that just about everybody faces. They are in your *Taking Care Participant Guidebooks.*" Indicate whether each one is never a problem for you, almost always a problem for you, or somewhere in the middle." These challenges include:

- Getting up, getting dressed and having breakfast.
- Getting to school on time.

- Attending all classes.
- Paying attention and doing assignments.
- Staying drug-free at school and away from school.
- Getting along with friends.
- Studying in school.
- Studying at home.
- Finding a place that's peaceful and quiet.
- Doing something relaxing every day, like reading or listening to music.
- Getting enough sleep.
- Getting enough to eat.
- Being left alone by pushy people — bullies — who want to control other people.

Discussion:

Facilitators can ask:
- "Which one do you worry about the most?"
- "Which ones are the most difficult for you to deal with?"

The facilitators can go around the circle quickly, finding out what each participant is most concerned about and writing the problem area on a chalkboard or flipchart. When participants bring up a problem that has already been mentioned, the facilitator can simply put a check near that problem.

After each participant has responded, the facilitator and the class can try to put the problems into broad categories and talk about general approaches to dealing with the issues. Participants can then brainstorm solutions to the problems under each category. People should not be allowed to criticize any suggestions made. The task of class participants, by themselves or by working with other class participants, will be to come up with their own specific ways of dealing with these daily hassles. The participants can also be asked:

- "Which of these can you actually do something about this week?"
- "What exactly can you do about each of them?"
- "Now, look at the things you cannot do anything about at the moment. Try to let go of them for now."
- "Write down how you feel."

Note: A "help-rejecting complainer" can tie up this exercise forever. Facilitators should make a participant aware of what he or she is doing if the person keeps rejecting suggestions without considering them at all.

Exercise:
"Pack Up Your Sorrows"

The facilitators can tell the participants:

"There is a song that goes, 'If, somehow, you could pack up your sorrows and give them all to me/ You would lose them, I know how to use them, give them all to me.' That's what we're going to do here. Pack up your sorrows.

"Read the Serenity Affirmation on page 147 again. Now, write down the things you cannot change, such as someone else's alcoholism or a teacher's angry mood. Next, put them in the sorrows pack which I'm passing around [any paper or cloth bag will do].

After the sorrows bag goes around the circle, the facilitator can ask someone to ceremoniously toss it into the waste basket. (Some facilitators have the class go outside and burn it.)

Discussion
The facilitators can ask:

• "How does it feel to put your sorrows into the bag?"

• "Can you think of other ways to keep the sorrows that you cannot change in a bag?"

The facilitator can point out that one way to do this is to make a designated worry time.

Exercise:
Make a "Designated Worry Time" for Yourself

Facilitators can explain "worry time" as follows: "One of the problems about anxiety and worry is that we tend to go over the same thoughts again and again. Although we unconsciously believe that worrying will somehow bring us an answer to a problem, that is seldom the case. Instead, we just repeat the same thoughts and we put the same stresses on our minds and bodies every time we repeat them.

"One very effective technique counselors use to help people who worry too much is to have them designate a special 'worry time' during the day. To do this, you pick a time of the day when you can sit down by yourself for at least fifteen minutes to a half hour. During that time, you will try to worry as hard as you possible can. You will write down all the things you are concerned about, you will go through them as many times as possible, and you will just try, as hard as possible, to feel as worried as you can.

"The other part of this technique is to not worry during other times of the day. If you start to worry about a problem, just jot that problem down on a piece of paper and tell yourself you will think about it during your 'worry time.'"

Exercise:
Role-Play on How to Tell a Friend About Family Problems

Sometimes young people spend a lot of energy trying to keep their friends from knowing about their problems at home: their parents' fights, their parents' separation, or alcoholism in the family, to name a few. Usually, it would take a great deal of stress off of these young people if they would simply tell their trusted friends about the problem. Here is a typical situation:

Fred has been over to his best-friend Joey's house many times. When Fred mentions that he has a neat video game at home, Joey says he'd like to go see it. Fred is very afraid of this because he knows the house will be a mess and his father will probably be intoxicated when they get there.

Discussion
After reading this scenario the facilitator can ask:

• "Has anyone ever been in a situation like this?"

• "Has anyone ever witnessed a situation likes this?"

• "What can Fred do?"

The facilitators can point out that Fred could get rid of a lot of stress if he simply told Joey about the problem. Participants could be asked to role-play the situation. After the role-play, facilitators could ask:

• "How did it feel to be Fred? Were you nervous about what Joey would say?"

• "How did it feel to be Joey?"

• "Do you think you would have wondered why you were never invited to your friend's house?"

• "How do you think most good friends would react if you did what Fred did?"

Role-plays can be enacted for any problems or situations the participants say are causing them stress.

Exercise:
Inventory of Stress-Reducers

The stress-reducers below are also listed in the *Taking Care Participant Guidebook* as an "Inventory of Stress-

Reducers." Stress-reducers are some simple things participants can do to help themselves feel less stressed and to cope better with the stresses they have. After participants have examined the list in their guidebooks, facilitators can ask them to name the stress-reducers that they are not doing and explain why not.

Some Basic Ways to Reduce Feelings of Stress:

- Eat right

- Get enough sleep.

- Develop some basic organizational plans: set priorities and avoid being distracted. (The "Moving On" material includes some basic approaches to time management. Facilitators could review some of that material now, if they think participants would be receptive. Like almost all LifeGuides material, repeating this material later in the process would still be beneficial.)

- Have at least one small place in your home that is organized and pleasing for you.

- Try keeping your room exceptionally neat for a week and see how that feels.

- Talk to people in this class and outside the class about your particular stresses.

- Don't think you are different because you have stress or feel stress. That is normal.

- Keep your values and goals in mind. Don't let others force their values on you.

- Find ways to relax without using alcohol or other drugs.

- Keep pictures of your favorite places and people in your room. Look at them and think about them when you need to relax and feel better.

- Read the affirmations in your guidebook.

- Write out your gratitude list (if you have made one).

- Get plenty of enjoyable exercise. Find some sport or activity that is fun for you to help you release your energy.

- Go to your favorite place. See it, smell it, hear it.

Exercise:
The Sixty-Second Tension Check

This is a simple technique participants can practice in class and use anywhere, anytime. Facilitators can give the following guidelines:

"Whenever you are feeling tense or anxious, **stop and take a deep breath. Breathe deeply for a few seconds.** Now:

- "Where in your body do you feel tension? Is it in your head, stomach, chest?"

- "Quickly, moving from your toes up, which muscles are you tensing?"

- "Shrug your shoulders and take deep breaths. Let the tension go."

- "Now close your eyes, and for a couple of minutes, think of a place you'd like to be."

Exercise:
Progressive Relaxation

The following is a basic relaxation exercise that facilitators can read to participants. The exercise can take between ten and twenty minutes.

In a classroom it is not always possible for people to get as comfortable as one would like for a relaxation exercise. A rug or pillows can help. In lieu of that, participants will just have to get as comfortable as possible. They can lie on the floor or sit at their desks. If they are sitting, they should close their eyes and put their hands on their laps. A facilitator, speaking softly and inserting long pauses at appropriate places, can say to the participants:

"You deserve to feel good, to feel relaxed, calm, and at rest. Take some time now to bring about a state of deep relaxation in yourself by following these guidelines:

"Sit or lie down in a comfortable place where unpleasant noises are at a minimum...loosen any tight clothes that restrict your circulation...take off your shoes... then close your eyes.

"Now be aware of how your body feels. Where is the tension?

"Wherever there is tension, you will release that tension through these exercises:

"Clench your fists tightly and maintain this for a few seconds...feel the discomfort in your hands...now relax your hands and notice the tension melt away. Enjoy this feeling for a few seconds...now stretch out your fingers as far as you can...feel the tension, then slowly relax your fingers...feel how good it is to be relaxed.

"Tighten the muscles in your arms and forearms...as this becomes painful, relax those muscles and feel the tension ooze away.

"Pull your shoulders back as far as you can and experience the tension in this posture...now relax these muscles...now hunch your shoulders forward as far as you can...feel how uncomfortable this is...now relax and be aware of how your shoulders feel as you relax.

"Turn your head far to the right, stretching your neck muscles...feel the tension as you do this...now let go and relax...Next turn your head to the left, stretching neck muscles in the other direction...feel the discomfort...now relax.

"Open your mouth as widely as you can...feel the strain...then relax...close your mouth as tightly as you can...feel the strain as you do this...now relax your mouth.

"Next, let your jaw fall forward as far as it can...as you feel the strain, let go and relax your jaw.

"Close your eyes as tightly as you can...feel your forehead grow tense...now relax your forehead.

"Next tighten your stomach muscles...draw them in toward your backbone...feel the tension...notice as you relax the air rushing out of your lungs...this is the tension leaving your body...notice that each time that you exhale you become more and more relaxed.

"Breath deeply...exhale the old air...bring in the new. [Pause for about 30 seconds.]

"Now make your stomach stick out as far as you can; be aware of the discomfort...now relax...Again, be aware of breathing.

"Tense your buttocks...now feel the strain relax.

"Now tense the muscles of your thighs by raising your legs off of the ground slightly...now relax.

"Point your toes away from you, stretching the calf muscles...after a few seconds, relax...point your toes toward your head, stretching calf and foot muscles in the opposite direction...feel the tension, now relax...now try to squeeze your toes together...when this becomes uncomfortable, relax.

"Be aware of any areas of tension that remain...take a few moments to tense and relax these muscles again, until relaxation can be felt.

"Be aware of your breathing. Allow yourself to take a slow, deep, full breath and feel your chest rise and fall...think of a wave of relaxation passing through you with each breath...now you are relaxed.

"The experience of deep muscular relaxation is a refreshing, energizing experience. It is like having a night of deep restful sleep. In a minute, I am going to count slowly backwards from five to one. When I reach the count of one, I want you to open your eyes and greet the day with renewed energy and vitality, while maintaining the ability to relax your muscles as you need to.

[Very slowly] "Five...four...three, waking up now, feeling refreshed...two, almost awake...one, open your eyes, stretch, and maintain confidence in yourself and your ability to relax as you need to.

"It is important that you practice relaxation every day. Try to set aside twenty minutes each day as a minimum. You deserve twenty minutes of each day to spend on yourself so be sure to take it.

"Relaxation is a skill that can be learned and that you are learning."

The LifeGuides Audiotapes

The lessons learned during the LifeGuides Program need to be reinforced outside of the classroom. They have to be repeated many times before participants really comprehend them on a basic, intuitive level. The LifeGuides audiotape series (available in 1990) is tailored to complement the LifeGuides curriculum. The tapes give participants an opportunity to hear some of the key points again and to practice basic techniques when they are not in the classroom. The LifeGuides audiotapes include:

• A progressive relaxation tape. Participants tune into their bodies, focus in on the tension in their bodies, and slowly let go of that tension.

• Relaxation through guided imagery. Participants are guided through a safe, serene, nurturing world that they create themselves in their minds.

• Counter-depression messages. This tape offers hope, positive thoughts, and other ideas, concepts, and images to counter depression.

Phase III: Moving On

Role Exploration

Where do I Fit In?

In describing the effects of parental alcoholism and other family problems on children, many writers have described certain system-based roles that children tend to fall into in order to compensate for a parent's impairment.

A discussion of family roles serves a useful purpose in helping participants examine their lives. The description of the typical family roles should not, however, become a rationale for labeling or creating self-fulfilling prophecies. Participants should not get the idea that they are locked into one pattern of behavior. They should also not be given the message that these roles give them permission to act out in a certain way because they are role-bound to do so.

These roles describe behaviors, not individuals. Certainly, in some extremely rigid and unhealthy family systems, people are locked into extremely rigid roles. But even in families profoundly affected by the impairment of one or both parents, children can adopt a variety of behaviors at different times.

A participant's behavior should not be considered negative simply because it appears to be related to problems in the family. It can be very shaming for a "class clown," who in fact is rather funny, to be told that his behavior is merely the result of family pathology and that he behaves that way primarily to distract people from their problems.

The point of discussing roles is to empower participants by giving them some tools to examine their lives, not to tell them that the way they are behaving is dysfunctional or based strictly on dysfunction.

The discussion of family roles occurs in this portion of the LifeGuides curriculum because, by this point in the program, there is less chance that participants will feel shame when considering whether their behavior is role-related.

Goals for Sessions on Roles

Goals for sessions in this subject area include:

- To help participants look at their behaviors at home, in school, and in their social lives.
- To help them assess the extent to which these behaviors are connected to their families or their families' problems.
- To help them determine whether or not these behaviors are beneficial to them within and outside of their family environment.
- To offer them suggestions on how they can change their patterns of behavior if they want to.

Affirmations on Looking at Who I Am

These affirmations can be used as warm-ups for each session in this subject area, or participants can read them daily during the week. The affirmations are found in the *Moving On Participant Guidebook*.

- I want to be aware.
- I am a part of a family.
- I am part of a family and I am an individual too.
- I recognize that my family has had much influence over how I behave at home and outside of the home.
- I accept that my family has helped make me who I am today.
- I will examine the roles I play in my family.
- I will decide which of those roles are healthy for me and for the other members of my family.

• I will decide which of those roles are not healthy and I will, with the help of other class participants, change those behaviors.

Overview

• Exercise: Through the Eyes of Others—How Do You Think Your Family Sees You?
• Exercise: The Family Circle
• Family Talk As It Might be Given in a LifeGuides Class
• Exercise: What's My Style?
• Exercise: Like Father, Like Son—My Mother, Myself
• Exercise: Family Sculpture Demonstration

Exercise:
Through the Eyes of Others — How Do You Think Your Family Sees You?

This exercise prepares participants for the task of examining their roles within their families. Looking at an issue from a different perspective — that of their parents — helps participants break their automatic inner monologue with themselves. Repetitious self-talk usually involves very self-critical statements.

To do the exercise, the facilitators simply have to ask the participants to describe themselves as they believe their parents would describe them. This can be done as a role-play. For instance, the participant could role-play her mother meeting a friend downtown. A facilitator can play the role of the friend and ask a series of questions such as:

• How is your daughter, Karen, doing?
• Is she enjoying school?
• How is she getting along with her little brother?
• Do you think she is going to go to college?

The facilitators will, of course, tailor the questions to fit a specific situation.

Discussion

To process the exercise, the facilitators can say:

• "How did it feel to play the role of your mother?"
• "Did that perspective give you any insights into how you look at your parent(s) or how they might look at you?"
• "Which of your mother's statements about you do you feel were inaccurate?"

• "Which of your mother's statements about you were accurate?"

Exercise:
The Family Circle

The "Family Circle" exercise is a simple way to introduce or remind participants of the concept of family systems. To do the exercise, some or all participants stand in a circle, then all turn to the right. Holding out their left arms so their hands are touching in the middle, each participant grasps the hand of the person directly opposite so that their arms serve as spokes to the wheel. The participants then walk slowly to the right.

The facilitator can point out how smoothly the circle works when people are in tune with each other: they are all walking in the same direction, holding hands across the circle. By each person taking care of himself or herself, they all are taking care of the circle.

The facilitator can then ask one of the participants to carry a chair as she continues walking with the circle. This will start to disrupt the family circle. The chair will get in other people's way; it will cause the person holding the chair to miss a step or tug on the others. These changes to the smooth rhythm of the circle can be pointed out to illustrate that one person's problems affect the whole family.

The facilitator could then ask the person to carry two chairs. This should be very disruptive to the family process. The facilitator can also ask another participant to help the person carry the chairs, which will, of course, further disrupt the circle.

The person carrying the chairs could be asked to sit down. One or two other members could try to get the person going in the circle again.

Discussion

The facilitator could comment:

"The chair was a problem for this family circle. It caused one person to slow down. Have you ever seen someone in a family develop a problem that slowed down the rest of the family?"

The facilitators can also use the Family Mobile, described on page 96, in "What's A Normal Family," to review the concept of family systems.

Family Talk As It Might be Given in a LifeGuides Class

Before starting the exercise on family roles, a facilitator may give a brief, informal talk about some of the typical roles that people assume in families with alcoholic parents or other disruptive problems. Here is an example of what this talk can sound like:

"Most of us get our basic needs met by our families — food, a place to sleep, and love, for example. We also get a lot of other things we've never probably thought about. Things that our families have taught us about who we are."

Families Teach Us Values

"I've found that much of who I am now has to do with how and what I learned from my family. For example, I learned neatness from my mother. She is very organized and has everything in its place. She taught me that to be clean, organized, and neat is important.

"I don't mean to say that being neat is either good or bad, or right or wrong; it is just a lesson I learned as a child. I can choose to be neat or not, but if I'm not thinking about how neat to be, I'm usually going to be neat. Also, if I don't think about it, I sometimes judge messy as being bad.

"My point is that our families teach us to make judgments about right and wrong. This is a very important function of families. It is something families must do. Our families teach us to make judgments about a lot of things besides neatness — having a job, going to college, being in the Army, who to hang around with, and so on. Quite often, when we make the judgments our families have taught us to make, we aren't even aware that we are making a judgment or that it is a judgment learned from our families."

Discussion

The facilitators can suggest that the participants take a moment and consider some of the judgments their families have taught them to make:

• "What are some of things that your family has taught you?" (At this point the facilitators can give the class a moment to come up with a few examples. Usually, these examples can expand on the idea that much of who they are is the result of what they learned from their families. In any event, the examples offered give an indication of the participants' understanding and acceptance of the notion, 'Yes, my family is teaching me to make judgments about people and behaviors without my really thinking carefully about those judgments.')

• "Considering what you have learned from your family, what do you value most?"

How Problems in the Family Affect What We Learn

"We learn from our families in many different ways. We learn from what they say and from what they show us by their actions. In a family where the parents abuse alcohol and other drugs, for instance, kids will learn a lot about alcohol and other drugs by watching how mom or dad use and what happens to them.

"When people have problems because of drug use, they seldom accept responsibility for their actions. Rather, they tend to blame both their drug use and the problems related to it on others. For instance, kids who get caught using might blame the pressures of school as the cause of their need to use drugs to relax, and they might blame the school administration for giving them consequences for that drug use.

"Parents who abuse alcohol or who are facing some other serious problems often act this way too. Their kids find that family life becomes pretty crazy. Sometimes moms and dads go from happy and friendly to mean and ugly after drinking. Sometimes they say things that hurt. Sometimes they blame their kids for bad things the kids didn't do, and sometimes they even do some pretty ugly things to their kids.

"Parents might blame lots of things — job pressures, the ills of society, their spouses, and even their kids — for their troubles. But they won't blame their own behavior or their own conflicts. They won't see their own behavior as the problem. That's delusion.

"When bad things start to happen in a family because of mom's or dad's problems, kids know on one level that the problem is not theirs, but their parent's. But on another level, kids don't really accept that the problem isn't theirs.

"When a parent's drug use starts to throw a family out of whack, kids often try to behave in ways that they believe — consciously or unconsciously — will make the family work better again."

Super Kids

"Some kids turn into family heroes or *Super Kids*. These are the kids who try to compensate for the crazy, mean, or ugly things that go on in their families by being the best: the best student, best worker, best football player, or whatever. Their job is to make the family seem less crazy. They think, 'If I'm doing this well, then all the crazy stuff I see going on around me can't be so bad.' Their parents usually agree, thinking, 'If I have raised one child who is so perfect, I must be doing great as a parent, regardless of how much drinking I do.'

"Super Kids tend to feel very responsible. They often become 'junior parents' — they take care of their younger brothers and sisters when mom or dad is drunk or they earn extra money to help the family out. They sometimes think they can fix mom's or dad's problems by helping the family in these ways, but they can't."

Rebels

"There's usually much to be angry about in a family with drug use problems. Unlike the Super Kid who can't do anything wrong, some kids in such families become *Rebels* who seem unable to do anything right. Their job in the family is to be the scapegoat, the one whom other family members can blame when things to wrong. Rebels are the ones who get in trouble in school or with the police. When they goof up, the family dumps their anger on them.

"The anger often has little to do with anything the Rebel has done, but is related to mom's or dad's chemical abuse. Families simply hold their anger back until the Rebel gives them an excuse for expressing it.

"When Rebels sense that feelings of anger are high in the family, they start to feel the expectation that they should act out in some way, get into trouble so the family can release its anger. I know that sounds crazy, like they're asking to get in trouble; but remember, we often learn to do things without being aware of exactly why we're doing them."

The Lonely Ones

"And then there are the kids who just don't seem to belong. They're the lost children, the **Lonely Ones.** They learn to get along in troubled families by staying out of the way, by escaping. They stay in their rooms reading books or listening to music. They withdraw to the corner or leave the room whenever there's a fight. They never make demands on their parents, brothers, or sisters. They escape the conflict and the immediate anger of the family, but they don't escape having hurt feelings and feeling neglected."

The Joker

"Another role in a chemical-abusing family is **The Joker,** the ones who always clown around. Unlike Rebels, who act out so that the parents' angry feelings get directed at them rather than at each other, Jokers try to make a joke or create a distraction when they sense tension in the family. The Joker is the comedian of the family.

"When kids play these roles, they actually do help their families avoid the crisis that takes place when family problems are faced directly. Avoiding the crisis, though, doesn't help solve the problems. The hurtful feelings are still there. The kids can't figure out what's wrong and think it's their fault. Meanwhile, nobody talks about what's happening. That's one of the strange rules about troubled families. Nobody talks about the main problems."

Developing Awareness

"The first thing people have to do when they are locked into roles that keep them from being happy is to be aware of just what roles they are playing. That's what the next exercise is about.

"We all tend to take on certain roles, certain ways we respond in our families, and there is nothing wrong with that. It is when these roles become too rigidly fixed and we can't get out of them that there is a problem. Let's first look at the roles we play in our families. Later, you can ask yourselves if your family role is a healthy position for you, or if it's something you want to change."

Exercise:
What's My Style?

At this point, facilitators can refer participants to their *Moving On Participant Guidebook.* In the exercise, "What's My Style?," there are four groups of statements; these are also listed below. Participants are to put an "X" next to all statements that apply to them. Next, participants should mark the **group** of statements that seems to fit them more than the other three by putting an "X" in the box at the top of that **group** of statements. Facilitators should let the participants know that they may fit into more than one category. Many kids have different traits.

When participants have finished, facilitators can give the names for each set of roles.

The Super Kid:
- Is very responsible.
- Is hard working.
- Seeks approval.
- Is successful in school.
- Is always volunteering.
- Is a class leader.
- Acts like a parent with other children.
- Needs to help others.
- Is bossy.
- Is very disappointed at losing.
- Acts superior when winning.

The Rebel:
- Stays away from adults.
- Is defiant.
- Is sullen.
- Acts up, gets into trouble.
- Uses drugs.
- If female, may get pregnant.

- Irritates adults.
- Is irresponsible.
- Gets into trouble with school authorities.
- Talks back to teachers.
- Hardly ever gets work done.

The Lonely One:

- Is withdrawn.
- Is aloof.
- Is quiet.
- Is distant.
- Feels rejected.
- Is sometimes seen as aloof or stuck up.
- Is not noticed in class.
- Never causes trouble.
- Has few friends.

The Joker:

- Clowns around.
- Tends to be hyperactive.
- Makes a lot of jokes.
- Attracts attention.
- Gets attention in class.
- Plays practical jokes.

During this exercise, facilitators can stress that these roles are not self-fulfilling prophecies and that children can adopt a variety of different roles at different times. Facilitators can say:

"We label behaviors, not people. Remember, you don't have to fall into any one category, and most people don't. Perhaps you are like the Rebel or more like the Super Kid than the other roles, but that doesn't mean you are only a Super Kid. The purpose of the names is not to label you, but to label general ways of behaving that you may or may not relate to. Everyone has combinations of these traits. In families with serious problems, kids can become locked tightly into these roles. Counseling can help you take a look at the role you have in your family in more detail."

Discussion

The facilitators can ask participants:

- "How do you show these behaviors at home?"
- "At school?"
- "On the job?"
- "With your friends?"
- "Which of these behaviors would you like to change?"

- "How can you take these behaviors, which are described in kind of a negative way, and make them positive; make them things that are helpful to you and for the people around you?"

Exercise:
Like Father, Like Son — My Mother, Myself

One of the most direct ways that people's families influence their behavior is for children to imitate their same-sex parent. Facilitators can ask participants:

"In what ways are you similar to your parents?"

- "For boys, in what ways are you similar to your father?"
- "For girls, in what ways are you similar to your mothers?"
- "Are you more, less, or approximately as responsible as your parents?"
- "In what ways do you express feelings differently from your parents? In what ways do you express feelings the same way?"
- "How are you similar to your parents in the way you treat other people? How are you different?"

Some participants will think of many ways in which they believe they are different from their parents and find it hard to conceive of any ways they are similar to them. If the facilitators have accumulated enough data about the participants' parents to make comparisons, they could try to make participants aware of any similarities or differences between them and their parents.

Exercise:
Family Sculpture Demonstration

Family sculpture is a method used by counselors and therapists to help clients better understand their families. It also helps them face their feelings caused by their families roles. While it would not be appropriate to attempt to sculpture the actual families of participants to help them work on their personal family issues, a demonstration family sculpture can be a safe and effective technique to teach family dynamics. To do this, the facilitator can read a simple description of a family. Here is an example:

"I am going to describe a family to you. First I am going to describe it with words, then we are all going to describe it together by doing what I call a family sculpture. There are six people in the Martin family. They are:

"**Dad.** The dad is a very successful executive. He works 60 to 70 hours per week. When he comes home, he is very demanding of both his wife and his children. He is not an alcoholic, but nonetheless, his moods are very intimidating. Once, a year ago, he slapped his wife and knocked her down. He has never done that since, but he still controls people with anger.

"**Mother.** The mother works part time at the local library but spends most of her time taking care of the home, planning social occasions, and overseeing the growth and development of her children. When dad is home, mom has to spend most of her time trying to keep the kids quiet and well-behaved so they do not bother him.

"**Van, the Super Kid.** Van has been very successful at football and is a good student. His father is pleased with him. When Van does not perform well in sports or in school, however, his father is extremely critical of him.

"**Linda, the Rebel.** Linda is a sophomore in high school and is doing poorly in school. She dates boys two or three years older than her and whom her father invariably hates. He forbids his daughter to date these young men. The daughter rebels but the mother covers up. The mom does not let the father know when Linda is acting out or getting in trouble.

"**Jan, the Lonely One.** Jan is quiet, shy, and no trouble to her parents. She spends most of her time in her room.

"**Mickey, the Joker.** Nine-year-old Mickey is always singing, making noise, and making jokes. He is very cute, has a winning smile, and tends to cheer up the rest of the family."

Now the facilitator will ask participants to play the roles. Perhaps a co-facilitator can play either the mother or father. If there are no volunteers for one of the spouses and the four children, the facilitator can select them. Facilitators should take care not to place people in roles similar or identical to their roles in real life. It is better for the demonstration if participants in the sculpture do not feel too exposed or too emotionally involved.

The family members are to be placed in relative position to each other and in poses which describe their roles. For instance:

- The father can be placed standing on a chair, arms folded, staring sternly across the room above the heads of the rest of the family members.

- The mother can be on one knee in front of the father with one hand reaching toward her husband. She

would be looking frightened and concerned at him. Her other hand would be positioned toward the kids in a manner that indicates "be quiet, stay away." Her goal is to protect the family from the father's anger and keep the children from irritating the father.

- The Super Kid could be standing with a big smile, facing his father, with arms outstretched. In one hand he could have a piece of paper with "A+" written on it (representing a report card) and in the other hand a football or something representing a football. He is showing off for his father and proving that he is a good performer. He could be about three feet from the father.

- The Rebel could be about six or seven feet away from the father, her body facing away, hands on hips, but turned around and giving the father the dirtiest look possible.

- The Lonely One will be about ten feet away, sitting on the floor, hunched over reading a book, facing away from everyone in the family.

- The Joker will be right next to the father, hanging on to his pant leg, trying to shake it, smiling up at the father, and trying to get his attention.

When placing the participants in position, the facilitator can say, "Just stand here for a second and wait. Think of how it would feel to be in this position in a family, to be in this role." This helps slow down the sculpture a bit and makes it less mechanistic than if the facilitators simply read off the information and stick somebody directly into the sculpture.

Once the sculpture is set up, each person in the sculpture can say a phrase that fits their role. For instance:

- The Super Kid: "I'm great, our family's great, we're going to make it. We're going to do real well."

- The Rebel: "This family stinks. I hate it in here. I want to get away from here. They blame me for everything. Get off my back."

- The Joker: "Hey, let's lighten up. Don't worry, be happy. We don't have to worry about our problems, we can just have fun."

The facilitators can ask those who are not part of the sculpture:

- "How do you feel when you look at the sculpture?"

- "How do you feel about Dad? Mom? Van? Linda? Mickey?"

- "What is each person getting out of their position."

- "What is each person not likely to get out of their position."

The facilitators can also ask each participant in the role-play:

- "How do you feel in that pose?"
- "What power do you have?"
- "What power are you giving away?"
- "What are you doing for the family?"
- "What is your family doing for you?"

Codependency and Codependent Behaviors

"Codependency" refers to the emotional and behavioral traits that those living with an alcoholic tend to take on as the drug use develops into chemical dependency. The definition of co-dependency varies, but three basic ingredients are usually present:

- **Enabling.** The codependent person engages in a variety of activities to protect the alcoholic from the effects of his or her drinking. The concern for another's needs often leads to the codependent person's neglect of his or her own needs.
- **Emotional dependency.** The codependent does not feel he or she has any worth unless the alcoholic loves her or unless she can help him live his life more effectively.
- **Lack of a separate identity.** Codependent people may have no concept of what their own needs or feelings are. They only feel sad when the alcoholic is sad or happy when the alcoholic happy; they have no concern about their own needs and only think of the alcoholic's needs.

Obviously, a person could be "codependent" on a person who is not an addict. People can enable, become emotionally dependent on, and give up their separate identities to almost any kind of person, whether that person is an addict or not, whether that person is healthy or unhealthy. But the most serious, destructive effects of co-dependency are seen when the codependent is trying to shape his or her life to meet the needs of an addicted or otherwise unhealthy person.

The "co" in codependency is there because it is presumed that the person on whom one is dependent is also a dependent person. That, of course, need not be the case. There are codependents who, having developed those behaviors in childhood, are codependent on healthy people. The term "dependent personality" was in use before the term "codependency" and is probably more accurate when describing relationships in which only one person is dependent. Since the term "codependency" is in such wide use, however, it will be used to describe the cluster of behaviors presented above: enabling, emotional dependency, and lack of a separate identity.

Over-Application of the Term "Codependency"

There are those in the field of chemical health/dependency who abhor the term "codependency" because it is slapped so automatically and indiscriminately on anyone whose life has been touched by alcoholism. It is often used in a very shaming rather than a helpful manner. As soon as anyone, especially a woman, is labeled "codependent," the person is automatically presumed to have acquired a whole host of traits. No need to ask whether a wife's supportive behavior was appropriate in a specific instance; she's obviously just an enabler. No need to listen to protests that she doesn't fit the mold the counselor has cast her in; she's just trying to "run her own program." It is preferable to avoid using the term "codependent" to label *people*. Rather, facilitators should refer to "codependent behaviors."

The same holds true for children of alcoholics. No child of an alcoholic should be presumed to be "just as sick as the alcoholic" simply by virtue of the fact that the child lives with an alcoholic. Not everyone living with an alcoholic is sick, and nobody should be considered codependent unless that person manifests the extreme behaviors that are characteristic of codependency.

Nonetheless, codependency is a very real and important concept. There are young people who do manifest enabling, emotional dependency, and a lack of separate identity in extreme forms. This is most easily seen in young women. Some young men express their codependency in reactive ways. Instead of becoming enablers, they might become hostile or violent toward others.

Goals for Sessions on Codependency

Goals for sessions in this subject area include:

- To help participants recognize their codependent behaviors.
- To let them know that they should not be labeled "codependent" simply because they live with an alcoholic.
- To help participants recognize the consequences of codependency.
- To prepare them for the future; to help them understand the risks they have for continuing codependent behaviors into adulthood.

Affirmations on My Own Unique Identity

These affirmations can be used as warm-ups for each session in this subject area, or participants can read the affirmations daily during the week. These affirmations are found in the *Moving On Participant Guidebook*.

- I'm an important person.
- I have my own feelings.
- I have my own life to lead and my own responsibilities.
- I can help another person without enabling that person.
- I can be concerned about another person without losing touch with my own feelings and my own needs.
- I can try to understand and be empathetic to another person without forgetting who I am.

Overview

- Exercise: Too Close for Comfort—The Codependency Inventory
- Exercise: The Pitfalls of Codependency

Exercise:
Too Close for Comfort — the Codependency Inventory

The "Codependency Inventory," in the *Moving On Participant Guidebook,* can be given several times during the LifeGuides process. To introduce the exercise facilitators can say:

"We're going to look at any codependent behaviors we might have. Think about a person in your life whose behavior has a tremendous impact on you or whom you are very concerned about right now. Keeping that person in mind, check 'yes' or 'no' on the statements on the codependency inventory in your workbooks."

Discussion

The facilitators can ask participants:

- "How many items did you check?"
- "How did you feel when you were going through the list?"
- "Have you ever asked yourself these questions?"
- "Were you able to be honest with yourself?"
- "Did you feel yourself 'editing' things out, holding back, not giving a totally honest response?"
- "Out of your responses, which ones do you think are the biggest problems for you?"
- "Let's look at each item. Who checked off the first one, 'My feelings about myself depend on how that person feels about me'? Can you give an example of that?"
- "How can you change some of the traits you checked that you would like to change?"

Exercise:
The Pitfalls of Codependency

Codependent behaviors lead to victimization. When people think only about the needs of other persons, live in fear of others' anger, and consider their own needs to be less important than other people's needs, they are setting themselves up for verbal or physical abuse. People who manifest codependent behaviors tend to believe they deserve what they get in life, including abuse. If a woman accepts physical abuse from a man, he also presumes that the woman deserves the abuse, accepts the abuse, and even needs the abuse to behave properly. This is a very disruptive, sick and self-energizing cycle. Victimization is just one of the possible consequences of co-dependency.

In the *Moving On Participant Guidebook* is a list, "The Pitfalls of Codependency." Participants should review this list and mark the ones they have experienced.

Discussion

Facilitators can ask:

- "How did you feel when reading through this list? Was it hard to do?"
- "Which of these pitfalls has the broadest consequences for you?"

• "Of the pitfalls you marked, which of them do you want
to try to change?"

Participants can be told to review this list as needed
between LifeGuides sessions.

Detachment

Letting Go to Catch On

For children of alcoholics, "detachment" means: they need not take responsibility for someone else's behavior; they do not feel guilty or ashamed because of what another person has done; and they do not try to control or change other people. Detachment is a very hard concept to grasp. It is difficult for most people to understand that a person can be detached from another person or that person's disease while remaining concerned about that person.

Detachment cannot be understood through a simple lesson nor learned in a single exercise. It is a concept that has to be returned to time and again. Opportunities for participants to learn about detachment will come up when the class works on day-to-day issues in relationships.

Goals for Sessions on Detachment

Goals for sessions in this subject area include:

- To help participants understand the concept of detachment.
- To help them learn the difference between detachment and callousness.
- To examine the role that forgiveness can play in helping them let go of the pain in their lives.
- To teach them the stages people go through in facing change and grieving for loss.

Affirmations on Letting Go

These affirmations can be used as warm-ups for each session in this subject area, or participants can read the affirmations daily during the week. These affirmations are found in the *Moving On Participant Guidebook*.

- I was not born to worry about the attitudes, feelings, or actions of other people.
- I am responsible for myself.

- I am responsible **to** certain other people in my life. I am not responsible **for** those people.
- I am going to stay detached from other people's pain and self-destructive life styles. I will also remain concerned about them.
- I know that I have not caused other people to have problems.
- I can face the losses in my life.
- I know that loss is inevitable. Everyone must face loss.
- I will be able to work through and accept those losses.
- I will be able to adjust and compensate for what was lost.

Overview

- Describing Detachment to Participants
- Exercise: Detachment Versus Callousness
- Forgiveness
- Exercise: Letting Go of Resentments, Anger, and Regret
- Exercise: Changing Expectations of Family Relationships and Letting Go.
- Grieving for Loss and Change
- Exercise: Examples of Loss and Change

Describing Detachment to Participants

In addition to the specific ways for describing detachment offered here, the facilitators can look for various manifestations of detachment, or the lack of it, in the behaviors of the participants. Pointing those out will deepen their understanding of this important concept.

People working in the field of alcoholism and drug abuse often talk about the "three Cs." This means that:

- No one can **cause** another person's drinking problems.
- No one can **control** another person's alcoholism; and
- No one can **cure** the disease of alcoholism.

The "three Cs" apply to issues other than alcoholism, for example, the issue of divorce:

- **Cause.** Children are not the cause of their parents' divorce. The divorce is the result of problems with the parents' relationship.
- **Cure.** Children will not be able to fix their parents' relationship, no matter how hard they try. Certainly, they can behave in ways that cause less stress for each parent, but only the parents can improve their relationship.
- **Control.** Trying to control parents or their relationship with each other can only backfire. It is futile for children to deliver information between the two parents or withhold information in the hope of making things work out the way the children want.

Exercise:
Detachment Versus Callousness

Facilitators can use the following examples and discussion to help participants understand the difference between detachment and callousness:

"Some people find the concept of detachment hard to grasp. They think that if you don't do everything you can to help a person you love, you are being callous and unloving. Let's look at the following situations and see what you think of them.

"Mary is very frightened about a speech she has to give in class today. She wants to talk to her boyfriend, Curt, about it. He says, 'Hey, that's your problem. You wanted to take a hard class, now you have to live with the consequences.' Then he walks away."

"What do you think of Curt's behavior? Is he concerned and detached? Co-dependent? Detached to the point of callousness?"

"Jan's father has been drinking all night. When he runs out of cigarettes, he asks his daughter to go to the store for him to buy more. He doesn't want to go there with liquor on his breath. Jan says she won't go. The next morning, Jan's father is sober but still shaky from the drinking. When he spills a pitcher of orange juice on the floor he asks Jan to help clean it up. Jan says, 'No way. If you weren't hung over, you wouldn't have dropped it!'"

"What do you think of Jan's behavior? The night before, was she appropriately detached, co-dependent, or callous? How about the next morning? Appropriately detached? Co-dependent? Callous? Can you think of some other options Jan could have tried?"

"Bill's father tends to get sentimental when he is drunk. He starts to tell his son about how tough things are for him in his life. Bill says, 'Don't tell me your problems. Your biggest problem is that you're a drunk' or 'Don't tell me you feel bad about the accident. You almost killed a couple of people.'"

"What about Bill's behavior? Detached? Co-dependent? Callous? What other approaches could Bill have tried to get his point across to his father?"

"One way we can tell that people have trouble with detachment is the amount of time they spend complaining about their parents. When we blame our parents for all the problems we have, it shows that we are still quite enmeshed with them. Even if our parents have caused us pain, complaining does not help."

Forgiveness

Here is an example of how facilitators can present information on forgiveness:

"When people have harmed us, holding resentments against them does not help us. Eventually, we have to let go of our anger and forget about the past. Often, it is best for us to forgive those who have harmed us. With alcoholics, especially those who have stopped drinking, we should consider forgiveness. However, do not let anybody tell you that you **should** forgive a person for past harms. If you still feel angry about it, that is your feeling. There is nothing wrong with that feeling. Forgiving another person can help you tremendously. However, do not forgive that person just to meet his or her needs. Forgive when it can help you the most.

"When forgiveness is not possible, you can try to forget, at least temporarily, the problems someone else has caused you. For instance, you may have had a destructive and upsetting argument one night with another family member. If you cannot forgive that person the next morning and are not in a position to resolve the conflict, you can try to forget about it for awhile. [The "thought stopping" technique described in "Stop That Stinkin' Thinkin'" on page 182 can be suggested here.]

"Sometimes, when adults get sober and also attend Alcoholics Anonymous, they become extremely optimistic. They have a natural tendency to want to put things in the past. This is because alcoholics who are part of

Alcoholics Anonymous want to take each day as a new day. Sometimes it seems as if they have forgotten what happened in the past and act as if the negative things did not happen. You may see it as an attempt to justify the past or run away from unresolved problems. But most often, it is their way of trying to make a new life for themselves.

"People in Alcoholics Anonymous are expected to make amends to those whom they have harmed. However, an apology does not make amends. It can take years to overcome some of the hurt and pain endured in childhood. LifeGuides participants whose parents are in recovery may feel pressure to put things in the past too quickly. Even if a parent has followed the Twelve Steps and has tried to make up for the harm done, it still may take a great deal of time for the wounds to heal."

Exercise:
Letting Go of Resentments, Anger, and Regret

This letter-writing exercise is like a role-play with paper and pencil rather than with words and actions. It is a way to work out anger and to share other feelings without taking the risks that talking directly to a person would entail. The exercise can be done in the classroom or assigned as homework. To begin the exercise facilitators can tell the participants:

"In this exercise, you will write a letter to someone in your life who has hurt you, disappointed you, or made you angry. Let that person know what it is they did to hurt you. Describe how you felt about it. Describe its effects on your life.

"Another way to start detaching is to write a letter to yourself. Think of the age you were when you first started facing the problems that most concern you now. Write a letter to that child, the child you were then. Tell your child that you know what was happening to the child. Let your child know that there was nothing he or she could have done about the problems, that they weren't his or her fault, and that the child was an innocent victim. Also, tell your child how you wish it would have been and what you are going to do to help that child — your child — have a better future."

Discussion
If this exercise is done in the classroom, the facilitators can look for reactions from the participants as they write. How do they look? Do the words flow or is it difficult for them to express themselves? What emotions are showing on their faces?

Not everyone will be able to finish their letters in a single session. Nevertheless, the facilitator can ask them to pause and then ask them the following question:

- "How hard or easy is it for you to write this letter?"
- "Did you know, immediately, who you wanted to write the letter to?"
- "Does anyone want to share what they wrote?"
- "If this exercise has raised feelings that you would like to talk to me about alone, please let me know."

Exercise:
Changing Expectations of Family Relationships and Letting Go

This exercise will help participants accept what their parents are able to give them and let go of unrealistic expectations for things their parents don't give them. It will also help participants consider what they want but have not gotten at home. Facilitators can have one or more boxes wrapped as gifts to use as props for the exercise.

To begin, participants can be asked to close their eyes and think about what kind of a gift they would like to receive from their parents. Facilitators can explain that this does not have to be something material, that it can be love, stability, or some other nontangible gift. As facilitators tell participants to imagine their parents walking into the room and dropping the gifts in their laps, facilitators can give the gifts to the participants. Then they can ask them to open their eyes.

Discussion
Facilitators can ask participants:

- "What will most likely be in that box?"
- "What do you want to be in that box?"

"Now think of your families. Instead of thinking about the problems, think of everything your mother or father has done for you, no matter how small. Think of the times they have shown you love and how they do it. Your job now is to:

- "Recognize the love that is there.
- "Accept the love that is there even if you have been angry. If you have rejected imperfect love, try to reconsider. Someone may love us even when they are mad at us, even when they are self-centered, even when they are preoccupied, and even when they do not know how to love because their parents were similarly distracted. Often, love is real but it is not consistent, not secure, not unconditional.

• "Determine what needs for love have not been met at home and are not likely to be met."

Grieving for Loss and Change

Children who are living in alcoholic or other disrupted home environments frequently have many losses in their lives:

• They may lose a parent through separation, divorce, abandonment, or death.

• They may lose their sense of security and happiness.

• Older children may lose many years of childhood to pain.

• They may lose their role as the children in the family and have to take on responsibilities of adults.

• They may lose friends, because some adults instruct their children to stay away from kids whose parents are divorced or "have too many problems."

• They may lose their ability to be high achievers because they spend their time keeping their home together rather than studying.

Here are some of the ways young people might deal with such losses:

• **Denial:** Many children will first deny that they have a problem. They will deny that their homes are any more disrupted than any other home or that the disruption has made them unhappy.

• **Anger:** People ask, "Why?" or "Why me? Why do I have to deal with this problem? I'm only a kid, I shouldn't have to deal with this. It's not fair!"

• **Bargaining or trying to control the situation:** "There must be something I can do. I will change my situation." Children will try to control the situation by trying to make alcoholics behave better or make parents stop fighting and get along better. When people realize that this will not work, they often fall into the next stage.

• **Depression:** People feel sad, hopeless, and worthless, and they give up.

• **Acceptance:** After children accept the losses that have come their way and realize that the past cannot be changed, then they can move out of sadness or depression and on to changing their lives.

People go through this process even for an everyday problem. A student who has flunked a course might first deny that it happened. He looks at the grade and says, "This must be a mistake, the teacher must have gotten my name mixed up with someone else." When the teacher shows the student his wrong answers on the final test, he becomes angry and says, "Well these are stupid questions. No one should be expected to know this kind of stupid detail!" Then bargaining or trying to control the situation, the student pleads, "Please, let me take the test again, I know I can do better this time." When the teacher says, "No, it's too late. Just try to do better next quarter," the student feels sad and depressed for a while, but finally accepts that he made the mistake and that he can do better next time. He sets his sights on the next quarter and gets a passing grade then.

Exercise:
Examples of Loss and Change

The following examples describe people who are facing loss or change. A facilitator or one of the participants can read the stories aloud to the class. As they listen to the stories, participants are to look for signs of denial, anger, bargaining or some other attempt to control the situation, depression, and acceptance. Participants can use the outline in their *Moving on Participant Guidebook*, "Facing Change, Dealing with Loss," to write down the various signs as they identify them.

Carl was a starting player on his high school's basketball team, but he was very unreliable. Although he had been warned many times by his coaches, he continued to miss practice at least once a week and to arrive late two or three other times. This week, he missed Thursday practice but showed up for the game at 7:30 on Friday night. The coach told him that he couldn't play and would be suspended for two weeks for missing practice. Carl laughed at first. He thought the coach was joking. "Gimme a break, coach. You know we need to win this one." He walked right by the coach and started to get dressed.

Then the coach said, "No, Carl, I'm not kidding. You can't play tonight. You're off the team for two weeks."

"Off the team!" he said. "You can't do that! You're just picking on me 'cause you never liked my old man." Carl slammed down his gym bag and started to walk out.

On his way out he saw the assistant coach and said, "Mr. Peterson, you gotta talk to the coach! Something's wrong with him. Tell him that I'm sorry and that I'll be real good from now on. Please, just tell that I'm ready to play now and there won't be anymore trouble!"

Mr. Peterson said he couldn't help him, that it was his own responsibility for not showing up for practice and he left. Carl walked out the building and sat in the car in the parking lot throughout the whole first half of the basketball game. During the second half, however, when he heard the crowd cheering, he went back in and watched the game. Even though he promised himself he wouldn't cheer for his own team, he couldn't help it. When they started to catch up with the other team, he jumped up and cheered with the rest of them.

Discussion

A facilitator can ask:

- "How did Carl indicate denial?"
- "Anger?"
- "Bargaining or trying to control the situation?"
- "Sadness?"
- "Acceptance?"
- "Have any of you had experiences like this?"
- "Can you describe some of the stages you went through to deal with your loss or change?"

When **Betty** came home from school yesterday, her mother and father looked very serious. They said they wanted to talk to her. They told her that they had decided that it would be better for Betty's father to leave. Betty knew that they had been fighting a lot, and her parents acknowledged that. They said they just couldn't agree on things anymore.

Betty didn't have much reaction. As a matter of fact, she didn't even think about what they said. All that night, Betty talked to her father about what they were going to do as a family, things they had already planned, like summer vacation. She presumed that all those things would still happen just as her parents said they would.

Two days later, when her father started to load his suitcase in the car, Betty broke down. "What are you doing! Why are you doing this to me! You can't go. You just can't!" She screamed at him, but very quickly her screams turned to tears. "Please, Daddy, don't go! I know you won't be happy anywhere else. Just stay one more night. We'll watch a movie together. You always like to do that."

But her father told her he couldn't stay, that he really had to leave. For several weeks after that Betty wouldn't talk to anybody, she wouldn't even visit her father in his new apartment. She wanted him to come over to visit her at her house. Finally, after two months, when her father asked her to go to a movie with him and then stay the weekend at his house, she said OK.

Discussion

A facilitator can ask:

- "How did Betty indicate denial?"
- "Anger?"
- "Bargaining or trying to control the situation?"
- "Sadness?"
- "Acceptance?"
- "Have any of you had experiences like this?"
- "Can you describe some of the stages you went through to deal with your loss or change?"

Interpersonal Skills

Finding Fulfillment in Relationships

Basic interpersonal skills such as initiating social interactions, complimenting others, and carrying on a conversation may be severely lacking in some LifeGuides Program participants. A person who has a very negative self-concept may be more likely to think and express negative rather than complimentary thoughts about others. A person who is very concerned about his or her survival is more likely to talk about that than show genuine interest in another person.

Any distorted patterns of communication and interaction in their family environment will impair the participants' abilities to begin and to sustain relationships. If a youth's place was "to be seen and not heard," he will likely find it difficult to meet people and carry on a conversation. If his parents were always extremely polite with each other and never talked about the negative events that had taken place, he is likely to turn people off by always being "nice" or being indirect and dishonest.

Goals for Sessions on Interpersonal Skills

Goals for sessions in this subject area include:

- To help participants review the qualities they like in their friends and in close relationships.
- To help participants consider and experiment with new ways of meeting people.
- To help participants assess their current relationships to determine if they are getting what they want and need from those relationships.

All LifeGuides sessions contribute to helping to improve a person's interpersonal skills. Becoming comfortable with the people they see every week in the class creates a solid foundation of personal support for participants. They must then go out and initiate social interactions at dances, in school, on the job, in job interviews, etc.

Affirmations on Finding Fulfillment in Relationships

These affirmations can be used as warm-ups for each session in this subject area, or participants can read the affirmations daily during the week. These affirmations are found in the *Moving On Participant Guidebook*.

- I can give love.
- I am sensitive to and considerate of the interests of others.
- I can find people I like and trust and who like and trust me.
- I enjoy people with different points of view, different backgrounds, and different capabilities.
- I am in control of my own life and do not let other people control me.
- There is more than one person or one group of people who can meet my needs for love, respect, and acceptance.

Overview

- Exercise: Finding Friendship
- Exercise: What Keeps You From Making More Friends?
- Exercise: Role-Play on Things to Do
- Exercise: Finding Places to Meet People
- Exercise: Initiating Conversation
- Exercise: An Honest Look at Intimate Relationships

Exercise: Finding Friendship

The "Finding Friendship" exercise offers participants an opportunity to think about what they like in a relationship and what keeps them from getting it. The participants can take several minutes to respond to the items listed in "Finding Friendship" in their *Moving On Participant Guidebook*. They can then meet in small groups or as a class to discuss their responses.

Discussion

The facilitators can ask:

- "What other qualities did you add to your lists?"
- "Which qualities did you mark 'Very Important'? Why?"
- "Which qualities did you mark 'Not very important'? Why?"
- "Do you think all your friends must have all the qualities you marked as very important? Can you choose some friends because they have certain qualities and others because they have different qualities?"
- "Are the qualities you look for in a friend also strong qualities in you?"
- "Do you ever look for qualities in a person that you lack or are not very strong in?"

Exercise:
What Keeps You From Making More Friends?

Participants can look at the exercise, "What Keeps You From Making More Friends?" in their *Moving On Participant Guidebooks* and fill out the form.

Discussion

The facilitators can ask:

- "What things did you add to the sheet?"
- "How many people marked that it's 'sometimes' or 'always' a problem to find places to meet people?"
- "How many for 'Starting conversations'?" (Facilitators should continue down the list.)
- "What can we do about those problems?"

The facilitators can help participants brainstorm ideas on how to solve each of the problems. Information on brainstorming is offered on page 182. Some ideas on finding places to meet people and initiating conversations are offered in the next two exercises.

Exercise:
Role-Play on Things to Do

To help participants come up with new ideas for things to do, facilitators can have them role-play a related situation. The class can be broken up into two or three small groups. They are then given ten minutes to plan a short skit in which they are talking about what to do on a Saturday night.

In all discussions about fun activities, facilitators should be prepared for the "help-rejecting" complainer. Whenever a person rejects ideas without any attempt to consider them further, their behavior should be pointed out and labelled appropriately.

Exercise:
Finding Places to Meet People

In the following exercise, facilitators can either list the suggestions given here on a board or flipchart or write down suggestions as they are given by participants. Facilitators can introduce the exercise as follows:

"To make new friends, you first have to go places where you would be likely to meet new people. You must also learn how to initiate conversations with the people you meet and feel comfortable letting those people get to know you. Think of all the places, events, and organizations where you can both enjoy yourself and meet people. Some ideas are:

- School
- Sports activities or teams
- Dances
- School activities other than sports
- Volunteer jobs and projects
- On the job
- The roller rink
- The swimming pool"

Discussion

When the class is done creating the list, a facilitator can say:

- "Look this list over. Are there any other places we should add to the list?"
- "What places would be your best opportunity to meet people?"
- "Are you running a risk of being pressured to use alcohol or other drugs at some of these places?"
- "What can you do about that?"
- "Are there people you'd feel comfortable with who could go with you to some of these places?"

Exercise:
Initiating Conversation

To introduce this role-play exercise facilitators can say:

"It is easier to initiate a conversation with a person if you are already participating in some shared activity or project. For instance, if you are volunteering at a nursing home and you see someone you would like to meet, you can begin by talking about the people in the nursing home. If you are working on a school project to prepare the gym for a dance, you have many ways to initiate a conversation such as: 'I'm having trouble with this. Can you help me?' Or, 'What do you think of this. Does it look OK?' 'Gee, I've never noticed that before!'

"It is much easier to do this type of initiating in a task-orientated activity than it is simply to meet someone new at a party and begin a conversation."

Role-Play

The facilitators can ask participants to think of situations in which they wanted to start a conversation but didn't. If they do not come up with ideas, the facilitator can suggest some of these:

Three boys are playing basketball and talking. If they had a fourth, they could start a game. The fourth person has to come along and start the conversation.

A girl sits down next to another girl on the bus. She would like to make a friend and has to start a conversation. (Try the same role-play with a boy meeting a boy.)

A boy sits down next to a girl on the bus and wants to start a conversation.

Two people are talking in a school cafeteria. A third one has seen these people before and would like to get to know them.

Each participant can try to role-play one of the situations. The rest of the class can reinforce the actions they think would work and offer suggestions for improvement.

Discussion

During these role-plays, those watching can give suggestions or even switch places in order to demonstrate a technique. If people get silly and act funny, that is all right too. Learning can still take place.

One helpful approach is for facilitators to suggest that the person in the role-play find out what the other person likes to do. "Do you like movies? Let's go see one." "Are you going to the dance this Saturday night? I'll see you there." "Are you going to be setting up for the dance? So am I."

Exercise:
An Honest Look at Intimate Relationships

Children from alcoholic and other disrupted family environments have not, as a rule, had an opportunity to witness or understand what a healthy marriage is like. They also may not know what it feels like to be loved. This can cause them to make many mistakes in developing close relationships. The LifeGuides Program cannot, of course, cover the development of intimate relationships in detail. But facilitators can remind participants of all the information they have acquired in class concerning the effects of family problems and ask them to consider how those effects could determine the nature of their intimate relationships.

This exercise provides an opportunity for participants to review what they are and are not getting out of their close relationships, along with the effects the relationship is having on them. Facilitators can begin by saying:

"Let's talk about boyfriends, girlfriends, and best friends. Think of the main relationship you have with a person — it can be with a friend of the same or of the opposite sex, it doesn't matter. Now ask yourself:

• "What does the person look like? Talk like? Act like?"

• "What do you give to the relationship?"

• "What does that person give to the relationship?"

• "What do each of you get from the relationship?"

• "How is your relationship with that person similar to and different from relationships in your family?"

• "How would you like things in that relationship to change?"

• "How realistic is it that those changes will come about?"

• "Think of the things we discussed about co-dependency. Are there things about your relationship that could be considered co-dependent?"

• "How is the relationship helping you grow? How is it keeping you from growing?"

Discussion

On the first go-around, participant responses are likely to be somewhat superficial. People will reveal that they think this person is nice, that they talk with him or her on the phone, they go shopping together, and so forth. On the next go-around, participants can be encouraged to talk about *why* they do those things with that *particular* person and not with all the other students in the school.

Participant feedback can also make the exercise more powerful. People may have observed the relationships of other participants outside of the class.

Facilitators should look for any parallels between participants' relationships with their closest friends and relationships with their parents.

Assertiveness Skills

Standing Up for Yourself

Because of problems with anger and co-dependency, appropriate assertiveness is difficult for many Life-Guides participants. For boys, anger and aggressiveness interfere with appropriate assertiveness. For many of the girls, dependency and playing the role of the victim interfere.

In addition to the specific exercises on assertive behavior suggested here, facilitators should constantly seek opportunities to point out the difference between non-assertive, assertive, and aggressive behavior.

Goals For Sessions On Assertiveness

Goals for sessions in this subject area include:

- Participants will learn the difference between aggressiveness and assertiveness.
- Participants will understand that assertiveness does not mean being self-centered.
- Participants will be given an opportunity to practice assertive behavior.
- Participants will learn to resolve conflicts productively.

Affirmations on Standing Up For Myself

These affirmations can be used as warm-ups for each session in this subject area, or participants can read the affirmations daily during the week. These affirmations are found in the *Moving On Participant Guidebook*.

- I will stand up for my rights.
- I will say yes and help people out when I want to.
- I will say no to people's requests when I want to.
- I will express anger in a way that helps both me and the person I am talking to.
- I will be assertive at school.

- I will be assertive at home.
- I will be assertive with my friends.
- I will seek to resolve conflict to the benefit of myself and the person I am in conflict with.
- I will be a responsible person.
- I will expect other people to be as responsible as I am.

Overview

- Exercise: Opportunities For Assertive Behavior
- Exercise: What's Assertive, What's Not?
- Exercise: Examples Of Non-assertive, Assertive, And Aggressive Behaviors
- Exercise: Resolving Conflicts
- Exercise: Imaging Assertiveness
- Empowerment Within The Family
- Exercise: Journal Assignment On Assertiveness.

Exercise: Opportunities for Assertive Behavior

This simple opening or warm-up exercise can be used to introduce the concepts of non-assertive, assertive, and aggressive behavior. Facilitators can say to participants: "Describe an incident when someone put you down and you handled it well?"

Discussion

The facilitators can ask:

- "What did you get out of the way you handled the situation?"
- "What didn't you get out of it?"
- "Would you have liked to have handled it differently?"

The facilitators can look for what participants think is a good way of handling put-downs. Some may think the best thing to do is respond sarcastically, others may opt for just holding one's tongue, and another may never speak to the person again. Each of the behaviors can be gently labeled as non-assertive, assertive, or aggressive.

The facilitators do not have to provide in-depth definitions of these labels at this time. They can simply say, "That's what I would call non-assertive. We're going to be talking about what I mean by non-assertive, assertive, and aggressive in a minute."

Exercise:
What's Assertive, What's Not?

Before discussing differences between non-assertive, assertive, and aggressive behavior, facilitators can have participants look at the list of behaviors under "What's Assertive, What's Not?" in their *Moving On Participant Guidebooks*. They can put an "N" next to the behaviors they consider to be definitely non-assertive, a "G" next to those they consider definitely aggressive, and an "A" next to those they consider assertive behaviors.

Discussion

The facilitators can ask a participant to read the behaviors he or she considered definitely non-assertive and then ask the class:

• "Does anybody have any others they would add?"

• "Does anyone believe that some of the traits that ___ read should not be considered non-assertive?"

The facilitators can follow the same line of questioning for assertive and aggressive traits.

After discussing "What's Assertive? What's Not?" facilitators can ask participants to turn to the page in the guidebook and look at "Non-assertive, Assertive, and Aggressive Behaviors." Facilitators can explain:

"Here is a list of the same behaviors, only this time they are organized in a way that many people believe is appropriate. One of the interesting things about a list like this is that we are all likely to be non-assertive sometimes and assertive at other times. Look the list over and then check off which behaviors under each of the three categories you think describe you best." After participants have completed this task facilitators can ask:

• "When do you behave that way? Can you give an example of when you behave in a certain way?"

• "Were you satisfied with that behavior?"

• "How would you like to change that?"

Exercise:
Examples of Non-assertive, Assertive, and Aggressive Behaviors

This exercise is another way to consider ways of acting appropriately assertive. Facilitators can say:

"Very few of us have been trained to be appropriately assertive. As children, we may have been told to be quiet or to stay in our place. On the streets we may have learned that the way to get what you want is to demand it, shout louder than anyone else, or be tougher than anyone else.

"Assertiveness means standing up for your own rights, opinions, and beliefs, while respecting the rights, opinions, and beliefs of others. Let's look at a few situations. Put yourself in each situation and think of a non-assertive response, an aggressive response, and a healthy and assertive response."

Facilitators can select some or all of the following examples for discussion.

Larry's mother has hit him many times when she was drunk. She recently started attending Alcoholics Anonymous and has since told him how sorry she is about hitting him. However, Larry still feels some anger. At the end of a talk in which she apologized to him for all the times she was abusive, his mom said to him, "You aren't mad anymore are you?"

"How could Larry respond in a non-assertive manner?"

• "In an assertive manner?"

• "In an aggressive manner?"

Some possible responses are: "Oh, sure, Mom, I'm not mad. How could I be?" (non-assertive); "I know that you're sorry for what you did and I know that the alcohol had something to do with that. I'm still angry, though. I'll need some time to get over that." (assertive); "After all you did, you think that you can just sit here and tell me you're sorry! You make me sick!" (aggressive).

JoAnne's father is attending AA. He believes it has changed his life and he is extremely grateful for what the program has given him. However, there is a problem for JoAnne. Her father quotes "recovery sayings" constantly. If JoAnne is worried about school her father says, "Just let go and let God." Or, "Easy does it," or "You'll just have to take one day at time." Once, when she wanted to talk to him about the problems she had with her tyrannical boss, her father just told her to say the Serenity Prayer. JoAnne felt like screaming at him. Tonight at supper, JoAnne was asking her brother some questions about his girlfriend. Her father interrupted and said, "Don't take his inventory!"

"How could JoAnne respond in a non-assertive manner?"

• "In an assertive manner?"
• "In an aggressive manner?"

Some options for JoAnne are: "I'm sorry" (non-assertive); "I'm just asking him some questions, Dad. There's nothing wrong with that. If he wants to answer he can." (assertive); "Why don't you just shut up! I'm sick and tired of hearing these proverbs of yours!" (aggressive).

Below are some other examples participants can look at. In each case, facilitators can ask them to consider how they could respond:

• In a non-assertive manner.
• In an assertive manner.
• In an aggressive manner.

You are the movies and are waiting in line to buy popcorn. The movie has just started and you are about to step up and make your order. Someone steps in front of you to place his order.

The teacher asks the class if anyone knows the answer. You are 60% sure you know the right answer.

You have a test the next day and you are very worried about it. You intend to study tonight. A friend calls up and says she feels lonely and would like to talk to you.

You make a mistake and a friend calls you an idiot.

You make a mistake and a teacher calls you stupid.

You make a mistake and a boss calls you stupid.

A parent calls you stupid.

You go into a store to buy a single shirt. The salesman is very aggressive. He pulls many shirts off the shelves and lays them there in front of you. You feel he has gone through a lot of work to show you these shirts. He is pushing three shirts very hard.

You go to a movie with a group of friends. They all agree that the movie was terrible. You thought the movie was very good.

You feel you have been mistreated by a teacher. You have been putting off talking to him about it and have been waiting for a chance to speak to him alone. As you walk by an open door, you look in and see that teacher by himself at his desk. What do you do?

Someone you know got very drunk the night before. While he was drunk he called you names and made fun of you. The next morning he tells you he is sorry. He says, "It wasn't me talking, it was the alcohol."

Exercise:
Resolving Conflicts

Here are some ways that different people react when they are in conflict with someone else.

• **Avoiding:** One or both people withdraw from the conflict situation.
• **Smoothing Over:** One or both people attempt to emphasize the positive aspects of the situation or of their relationship rather than focusing on the main issue. This could be either postponing resolution of the conflict or ignoring it, letting it simmer.
• **Compromising:** Both parties get part of what they want.
• **Problem-Solving:** Coming up with an alternative not previously considered.
• **Power Struggles:** Both people try to win over the other person.

The facilitator can ask the participants to look these over in their *Moving On Participant Guidebooks* and say:

"Consider which of these describes your ways of dealing with conflict. Which ways are non-assertive? Assertive? Aggressive?"

Participants can now consider situations that involve conflict. Facilitators can select one or more of the following situations to present and then ask the discussion questions.

You and your friend have just met a girl you like. You think that she may like you, too. Your friend tells you that he likes her and is going to ask her for a date.

You have a test and your boss says he would like you to work late because someone else has not shown up for work.

You are with a group of friends and somebody says something very hostile and negative about a person you know and like. Everyone else agrees with the hostile and negative statement.

Discussion

The facilitator can point out the conflict resolution styles in the guidebook and say:

- "What behaviors are you likely to use?"
- "Will you use more than one of these approaches?"
- "Think of the family roles we talked of before. Which one of these approaches fits the Super Kid? The Rebel? The Lonely One? The Joker?"

Exercise:
Imaging Assertiveness

This a brief exercise to help participants role-play assertiveness in their minds. Facilitators can ask participants to close their eyes while a facilitator reads the following:

"Imagine, right now, a person who intimidates you, who can make you feel bad about yourself by a word or even a look. Now say to yourself, 'I am a good person, I am a worthy person, I have a right to respect, I will stand up for myself, I will not be intimidated, I will not be afraid.'

"Now imagine that person saying something to put you down. [Give participants a few seconds.]

"Now, say something assertive, but not aggressive to that person."

Facilitators can then ask participants to describe the scene they had in their minds. They do not have to name the person they imagined. Discussion of the scene will assist participants in thinking of assertive ways of acting and speaking. When a participant describes the scene, facilitators and other participants can try to help that person improve his or her assertive thoughts and behavior. After everyone in the class has described a situation, a facilitator can walk them all through the exercise again. Participants can then be asked to work on that positive imaging every day of the following week and report at the beginning of the next class on any changes they felt.

Empowerment Within the Family

Children from alcoholic and other disrupted family environments are concerned first and foremost with surviving within their families. They are taught through the LifeGuides class that they are not responsible for their parents' problems or the general behavior of their families. Nonetheless, they are active members of their families and can affect their families in a healthy manner without becoming enmeshed with the family or feeling responsible for their families' well-being.

Researchers have found that even when only one person in a family is in counseling, other members change as well. Facilitators could summarize these examples:

In New York state, a social service agency offered individual and group counseling to children with an alcoholic parent. In at least 50% of the cases, the child's participation in treatment motivated the alcoholic parent to seek help. (Services for Children of Alcoholics, NIAAA Research Monograph-4, 1981).

In a school-based drug prevention program, all of the participants talked to their non-alcoholic parent about their experiences in a support group. In several cases, the non-alcoholic parent began attending Al-Anon, a self-help group for the spouses of alcoholics (ibid.).

Other authors (Szapocznik J, et. al.,1983) found that involving one member of a family intensely and in one-person family therapy (therapy with only one family member present for most sessions) was as effective as having the entire family present at all sessions.

These three examples demonstrate how programs for children from chemically dependent families can begin the process of intervention into the family's cycle of problem drinking. Counselors find that when just one member of a family system begins to change his or her behavior, as usually happens when a young person joins a LifeGuides class, the dynamics of the family can change. Intervention into the family's problem of alcoholism or other problem behaviors then begins in a very natural fashion.

After summarizing the research articles for the class, facilitators can ask them:

- "Have you seen any changes like this in your families?"
- "Do you believe it is even possible?"

Being Responsible is Empowering

When people take care of their responsibilities to themselves and to others they are empowering themselves. People behave responsibly toward themselves when they do the tasks they need to do to learn, grow, and feel good about themselves. When they are responsible to others they earn the right to be respected and to be listened to.

If someone is never reliable, it is more difficult for that person to demand that others be reliable as well.

Certain patterns of communication are also empowering. If a child tends to cry or whine when she doesn't get her way, people may discount her. But if she were very clear about what she wanted, why she wanted it, and why she thought she deserved it, she would more likely to earn what it was she wanted.

Discussion on Empowerment Within the Family

Facilitators can ask:

- "Which of your behaviors allow your family or others to look at you as a kid rather than an adult?"

- "How can you change this?"

- "Make a commitment to change one of these behaviors before the next session."

Families are not the only systems affected by the behavior of one or two actors in a system. Schools, classrooms, peer groups, and work situations can all be affected by the behavior of a single person. Participants can be asked to think about what happens when one person enters any of those systems and is in a very foul mood. It makes the system take on a negative tone. The more powerful the person is in a system, the more noticeable will be the effect. Participants can also consider how a person who is assertive, kind, and helpful can change the tone of an entire system.

When a participant talks about some way he or she is disregarded at home, or in another context, the other participants will say, "The way they treat you is not right," or "They should have listened to you on that." Hearing this from other participants helps these children learn that they deserve to be listened to. That is the first step in actually being listened to or being regarded with respect.

Examples of Empowerment Within the Family

The facilitators can read some or all of the following examples to the class. After each one the facilitator can ask, "What reaction is going to earn the person more respect, more power in the family?"

Betty

Betty came home 20 minutes last night because her girlfriend ran out of gas. Her father grounded her for a month and Betty thought it was very unfair. Betty can:

a. Scream, yell, and smash the mirror in her bedroom because she is so mad.

b. Take the consequence that night, and talk to her father in the morning, when she can explain to him the effort she made to get home on time, tell him why they were late, give evidence to support her case, and offer an alternative of one-week grounding only.

Mike

Mike's father always likes to take a two-week summer vacation at an isolated cabin. There the father can fish, but the children have nothing that they like to do. Mike can:

a. Do what he usually does, go to the cabin and be angry all or most of the time. He generally fights with his father, mother, and his sister the entire time he is there.

b. Explain clearly to his father and mother why he doesn't like going to the cabin anymore. Suggest an alternative of one week at the cabin and one week at a place with more recreational activities.

Facilitators can reflect back to family roles if participants have already been introduced to them.

The facilitators can also tell participants: "For the most part, if you behave in a predictable fashion, you are less likely get what you want. If you do something different, you will get the attention you want. For instance, a Rebel might always argue and fight when he doesn't get his way and then run out of the house. If he instead stays in the house and gives rational reasons to the parents, he will be more likely to get what he wants."

Marlene has been planning all week to go out with her friend on Friday night. That afternoon her parents tell her that they have received a special invitation to her father's boss's house and they have to go. They tell Marlene that she has to babysit for them.

a. Marlene could become hurt, angry, and abusive to her parents. She could call them stupid, selfish slobs and go to her room, slamming her door behind her.

b. She could say, "Wait a minute, I don't think that what you're doing is fair. I have a compromise though. I know some kids who can babysit for us and I'll take care of it."

Even though Marlene didn't win an argument and still had to do work — hire the babysitter — which perhaps she shouldn't have had to do, she got what she wanted. She did not get to prove that she was right, but she did get to have a good time.

Exercise: Journal Assignment On Assertiveness

Facilitators can ask participants to look over the list of assertive behaviors during the week and try to act on as many of these as possible. Participants can then write down what happened and how they felt about it.

Taking Care of Business

Problem-solving, Decision-making, and Goal-setting

All of the work done prior to this session will have a bearing on problem-solving and decision-making skills. Depression and co-dependency, for instance, can greatly impair a person's ability to solve problems and make decisions.

For students whose family environment has become disorganized due to alcoholism or other family problems, it is quite likely that they have not had much opportunity to set or to observe someone else set goals. They may have no concept of how goals can help them feel better about themselves. (There will be some participants who are overly responsible and perhaps quite good at goal setting. Their skills will be a help to others during sessions in this subject area.)

Through the exercises in this subject area, participants will be presented with realistic, relevant situations. They will be asked to brainstorm solutions to problems posed and employ a systematic decision-making process to pick a course of action.

Goals For Sessions on Taking Care of Business

Goals for sessions in this subject area include:

- Participants will examine the attitudes and ideas that keep them from being more productive.
- Participants will learn the basic steps in problem-solving and decision-making.
- Each participant will establish at least one goal for school, for home, for personal growth, and for exercising or having fun.
- Participants will have a written plan for achieving each goal.

Affirmations on Taking Care of Business

These affirmations can be used as warm-ups for each session in this subject area, or participants can read the affirmations daily during the week. These affirmations are in the *Moving On Participant Guidebook*.

- I can develop the serenity to accept the things in my life that cannot be changed, the courage to change the things I can, and the wisdom to know the difference.
- I can accept responsibility.
- I can plan my life but accept surprises as well.
- I can set realistic, meaningful goals for myself.
- I can make the decisions I must make.
- I will try, very hard, to make life better for myself and those around me.
- It is OK for me to make mistakes.
- It is OK for me to do something less than perfectly.
- If I enjoy doing something, it doesn't matter if others think I do it well.
- If doing something gives me satisfaction, that is enough reward. I do not have to have everyone like what I do or how I do it.

Overview

- Films: "The Bizarre Trial of the Pressured Peer" and "Why Is It Always Me?"
- Exercise: Stop That Stinkin 'Thinkin'!
- Basic Steps in Problem-solving and Decision-making
- Exercise: Case Examples for Problem-solving

• Goals Work For Task-oriented *AND* Personal Problems

• Exercise: Practice in Goal-setting

• Homework Exercise: Time Management

Films

"The Bizarre Trial of the Pressured Peer" and "Why is it Always Me?" are two films that consider decision-making and conflict resolution for adolescents. They are described in Appendix B on pages 196 and 197.

Exercise: Stop that Stinkin' Thinkin'!

This section looks at some ways to help participants plan their lives better. Before discussing techniques that can be used to do this, facilitators can review the kind of negative, self-defeating thoughts that keep people from succeeding. Participants should complete the exercise "Stop That Stinkin' Thinkin'!" in their *Moving On Participant Guidebook*.

Discussion

After participants have filled in the positive self-talk statements, facilitators can say:

"In the lefthand column are the ideas that keep us stuck. They are thoughts that we keep on little tapes in the back of our minds and play again and again. Much of what we have done so far in the class has to do with examining what's beneath the thoughts that keep us believing we are less worthy than others."

Facilitators can ask participants to look at their completed exercise, and ask:

• "How did you feel about filling in the positive statements?"

• "Did you feel any sense of phoniness when you did it?"

• "Now let's each read those statements to each other."

Acting "As If"

The facilitators can tell participants that it's OK if they don't feel completely confident reading their positive self-talk statements. This is a chance for the participants to act "as if" they felt confident and optimistic about those statements. Facilitators can tell them that it is a well-known fact that when people say positive things to themselves, they're more likely to behave in a positive, productive, and effective way.

Thought Stopping

"To start a task or make plans, we have to get down to business. We can't always stop to analyze why we feel a certain way. What we can do, however, is recognize that our negative thoughts are invalid and non-productive. We want to stop them whenever we start thinking them. **Thought stopping** is a simple process. Whenever you start thinking a repetitive, negative thought, you say in your mind, 'Stop!' You may have to do that 50 times an hour the first time you do it, but you must keep at it. You don't have to try to replace the negative thought with another thought. Your mind will do that automatically. You simply stop the negative thought. You can also wear a rubberband on your wrist and snap it every time you say, 'Stop!' in your mind. That helps you snap out of a negative cycle of thinking."

Basic Steps in Problem-solving and Decision-making

When people are faced with a problem, they often become confused. If a person just accepts this state of confusion and wanders around thinking about the problem, the confusion increases and the person falls back on old ways of solving problems. For example, if someone drank alcohol in the past when she felt lonely, she is likely to do that again unless she stops and looks at the problem she is facing. There are some key steps that participants can use to solve problems without falling back into old behaviors. These are found under "Basic Steps in Problem-solving and Decision-making" in the *Moving On Participant Guidebook*. The following is an example of how facilitators can explain these key steps:

"Recognize and Accept the Need for Change. Sometimes this does not come easily. A person who is doing poorly may believe that that's the way kids from his family perform; it has always been that way and always will be that way. There is no need to change. Alcoholics can believe this too. They may think that their lives are going fine, or they may know that their lives are terrible, but think that that's the way it was for their parents and it will always be that way for them. However, with some confrontation and a dose of reality from our friends, we usually do see and accept the need for change.

"Determine What is Possible to be Changed. If a young person is doing poorly in school and getting in trouble because he is not doing his homework, he may feel that the best option is to have the teachers in the school district change their approach. However, it is not likely that the student will be able to change his environment to that extent. Therefore, he will probably want to narrow down his options to things that will help him perform better in school.

"Brainstorming. Sometimes people have a lot of difficulty solving problems because they only think of one or two distasteful solutions. Usually, this involves a 'win/lose' situation in which somebody must lose for someone else to win. Those who can think of entirely new alternatives do best in problem solving. Brainstorming can help us come up with new alternatives to old problems. In a few minutes I'm going to give you some case examples so you can practice solving problems by following these key steps. When you're doing that exercise try to brainstorm a wide range of possibilities about what can be done. If you have trouble coming up with alternatives, it may be that you are unconsciously limiting yourself in some way. If so, examine the brainstorming you are doing. How rigid and inflexible is it? How can we loosen it up?

"Here are some things to think about that may help you come up with a new solution:

- **"People.** Think of some person that could help the youth in your example solve his or her problems. What people could he or she go to for help?

- **"Models for change.** Who do you know who has faced similar situations? How did that person or persons deal with this type of problem?

- **"Organizations.** What organizations would help solve the problem?

- **"Programs.** What special programs, whether they are within an organization (for example, AA) or not, could help solve the problem?

- **"Narrow Down your Options**. Of all the possible options you have brainstormed, which are within the realm of possibility and have some chance of success?

- **"Consider the Consequences of Each of the Remaining Options.** List all of the consequences of the remaining options.

- **"State the Actual Goal You Would Like to Attain.** State exactly what you want to change and list what steps you must take to achieve that goal — daily, weekly, monthly, and/or long-term.

"For each of those steps, state some observable, time-limited criteria for taking that step. For instance, if a person has decided he will move out of his parents' house, he must then find out what other places to live are available and how much it will cost, decide how to pay for it, decide about furniture, and so forth. When listing those steps, he should set a time for accomplishing each; for example, he may give himself a deadline of two weeks to find out what his options are for other places to live.

"Now lets look at some real life situations."

Exercise: Case Examples for Problem-solving

The facilitators can choose one, two, or all three of the following situations and present them to the class. Or the class can break up into two or three groups, each group taking one of the cases presented. The participants should refer to the "Basic Steps in Problem-solving and Decision-making" in their *Moving On Participant Guidebooks.*

A seventeen-year-old boy lives at home with his verbally abusive, alcoholic father and depressed mother. He is a junior in high school and gets average grades. He would like to finish high school because he wants to go on and get a two-year degree in mechanical drafting. However, his best friend is taking a job at a local factory that pays $8.50 an hour and he knows he could get a similar job. If the boy takes the job, he will be able to get his own apartment and move away from his family.

A twelve-year-old girl is being pressured by her stepfather to sit on his lap and kiss him. She is afraid of this and has been telling him no. He has told her that she had better not resist or tell anybody, or else he will beat her up.

A fifteen-year-old girl has had a best friend for several years. Her friend has starting using drugs and is hanging around with other drug users. Rather than abandoning her, her friend invited her to join the new group. Today they plan to cruise through the department stores and do some shoplifting. She knows she must do this in order to be accepted.

Goals Work for Task-oriented *AND* Personal Problems

Many participants may believe that goals will work fine for task-orientated challenges but not for personal problems, such as overeating, drug use, and enabling. Facilitators can show how the same steps work just as well for personal problems with the following example:

"Suppose a person wants to stop enabling. He or she can:

- **"Clarify and accept the need for change.** This is a very big step for enablers. Often they do not believe that their behavior has to change; rather, they believe their behavior is doing a lot of good. Sometimes it takes a long time to realize that enabling is not always helpful.

- **"Determine what is possible to change.** Enablers often spend time trying to get the other person to change rather than changing themselves. Clearly, their focus must be on changing **their own behavior,** not someone else's.

- **"Determine what you can change.** This step in the goal-setting process goes back to the Serenity Prayer—the courage to change the things that can be changed and the wisdom to know the difference. For example: Ken has a younger brother who is sniffing glue. His brother is out of it a lot and needs help with his homework. Ken doesn't want his brother to get into trouble because of his poor achievement in school so he helps him with his homework. Ken also has been trying to find and lock up all the volatile substances in the house so his younger brother can't get to them. Both activities could be considered enabling. However, Ken may want to keep the volatile substances out of reach because they are extremely dangerous to his younger brother. Meanwhile, he begins an intervention process by not enabling his brother by doing his homework for him.

- **"Determine the consequences of each action.** Clearly, Ken has reviewed the consequences of stopping both types of enabling. He decided that, for the immediate future, the consequences of letting his brother have access to volatile substances was too dangerous and he would not do it.

- **"State the goal.** A goal may be either more or less inclusive. For instance, Ken's goal may be to stop his brother from using drugs. In that case, a number of steps would follow. If Ken's only goal is to save himself more time for his own homework, then the goal will be less inclusive."

If time allows, facilitators can ask participants to suggest steps Ken can take to stop his brother's drug use.

Exercise:
Practice In Goal-setting

In this exercise, participants will work on setting goals in four areas: school, family, friends, and having fun. Participants can turn to their *Moving On Participant Guidebooks,* find the goal area for school, and write down one verifiable and measurable goal. In other words, rather than, "I want to be more responsible in school," a participant might write, "I will hand in my homework on time for all of my subjects this week." Under the column "Things That Must Be Accomplished," participants would write down the number of homework assignments due this week, and then under "By When?"

they would write "this time next week." Participants can then do the same kind of verifiable, measurable goals for the other categories.

At first, participants should set one-week goals. After they have tried this several times, they can make goals for the school year. The larger, long-range goals become meaningless, however, unless there are short-term goals to help them reach them.

Homework Exercise:
Time Management

Facilitators can give the following instructions:

One of the most important things we can do to achieve our goals is to manage our time better. To do this we must look at two things: priorities and distractions.

"Every day this week, make a list of the things you have to do. Use the 'Time Management Guide,' in your *Moving On Participant Guidebooks.* After you have looked the list over, put an 'A' next to the things that absolutely must be done, a 'B' next to the things of secondary importance, and a 'C' next to those of even less importance. Then start with the As. Plan your day around accomplishing them. If at the end of the day you haven't finished all your As and you can still do them tomorrow, move them to the next day. Keep track of your activities for a week.

Distractions

"Think about how you went about trying to achieve your goals in the preceding week. What distractions do you most often indulge in: Television? Talking on the telephone? Hanging out and talking with friends? Eating? For starters, after you have listed your priorities for the day, allow yourself none of your favorite distractions until all your As have been accomplished."

Discussion

At the end of the week or at the next LifeGuides session, the facilitators can ask:

- "Did you use your time-management grid this week?"
- "Did it help to prioritize your tasks?"
- "Were you able to ignore distractions any better this week?"
- "When you prioritized your tasks, did you have trouble being assertive? Did you give something a higher priority because you were afraid that other people would give it a higher priority?"
- "Give some examples of your As."
- "Give some examples of your Cs."

Taking Care of Ourselves, Having Fun

The absence of sad feelings does not automatically mean the presence of happy ones. Children from disrupted family environments often have not had the time, the role models, or the freedom from fear or sadness to explore ways to have fun.

Have fun, lighten up

The facilitators can model good humor and having fun. It is all right for them to joke with each other and with participants, to not take themselves too seriously, and to act out in a good-natured way.

They can let participants know that it is OK to joke sometimes and to have fun as long as it is not used to distract the class from important business. Humor can be very facilitating to the class process and to the whole process of growth and development of LifeGuides participants.

The more interests the facilitators have, the more they will be able to refer to those interests and to the enjoyment they provide. For example, they can mention to the class: "When I feel tense, I like to play basketball" (or take a hot bath, play tennis, play sports, go to a movie, etc.). Or, "One of the most challenging things I ever did was rock climbing," or "Visiting the museum last week was a lot of fun for me."

Goals for Sessions on Taking Care of Ourselves

Goals for sessions in this subject area include:
- To experience having fun in the class.
- To help participants find healthy activities that they really enjoy.
- To examine what keeps participants from having fun.
- To plan ways to have fun during the day, during the week, and on the weekends.

Affirmations on Taking Care of Ourselves

- There is joy in life.
- I **deserve** to have fun in my life.
- I **need** to have fun in my life.
- I **will** have fun in my life.
- I will have fun even when it first involves some risk.
- I will have fun and I will take the time to do it.
- I can enjoy part of my day even if my entire day is not all joy or all fun.

Overview

- Trying New Activities
- Exercise: What Keeps Me From Having Fun?
- Exercise: How To Be a Kid Again
- Exercise: The Gift Exchange
- Tradition and Rituals: A Way for Having Classroom Fun

Trying New Activities

Facilitators can introduce this subject areas as follows:

"It's hard for anyone — kids and adults — to break out of a rut. For some reason, most of us prefer the comfort of boredom to the effort and risks we must take to get some excitement and fun back into our lives. You've seen this. Take a bunch of kids who are bummed out because they can't watch their favorite music video for some reason. If you suggest that they just forget it and go play softball instead, you'll get jeers, boos, and hisses. Get those kids into the game for five minutes and they won't want to quit.

"This happens all the time. People don't think they'll enjoy doing something different or something new until they try it, until they get into it for a while. I could provide you with a list of 'alternative highs,' but it would be just another list, nothing more. Things don't look like they'll be fun when you see them written down. If you need something in your life to replace the highs that drugs seem to offer, you'll have to experiment:

• Join something.
• Sing something.
• Play some new sport.
• Listen to something.
• Help someone.

"We can't tell you what the 'somethings' are, who the 'someones' are, where the 'somewheres' are. You have to find this out, not just by thinking about it, but by doing things. Don't worry if you can't think of anything fun or new right this moment. Keep your eyes and ears open during the next week and you'll see that there are things you have automatically written off in the past that you may want to take a closer look at.

"Don't be too rigid in the way you look at and react to new ideas for fun. One way of being rigid is to divide everything into what's 'cool' and trendy and what's 'corny' and 'dumb'. Risk not being cool sometimes and you'll find there are a lot of fun things that 'cool' kids rule out of their lives."

Exercise:
What Keeps Me from Having Fun?

The participants can be told to look in their *Moving On Participant Guidebooks* to review "What Keeps Me from Having Fun?" On that page there are several attitudes participants may have that prevent them from trying new activities. They include:

• I don't have any time because I'm working.
• I have to take care of too many things at home.
• I'm too shy to meet people
• I am not a very enjoyable person.
• I don't think people will like me.
• I don't know how to (dance, play sports, act, etc.).
• I'm afraid of looking dumb if I try something new.
• I'm just too tired to try anything.
• I can never find the money to do something new.

Participants can pick the ones they think are the most serious for them, the ones that most commonly run through their minds. Next they should consider when those thoughts usually arise and be prepared to give an example to the LifeGuides class.

Discussion

After a participant has given his example, facilitators can say:

• "What do you think of John's reasons for not having fun? Are they realistic?" (The facilitator should not allow the class to discount all of the reasons the participant presents. Some of them may be valid and very serious problems. Participants must take each other seriously and attempt to help the person who has given his example to overcome the problem. In some instances, the reason will be superficial and, if the class is a trusting and safe place, the person can be confronted on that.)
• "What could John do about this problem that keeps coming up in his life?"
• "Does anyone else feel the same way? Do you have the same problem occurring again and again for you?"

Exercise:
How To Be a Kid Again

In the *Moving On Participant Guidebook* there is an exercise called "How to Be a Kid Again." This gives participants an opportunity to look over all the things they have ever done that made them feel good. Facilitators can give the following instructions:

"In the lefthand column, write down all the things that you have done that you have enjoyed. Include the things you did when you were young. Write down things that were healthy, relatively safe, and did not involve alcohol or other drugs. In the column next to it, write down how you can do that same activity or something like that activity today."

Discussion

After participants have had a few minutes to fill in this form, facilitators can tell them to review it and see if there is anything they need to do differently to be able to do some of the fun activities. Facilitators can ask:

• "How do your family problems interfere with your ability to have a good time?"
• "How does school interfere with your ability to have a good time?"
• "How do your own feelings of shyness, inadequacy, or co-dependency interfere with your having a good time?"

Participants can use this page to keep a list of fun things to do, places to go, and people to contact. Facilitators might want to give participants the ongoing assignment of contributing something new to the page each week.

Exercise:
The Gift Exchange

In this exercise, participants are asked to bring some object home that their parents are willing to give up: an inexpensive object or one in which the family has lost interest in, such as an old record or music tape. The facilitator will also provide some useful but inexpensive prizes, such as colored erasers, colored pens, and so forth. Participants are to bring their gifts wrapped in gift paper or newspaper.

To start the exercise, facilitators will say:

"Starting around the room on my right, each of you will ask for a gift from somebody else in the class. You can ask for any gift, even one that someone has already asked for. You can change the gift you have for one in the middle. After we have gone around the circle once, we will all open our gifts. Then I will set a timer, but I will not tell you how much time we have. Going around the group again, you can trade for whatever prize you want most. But the next person can trade you back for it if he or she wants to. The exchanges stop and you keep what you have when the timer goes off."

In this game, even the most rational people can get absurdly and humorously invested in one of the gifts.

Traditions and Rituals: A Way for Having Classroom Fun

Birthdays, holidays, graduations, sobriety dates, and other opportunities for gift-giving or recognition should all be taken advantage of in the LifeGuides Program.

It would be helpful for facilitators to keep track of every participant's birthday and sobriety day (if applicable). Also, if a participant is about to reach a major milestone — such as graduating, passing a difficult exam, or getting a driver's license — the class can take time out to give that person recognition.

Facilitators can even send birthday cards to the participants at home. This not only adds to the person's sense of well-being and of being supported, but it helps maintain rituals that may have been dropped from the person's life.

Appendix A

Reading Material on Subjects Relevant to the LifeGuides Program

Child Abuse

National Committee for Prevention of Child Abuse, P.O. Box 94283, Chicago, IL 60690

This organization provides a wide variety of short, practical, low-cost publications on all aspects of child abuse. Catalogue available.

Children of Alcoholics

Broken Bottles, Broken Dreams: Understanding and Helping the Children of Alcoholics
C. Deutsch
New York: Teachers College Press, Columbia University, 1982, 213 pages

Written primarily for adults who work with young people in schools, social service agencies or the juvenile justice system, this book develops the reader's awareness of the problems, increases empathy for those who are suffering, and engenders in the reader a willingness to take action on their behalf. The first section of the book, "The Children," provides the basic background information necessary for constructing the "blueprint for action" described in the second section. Part Two, "Helping," contains some practical, realistic ways to help the children of alcoholics. The suggestions provided usually involve one-to-one approaches that teachers and social service professionals can integrate into their current daily activities. The section on "Community Strategies" describes some practical issues in getting community-wide cooperation to help children of alcoholics. The book would be useful for those planning for inservice training on the LifeGuides curriculum and the need for staff cooperation.

Children of Alcoholics: A Guide for Parents, Educators, and Therapists
R. J. Ackerman
New York: Simon & Schuster, Inc., 2nd edition, 1987, 199 pages

Describes the effects that parental alcoholism has on children — how these children look at the world and how they develop emotionally and socially. The book also includes practical suggestions for educators, therapists, and concerned parents.

Mom and Me
K. Crosbie
Minneapolis, MN: Community Intervention™, Inc., 1989, 20 pages.

David is in the seventh grade. He is bright, clever, and is starting to learn about alcoholism — his mother's alcoholism. This fictional account about the effects of a parent's alcoholism on a child is a sensitive look at a family's secret, as told by young David. Through the efforts and explanations of a school counselor, David comes to understand that his mother has an illness, that she can be helped through treatment, and that, with time, she can become well again.

Eating Disorders

Bulimia: A Guide To Recovery
L. Cohn
Carlsbad, CA: Gurze Books, 1986, 158 pages

This book combines graphic case histories with specific research-based information to give a useful introduction and broad overview to the problem of bulimia. Much of the book is devoted to practical ways to overcome bulimia.

The Golden Cage: The Enigma of Anorexia Nervosa

H. Bruch
Cambridge, MA: Harvard University Press, 1978, 149 pages

Dr. Bruch is one of the pioneers in the area of eating disorders. Her earlier book, *Eating Disorders: Obesity, Anorexia Nervosa, and The Person Within* appeared in 1973. *The Golden Cage* provides a solid description of the disease of anorexia nervosa as well as speculations on its causes. The author believes that, in most incidents, the anorexic must break free of what she (the vast majority of anorexics are female) feels are the high expectations of her family. While LifeGuides facilitators cannot take it on themselves to intervene into anorexia nervosa by themselves, the therapeutic techniques described by Dr. Bruch will be of interest and shed some light on to the kinds of support these girls need as they struggle to change with the help of professional treatment.

Loss and Change

Helping Children Cope with Separation and Loss

C. L. Jewett
Harvard, MA: The Harvard Common Press, 1982, 146 pages

This book is written for adults who live or work with children who are facing a recent loss or trying to make sense of past losses. The first chapter, "Telling a child about a loss," prepares adults for what might be a very difficult task, depending on the nature of the loss in question. The author describes how to work with children on a one-to-one basis rather than in a classroom situation.

Perspectives on Loss: A Manual for Educators

B. A. Bebensee
TLC Publications: Arvad, Colorado, 1985, 125 pages.

This book provides classroom teachers with exercises to help students recognize the obvious and not so obvious losses they have faced in their lives and to consider the many ways those losses may be affecting them. Students are taught a basic model of what happens when loss occurs and how people generally recover from losses.

Meditation Guides

The Promise of a New Day

K. Casey and M. Vanceburg
Center City, MN: Hazelden Educational Material, 400 pages

Twenty-Four Hours a Day for Everyone

A. L. Roeck
Center City, MN: Hazelden Educational Material, 383 pages

These books provide succinct, one-page readings on a wide variety of feelings and issues related to personal growth and emotional well-being.

Safety, Violence in Relationships

Coping with Dating Violence

N. Rue
New York: The Rosen Publishing Group, 1989, 140 pages

It is likely that many of the girls in a LifeGuides class will be involved in unhealthy relationships. A particularly powerful aspect of such relationships is physical abuse. This book describes patterns of abuse manifested among teenagers who are dating. It contains real-life examples, research and background information, and insights into the dynamics of abuse among adolescents. It also provides many practical suggestions that can be used in a LifeGuides class or personal counseling sessions to help girls avoid abusive relationships.

How To Raise A Street-Smart Child

G. Hechinger
Facts on File Publications: New York, 1984, 160 pages

The book is written for parents and other adults who are concerned about the safety of children. It is a practical and very detailed description of the kind of information elementary and junior and senior high school students must have to conduct themselves safely in today's society. While many of the specific guidelines suggested apply primarily to urban settings, the abundance of information provided ensures that those from non-urban settings will be able to make use of the book as well. The author describes how to help children think about safety and danger in their daily lives, how to avoid dangerous situations, how to deal with dangerous situations when they arise, and how to report crimes and face the feelings that those crimes cause in young people.

No More Secrets: Protecting Your Child from Sexual Assault

C. Adams and J. Fay
San Luis Obispo, CA: Impact Publishers, 1981, 90 pages

This book is based on the proven premise that strangers account for only 10 to 15 percent of the sexual offenses against children. The authors describe a wide variety of myths that parents and other adults believe about sexual assault and suggest appropriate ways to protect children from those assaults. Many different techniques used by perpetrators are described. Several anecdotes are offered on every page, not to describe the horrors of sexual assault but to describe specific situations in which children are pressured to touch or to be touched by an adult. The book is an excellent resource for Life-Guides facilitators. Those who become familiar with each of the chapters will be able to draw upon useful, focused information when the need arises.

Sexual Identity

Gay Youth: A Positive Approach for Parents and Siblings

M. Brownley
Minneapolis, MN: Community Intervention™, Inc., 1988, 25 pages

As more and more gay and lesbian youths recognize their sexuality, their families need to deal with their own emotions concerning these young people. This book guides family members through the fears, myths, and confusion that can attend the subject of homosexuality. It examines the struggles behind an adolescent's decision to "come out" and suggests ways in which families can respond to that decision. It offers intelligent ways to handle religious conflicts, fears of telling others, feelings of isolation, and more. Although it is written primarily for parents, the discussion of the common myths surrounding homosexuality and the problems faced by young gays and lesbians and their parents would be appropriate for LifeGuides class facilitators, student assistance program counselors, staff members, and all those who work with youth on a daily bases.

Suicide

Adolescent Suicide: Identification and Intervention

Minneapolis, MN: Community Intervention™, Inc., 1987, 40 pages

This booklet provides a brief, fact-filled overview of key issues in adolescent suicide and suicide prevention: current rates of adolescent suicide, some of the reasons for suicide, indications that a youth is considering suicide, and what to do if you are concerned about a particular youth.

Suicide and Its Aftermath: Understanding and Counseling the Survivors

E. J. Dunne, J. L. McIntosh, K. Dunne-Maxim, eds.
New York: W.W. Norton & Company, 1987, 352 pages

This book touches all the bases. It provides research findings, offers personal accounts of people who have experienced suicide in their lives, describes therapeutic programs, and suggests specific one-to-interventions for those working with youth at risk for suicide. Although it is addressed primarily to therapists, the information can be useful for LifeGuides facilitators, program planners, and those providing inservice training to staff members.

Appendix B

Audiovisual Resources for the LifeGuides Program

The following films can be used in a variety of ways in LifeGuides classes.

Facilitators should, of course, review each film before showing it to a class. In most instances, review copies can be obtained for the cost of shipping and handling, or rental fees can be deducted from the purchase price if the film is purchased within ninety days.

Although many of the films come with a discussion guide, LifeGuides facilitators will most often want participants to consider aspects of the film the guide does not address. Several of these films, for instance, focus on adult behaviors and the discussion guides presume that the audiences will be made up of adults. In the context of a LifeGuides class, however, the junior and senior high school students may be viewing the behavior of the adults with an eye to considering what effects the adult behavior would likely have on their children or other family members.

When using a film to help describe problems or stimulate discussions on a particular subject area, the facilitators can review some of the LifeGuides exercises listed under that subject area. Some of the questions used to guide discussions for the exercises could also be adapted for discussing the films. The more familiar facilitators are with the LifeGuides materials, the better prepared they will be to draw up a list of appropriate statements and questions to guide discussions in a manner that furthers the goals of the LifeGuides Program.

Child Abuse, Sexual Abuse

Important: Facilitators who wish to show any of these videos must feel confident that they will be able to aid newly identified abuse victims in the class to get the protection and help they need. It may be helpful to have present a person who has had experience in intervention and referral of child abuse cases.

No Easy Answers

Audience: Junior/senior high students
Time: 32 minutes
An Illusion Theater Production
Distributor: 1-800-862-8900

This videotape focuses on prevention and intervention into sexual abuse. Actors from the Illusion Theater in Minneapolis perform brief scenes and dramatize healthy and unhealthy relationships and interactions. A moderator facilitates discussions with teenagers who are asked to consider a wide range of issues relating to sexuality and personal rights.

Among the topics touched on are the differences between sex and sexual abuse, how to talk about sex, and how to differentiate between touch that feels good and touch that is shameful or threatening. Some typical scenes of sexual abuse are portrayed by the actors: a girl being pressured by her boyfriend in a car, a babysitter who is kissed and fondled by the father of the child she was taking care of, a coach who touches one of his athletes in a sexual manner, an acquaintance rape. In one scene, a family of three talks about problems caused by incest.

All of the dramatizations are handled quite well. The actors provide a sense of the fear and shame they feel in the different situations, but the sexual actions are never explicit or in any way sensational. A moderator helps students discuss their feelings about the incidents portrayed and what they believe they would or should do in such a situation. Some "Facts on Sexual Abuse" are emphasized: sexual abuse is not the victim's fault, sex offenders can be almost anyone, alcohol and other drugs are not an excuse for sexual abuse, rape is not the only kind of sexual abuse, and there are people in programs who can help both victims and perpetrators.

Come In from the Storm
Part I: China Doll

Audience: Elementary/junior/senior high students
10 minutes
Team Entertainment Education Production
Distributor: 619-698-9567

"China Doll" is designed to help children begin to get in touch with their feelings by exploring emotions such as anger, fear, sadness, and happiness. It helps clarify the sources of conflicting feelings in families, since the subject is conflict and emotional abuse by a mother who clearly loves her daughter.

The film is apparently aimed at children in elementary school. It portrays a seven-year-old child who is verbally abused by her divorced mother. When the daughter is playing with her doll one day, the mother overhears her daughter verbally attacking the doll in the same way that the mother attacks her daughter.

Although LifeGuides participants are older than the daughter in the film, they will be able to identify with the girl's experience. Furthermore, the younger daughter can help play the "child" inside the participants. How the participants feel about that girl is probably very much how they feel about the vulnerable "child" in themselves. An excellent discussion guide is provided with the "Come In from the Storm" series.

Come In from the Storm
Part II: The Diary

Audience: Elementary/junior/senior high students
18 minutes
Team Entertainment Education Production
Distributor: 619-698-9567

"The Diary" is designed to help children begin to understand what is meant by "child abuse" and the different kinds of feelings that abused children experience, such as guilt, loyalty, fear, and confusion. The major message of the film is that, if abused children do not tell someone and get help, they are very likely to become abusing parents themselves.

In this film, Bryan, an eleven-year-old boy, is a victim of emotional and physical abuse. No violence is portrayed on the screen, but incidents are described through Bryan's diary. These include: being thrown down the stairs, his father beating his mother, being beaten with a belt, having a tooth cracked, and having a broken ankle.

In the middle of the night Bryan is visited by his future son, who has traveled back in time. After a comedic introduction, the two settle down to a sobering conversation about Bryan's feelings and options.

Come In from the Storm
Part III: The Necklace

Audience: Elementary/junior/senior high students
18 minutes
A Team Entertainment Education Production
Distributor: 619-698-9567

The focus of this film is incest and other forms of familial sexual abuse. Karen, an enthusiastic, well-adjusted twelve-year-old girl, has a problem. Her best friend, Jessica, has shared a terrible secret—her dad is sexually abusing her.

Karen has great trust and confidence in her own father and seeks his advice. This wise father guides Karen to a better understanding of sexual abuse and together they decide the best way for Karen to approach the problem.

When Karen describes to her father what Jessica has been experiencing, there is a dramatization of the kind of verbal seduction and veiled threats that fathers use to pressure their daughters into cooperating in the abuse and keeping the secret.

One of the approaches used by the producers of this film is to contrast an ideal, healthy adult/child relationship with an inappropriate relationship. They hope that most children will focus on and relate to the positive relationship. From this safe perspective, the adult showing the film can teach children about the awful realities of abuse while, at the same time, reinforcing and preserving good adult/child relationships. On the other hand, an abused child will focus on and relate to the negative relationship.

The ideal relationship is, perhaps, a bit too ideal. Karen's father is almost too warm and friendly and their home is almost too beautiful. Even as he is rushing off to work, father and daughter walk into the living room to talk by a fireplace with a fire that's already burning. The idea that good families must be "perfect families" is reinforced by this approach. Facilitators can ask participants to comment on this problem.

Children of Alcoholics

Lots of Kids Like Us
28 minutes
A Gerald T. Rogers Production
Distributor: Commuity Intervention, Inc.
1-800-328-0417

A note on appropriate audiences: Although **"Lots of Kids Like Us"** focuses on the lives of a pre-schooler and a child in elementary school, junior and senior high school students are able to relate to this film easily. A goal of the LifeGuides Program is to help participants look at how they were affected as younger children. This film will help them get in touch with those experiences and feelings.

This film tells the story of Ben and Laurie, who are trying to cope with their father's alcoholism. Ben and Laurie are burdened by tremendous feelings of guilt and are often exposed to physical and emotional abuse as they suffer in silence out of their need to keep the "family secret." "You aren't alone" and "it isn't your fault" are major messages of the film. **"Lots of Kids Like Us"** does not describe the processes of addiction or enabling. Rather, it focuses on the effects of alcoholism on children and the feelings of those children. Some of the content includes:

- The loneliness and withdrawal of many children of alcoholics.
- How the anxiety, preoccupation and fears of the non-alcoholic spouse cause trouble for the children.
- The effects on the children of the parents' fighting and children's fears of a parent leaving.
- The practical problems of living with an alcoholic, especially how to avoid riding home with a parent who is drunk.
- How to find alternative ways of getting one's needs met.
- Reaching out and getting support from peers and other adults.

Facilitators questions can focus on who the LifeGuides participants identified with in the film, what feelings they had while watching the film, how their families are similar to or different than the family in the film, and what specific incidents seemed most real to them.

Children of Alcoholics, Risks of Addiction

My Father's Son
Audience: Junior/senior high students
33 minutes
A Gerald T. Rogers Production
Distributor: Community Intervention, Inc.
1-800-328-0417

This film describes the effects of alcoholism and chemical dependency on a family. The film also shows how chemical dependency is transmitted from generation to generation. The dramatic action is focused primarily on a senior high school boy who watches his mother protect and enable his father's drinking while his brother becomes increasingly more fearful. Some of the topics touched on in the film include:

- The embarrassment that children of alcoholics feel about their parents' drinking.
- The great amount of denial that goes on in alcoholic homes.
- The feelings of anger, depression, and isolation felt by children of alcoholics.
- The risks for addiction that children of alcoholics face.

The film is accompanied by a discussion guide that provides suggestions for preparing a group to watch the film and processing questions and comments for discussion following the film.

Communication Problems, Denial, Enabling

Open Secrets
Audience: Junior/senior high students
25 minutes
Distributor: Community Intervention, Inc.
1-800-328-0417

"Open Secrets" is about a family whose inability to talk openly about alcohol and drugs leads to tragedy. The film opens in a hospital room where three members of the family — the mother (Pat), the father (Frank), the sister who is in twelfth grade (Alison) — are waiting to find out what has happened to the younger brother, Mike, who is in tenth grade. Mike has just been seriously injured in a drunk-driving accident. He was not the driver. The mother, father, and daughter each address the camera directly. They describe their current feelings and the events that took place at home that day. As each character talks, it becomes clear that their inability to express their feelings directly and to communicate information clearly has contributed to the current problem they face.

This film touches on three issues of concern to Life-Guides participants: denial, enabling, and problems in communication.

Denial. Before showing the film, the facilitators can ask participants to look for any signs of denial (or enabling or communication problems, depending on the focus of the class for that session). Some examples of denial in this film are:

- Pat, the mother, states her belief that her son, Mike, couldn't possibly be involved in any serious drinking or drug use.
- She also believes that her daughter's use of drugs indicates that Alison is "just going through a stage."
- Although the mother is very concerned about drugs, she is a smoker and perhaps a heavy smoker.
- Frank, the father, indicates that he thinks it is normal for all kids to use alcohol, that it is just a phase kids must go through.
- The father, feeling defensive about his own drinking, minimizes his children's use of alcohol. He even believes marijuana is not a very serious problem since it is not one of the "hard drugs."

- Mike, the son, tells his parents that only one or two "burnouts" have ever gotten into trouble with drugs in his school.
- Alison, the daughter, states that it is only the younger kids in the high school who have trouble with drinking because they don't know how to handle it well.

Enabling. Some examples of enabling in the films are:
- Pat, the mother, does not confront her daughter about the stash her daughter kept in her room.
- Pat is very indirect with her husband because she does not want to upset him. She does not tell him about the stash of drugs and alcohol she found in her daughter's bedroom.
- Alison gets her boyfriend to buy beer for Mike.
- The father focuses attention strictly on drug problems, giving the impression that alcohol use is all right.

Communication Problems. The entire film is about indirect and unclear communication. Simply by asking participants to note how each person in the film communicates indirectly and incompletely, many examples will be easily identified.

Decision-making, Peer Pressure

The Bizarre Trial of the Pressured Peer
Audience: Junior/senior high students.
29 minutes
A Gerald T. Rogers Production
Distributor: Community Intervention, Inc.
1-800-328-0417

This fast-paced, entertaining film provides an introduction to problem-solving skills and how they can be used to deal with negative peer pressure. Barbara Barnes, sixteen years old, is becoming increasingly aware of the negative consequences of her actions, especially those influenced by her new "friends." With the assistance of a very helpful substitute teacher and a wild nightmare where she's accused of "D.U.I.—Deciding Under the Influence"—Barbara begins to learn the process of making decisions based on what is right for her. A discussion guide is included.

Why Is It Always Me?

Audience: Junior high students.
14 minutes
A Gerald T. Rogers Production
Distributor: Community Intervention, Inc.
1-800-328-0417

Mike seems to have more problems than anyone else. Like many kids, Mike needs to learn problem-solving skills. In this film, Mike learns five simple steps to problem-solving and conflict resolution. Using a humorous approach, the film is both entertaining and educational. Each of the problems presented in the film involves both conflict resolution and dealing with anger in a productive way. Typical unreliable and ineffective ways of trying to resolve conflicts or deal with anger are also presented. A discussion guide is included with the film.

Depression, Suicide Prevention

Friends For Life

Audience: Junior/senior high students
22 minutes
A Gerald T. Rogers Production
Distributor: Community Intervention, Inc.
1-800-328-0417

Research has shown that when a young person is feeling depressed or suicidal, he or she is much more likely to tell a friend than a parent or other adult. This film makes young people aware of this fact and provides guidance as to what to do when they are concerned about one of their peers.

Without portraying any individual who might be suicidal, **"Friends for Life"** illustrates how several young people take steps to confront friends who are depressed and might be candidates for suicide attempts. Five different situations are shown. In one them, three friends discuss the role that drugs may have played in the suicide of a friend. The other four situations portray different ways of confronting and offering help to a sad or depressed friend. Through these dramatic interchanges, the relationships of depression to drug use, family problems, parental alcoholism, and divorce are raised. The viewers are also given the warning signs of suicide and practical suggestions about what to do when they think a friend is depressed or suicidal.

Divorce

No Fault Kids: A Focus on Kids with Divorced Parents.

Audience: Junior/senior high students
27 minutes
A United Learning Production
Distributor: Community Intervention, Inc.
1-800-328-0417

This film was designed for junior and senior high school students and has also been used effectively with groups of parents. It uses a documentary approach that focuses on the problems facing youth with divorced parents. The young people interviewed talk about their parents' divorces and the isolation, embarrassment, anger, and guilt that they feel. They also discuss many of the practical problems divorce has caused them:

- What it's like to be caught in the middle of their parents' arguments.
- How they feel when the parent they are living with ignores the need for them to have both a mother and a father.
- What happens to them when a "congenial" divorce turns angry and hostile.
- How they feel about being used by one parent to provide information about the other parent.
- What they and children like them can get from a support group.
- What practical steps young people can take to lessen the impact of divorce on their lives.
- A discussion leader's guide is included with the film.

Drinking and Drug Use

Friday Night: Five
27 minutes
A Gerald T. Rogers Production
Distributor: Community Intervention™, Inc.
1-800-328-0417

Special note on audiences: **"Friday Night: Five"** is a film primarily for and about alcoholics. However, in the context of a LifeGuides class, this film presents a range of adult drinking behaviors for participants to comment on. LifeGuides facilitators can use the film in sessions related to the material on "Drug and Alcohol Use: What's Normal, What's Not?" The film comes with a discussion guide that describes the symptoms of a range of drinking behaviors. The five different adults portrayed in the film give participants a chance to consider and comment on what they believe to be appropriate or inappropriate drinking.

Drug Abuse

"Are You Talking To Me?"
29 minutes
Audience: Junior/senior high students
Young Star Productions, Thomas Van Dyke-Producer
Distributor: Community Intervention™, Inc.
1-800-328-0417

This is a broadly-focused film that touches on issues in prevention and intervention for drug use. Teenage pregnancy, suicide, peer pressure, family relationships, and the harsh realities of criminal action are also depicted.

The film can be used along with LifeGuides sessions related to "Alcoholism and Drug Dependency: When Use Goes Out of Control."

A detailed, scene-by-scene breakdown of the film is included in the discussion guide to help facilitators refer to specific scenes in the film.

Drug Abuse, Peer Support, Peer Intervention

The Invisible Line
Audience: Junior/senior high students
31 minutes
A Gerald T. Rogers Production
Distributor: Community Intervention™, Inc.
1-800-328-0417

This is the story about a teenager, Jason, who started drinking beer and wine, advanced to pot, then pills, and finally cocaine. After his death, his brother talks to Jason's closest friends to find out about Jason's drug use. Each person asks him or herself, "What could I have done to help Jason? Why didn't I do it?" This film gives LifeGuides participants a lot to think about concerning their own drug use and their responsibilities to drug-using friends.

Bibliography for LifeGuides Materials

Behling, DW. Alcohol abuse as encountered in fifty-one instances of reported child abuse. *Clinical Pediatrics* 1979; 18:87-88, 90-91

Benson, PA, Wook PK, Johnson AL, et al. 1983 Minnesota survey on drug use and drug-related attitudes. Minneapolis: Search Institute, October 25, 1983

Booz-Allen and Hamilton, Incorporated. An assessment of the needs of and resources for children of alcoholic parents. Final report prepared for National Institute on Alcohol Abuse and Alcoholism, Springville, VA: National Technical Information Service, 1974; Grant No. (ADM) 41-74-0017

Brody GH. Prepared statement of Gene H. Brody, Ph.D., Program for the Study of Competence in Children and Families, Department of Child and Family Development, University of Georgia. In: U.S. Congress. House. Select Committee on Children, Youth and Families Hearings on Divorce: The Impact on Children and Families, June 19, 1986. Washington D.C.: U.S. Government Printing Office, 1987

Burke RJ, Wolpin J. The increasing need for counseling services in the eighties. *Guidance and Counseling* 1985; 1(1): 23-31

Clair DJ, Genest M. Variables associated with the adjustment of offspring of alcoholic fathers. Conference paper, 92nd annual convention of the American Psychological Association, Toronto, August 1984

Cork RN. *The Forgotten Children: A Study of Children with Alcoholic Parents.* Toronto: PaperJacks, 1969 (reprinted June 1987)

Dean AE. *Once a Upon a Time: Stories From Adult Children of Alcoholic and Other Dysfunctional Families.* Center City, MN: Hazelden Educational Materials, 1987

Deutsch C. *Broken Bottles, Broken Dreams.* New York: Teachers College Press, 1982

Efron D, Vednendaal K. Video taping and groups for children of substance abusers: a strategy for emotionally disturbed, acting out children. *Alcoholism Treatment Quarterly* Summer 1987, 4(2): 71-85

Egan G. *The Skilled Helper: Model, Skills, and Methods for Effective Helping.* 2nd ed. Monterey, CA: Brooks/Cole Publishing, 1982

Fialkov MJ. Biologic and social determinants in the etiology of alcholism. In: Tarter RE, VanThiel DH, eds. *Alcohol and the Brain: Chronic Effects.* New York: Plenum Press, 1985; 245-263

Ficula TV, Gelfand DM, Richards G, Ulloa A. Factors associated with school refusal in adolescents: some preliminary results. Paper presented at the annual convention of the American Psychological Association, Anaheim, CA, August 1983

Finkelhor D. In: Hechinger G. *How To Raise A Street-Smart Child.* New York: Facts on File Publications, 1984; 91

Gwinn DG. Poor school performance: contributing factors and consequences, with emphasis on the non-white child. Paper presented at the annual international convention, the Council for Exceptional Children, Chicago, April 1976

Hamilton CJ, and Collins JJ. The role of alcohol in wife beating and child abuse: a review of the literature. In: Collins JJ, ed. *Drinking and Crime.* New York: Guilford Press, 1981

Hastings JM, Typpo MH. *An Elephant in the Living Room: The Children's Book.* Minneapolis, MN: Comp-Care Publications, 1984

Hechinger G. *How To Raise A Street-Smart Child.* New York: Facts on File Publications, 1984

Kaufman G. *Shame: The Power of Caring.* Kingbridge, MA: Schenkman Publishing Company, Inc., 1980

Lund CA, Landesnan-Dwyer S. Pre-delinquent and disturbed adolescents: the role of parental alcoholism. *Currents in Alcoholism* 1979; 5:339-348

Muldoon J, Crowley J. *One Step Ahead: Early-Intervention Strategies for Adolescent Drug Problems.* Minneapolis, MN: Community Intervention, Inc., 1986

Muldoon J. *Facilitator's Guide for the Insight Class Program.* Minneapolis, MN: Community Intervention, Inc., 1987

Naiditch B. Rekindled spirit of a child: Intervention's strategies for shame with elementary age children of alcoholics, *Alcoholism Treatment Quarterly;* 4 (2) Summer, 1987, 57-69.

Namakkal S, Mangen DJ. Ninth-12th grade chemical use survey, 1979. Unpublished final report prepared for State of Minnesota, Department of Public Welfare, Prevention Branch, Chemical Dependency Program Division

National Institute on Alcohol Abuse and Alcoholism. Services for Children of Alcoholics, Research Monograph -4. Rockville, MD: NIAAA, 1981; DHHS Publication No. (ADM) 81-1007

O'Gorman P, Ross RA. A review of intake information from a 232 bed, non-secure residential treatment facility for adjudicated male offenders. In: Ackerman RJ, *Growing in the Shadow: Children of Alcoholics.* Pampano Beach, FL: Health Communications Inc., 1986

Smart RG. *The New Drinkers: Teenage Use and Abuse of Alcohol.* Toronto: Alcoholism and Drug Addiction Research Foundation, 1980

Szapocznik J, Kurtines WM, Foote FH, Perez-Vidal A, Hervis O. Conjoint versus one-person family therapy: some evidence for the effectiveness of conducting family therapy through one person. *Journal of Consulting and Clinical Psychology* 1983; 51(6): 889-899

Tarpley MR, Moorehouse ER, Seixas JS, Kern JC. Psychosocial assessment and intervention with children of alcoholic parents. In: Cook D, Fewell C, Riolo J, eds. Social Work Treatment of Alcohol Problems. New Brunswick, NJ: *Journal of Studies on Alcohol, Inc.,* 1983; 131-142

U.S. Bureau of Census. Statistical Abstract of the United States, 1988. 108th ed. Washington, D.C.: U.S. Bureau of Census, 1987

U.S. Congress. House. Select Committee on Children, Youth and Families Hearings on Divorce: The Impact on Children and Families, June 19, 1986. Washington, D.C.: U.S. Government Printing Office 1987

U.S. Department of Health and Human Services. Executive supplement: National study on the incidence and the severity of child abuse and neglect. Rockville, MD: DHHS, 1981; DHHS Publication No. (OHDS) 81-30329

Vaillant GE, Milofsky ES. The etiology of alcoholism: a prospective viewpoint. *American Psychologist* 1982; 37(5):494-503

Williams G. Epidemiologic Bulletin No. 15: Demographic Trends, Alcohol Abuse and Alcoholism, 1985-1995. *Alcohol Health and Research World* Spring 1987; Rockville, MD: National Institute on Alcohol Abuse and Alcoholism

Woititz JG. Guidelines for Support Groups: Adult Children of Alcoholics and Others Who Identify. Pompano Beach, FL; Health Communication, Inc., 1986, 37 pages

Woodson AL. A method for identification of persons with problem-drinking parents. Paper presented at 27th annual meeting of the Alcohol and Drug Problems Association of North America, New Orleans, September 1976. Cited in Biek JE, Screening test for identifying adolescents adversely affected by a parental drinking problem. *Journal of Adolescent Health Care* 1981; 2:107-13

Younes RP, Web G. Initial computer analysis: 201 children with learning disabilities. Paper presented at the international scientific conference of IFLD, Montreal, Canada, August 1976